State of Paralysis

More Works by John Elsom:

Plays

Peacemaker
Maui
One More Bull
How I Coped
Malone Dies
The Well-Intentioned Builder
The Man of the Future is Dead
Second Time Round
Old Boy
World Within

Books

Theatre Outside London
Erotic Theatre
Post-War British Theatre
The History of the National Theatre
Post-War British Theatre Criticism (Ed.)
Cold War Theatre
Is Shakespeare still our Contemporary? (Ed.)

His Works with The Lutterworth Press:

Missing The Point
State of Paralysis

State of Paralysis

A Cultural History of Brexit

John Elsom

(L)
The Lutterworth Press

The Lutterworth Press
P.O. Box 60
Cambridge
CB1 2NT
United Kingdom

www.lutterworth.com
publishing@lutterworth.com

Paperback ISBN: 978 0 7188 9517 4
PDF ISBN: 978 0 7188 4730 2
ePub ISBN: 978 0 7188 4731 9
Kindle ISBN: 978 0 7188 4732 6

British Library Cataloguing in Publication Data
A record is available from the British Library

First published by The Lutterworth Press, 2019

Cover credits:
(front) David Holt, *London October 20 2017 (50) Scaffolding Big Ben*;
(back) Freepik, *London Skyline* and *Illustration of UK flag Vector.*

Contents

Acknowledgements

This has not been an easy book to write. I have needed help and support from many people. Top of the list has been the constant encouragement that I have received from Judith Elliott, a former BBC producer with an eagle-eye for errors. She read the drafts, helped to compile the Index and the Appendix, and checked the proofs. Many friends read the typescript and discussed the contents with me, among them Roger Jeal, Paul Medlicott, Peter O'Hagan, John Pick and David Warwick. I was always able to contact my colleagues in the International Association of Theatre Critics to gain their non-British views on what became a humiliating episode in our national life. My son, Jon, a systems analyst, gave me his professional advice on the Internet. The team at The Lutterworth Press, including my Euro-sceptic editor, Adrian Brink, and the design and content editor, Debora Nicosia, were helpful throughout and skilfully adjusted to the sliding time-scales.

Finally, I would like to thank someone, who will never read this book but was physically present while much of it was being written. Shortly after I received the contract, my wife, Sally Mays, was diagnosed with lung cancer from asbestos poisoning. She had only a few months to live. Her courage and spiritual strength acted as a constant reminder that, however serious the issues that surrounded Brexit might seem, they paled into insignificance beside the life-and-death struggles of our daily lives, everywhere.

John Elsom

Chapter One
Never Again

(i)

I was nine years old during the days of the Normandy invasion and can remember kneeling beside my bed, praying for the Allies to win. I used to watch the shadows of leaves, cast through the window and playing upon the sheet, and pretend that these were the shifting front lines of the opposing armies. Even as a child I knew what was at stake. In June 1944, we were accustomed to the disciplines of war: rationing, sirens and blackouts. I was always sent to bed before the BBC Nine O'Clock News but I could guess from the tone of the voices downstairs whether the news was good, bad or simply terrible. The BBC had gravitas. It was careful not to be alarmist or over-cheerful, and to keep its emotions in check at all times, for there could be no victory without sacrifice. The formal voice suppressed the anxiety.

But D-Day was different. We were on the front foot and not the back, to use a phrase from cricket, attacking not defending; but this push towards victory held many risks. We were throwing hundreds of thousands of men against a well-fortified coast across the Channel and nobody knew what would happen next. In Cheltenham, the garrison town to which my family were evacuated, wards in the hospital were cleared of all but emergency patients. That was how we knew that something was going to happen but 'Careless Talk Costs Lives', as the posters said, and so we kept quiet and said nothing, and waited for the BBC Nine O'Clock News.

This book is not intended to be about my personal memories but about the climate of opinion in Britain, our changing culture, that led to Brexit and the out-in-out relationship with our continental neighbours that upset what had seemed to be the world order in 2016. But memories do play a part. Within the mixture of motives and facts, legends and myths, that characterised the European Union (EU) Referendum in 2016, there were many echoes of World War II, and the time when Britain stood alone, and then not quite alone and, finally, with the help of the Americans, Canadians, Poles, Australians and divisions from what was still the British Empire, we managed to push back the Axis forces and won a glorious victory.

That is now the national narrative, celebrated in books, films and YouTube clips, and passed down from parent to child in what has become a collective memory. It is not exactly false or fake but censored here and there, simplified and turned into a ripping yarn. The facts stay the same but certain elements are missing, which prevent the well-documented history from sounding wholly truthful, all Brylcream and stiff upper lips. From my stock of childhood memories, however, I can still remember the ferocious uncertainty, expressed in the voices downstairs, the fear and over-determination, repeated twice a day at school and at bedtime, to believe that God was on our side and would eventually prevail.

This narrative is woven into the fabric of British culture, a distinctive feature, which we take for granted, but from a few miles away, across the English Channel, may seem one-sided and even complacent. That is what a national narrative is like. It offers a useful framework, part history, part legend, in which we can place who we are, where we come from and what our native qualities may be. But when we examine this structure closely, we can notice how fragile it is, how much guesswork went into its making and how under pressure, it can buckle and snap, leaving us with little sense of national identity at all. Where was the Battle of Stalingrad in the British narrative of how we won the war? Just outside the frame.

In his Preface to *A History of the English-speaking Peoples* (1956),[i] Sir Winston Churchill wrote that: 'For the second time in the present century, the British Empire and the United States have stood together, facing the perils of war on the largest scale known among men . . . and [we] have become more conscious of our common duty to the human race.' The special relationship was born, and handed down to Macmillan and Kennedy, Thatcher and Reagan, Blair and Bush, May and Trump. Although his vision was less than messianic and did not preclude 'the erection of other structures like United Europe', Churchill expressed his belief that the English-speaking peoples with the common 'language, law and processes by which we have come into being, already afforded a unique foundation for drawing together and portraying a concerted task', which was to create, although he did not exactly say so, the New World Order.

And so another thread was woven into the fabric, the 'English-speaking peoples', but General de Gaulle, isolated in his country retreat in France, might well have been irritated by the way in which Churchill with such becoming modesty sought the leadership of the Free World for the English-speaking peoples and won a Nobel Prize for doing so. In his *War Memoirs*, published in the same year, de Gaulle complained that during the war he was kept away from the top-level meetings between the US President, Franklin Delano Roosevelt, and Churchill, although he was the Commander-in-Chief of the Free French Forces and the head of the French Committee of National Liberation, the provisional French government-in-waiting. De Gaulle's resentment was not only personal, but felt as a snub to France itself, whose language, laws and culture were in danger of being side-lined after the war, although they too had influenced 'the destiny of the world'.

'Culture' is one of those awkward words which can be used to cover almost anything. In English, it can mean something broad and generic, like 'Chinese culture', or something rather narrow, to indicate 'the arts', which are supposed to be cultural, as opposed to mere entertainment, which is not. In Eastern Europe under Communism, the ministries of culture were the censors-in-chief as well as being responsible for the churches and appointments to bishoprics and sees, for which they as atheists were the state guardians.

In this book, I will be using the word culture in an equally all-embracing fashion to mean the way in which we as humans think – our habits of mind rather than the neurological functioning of the brain. I would like to be more precise and to demonstrate with the certainty of a phrenological chart that the right side of the brain controls the imagination, while the left organises reason and mathematics. But culture is not like that. It is acquired, rather than innate, and comes from many sources, some of which are derived from society at large, such as a national narrative, while others are very personal.

A culture may contain assumptions or myths that we take for granted, although we cannot prove that they are factually 'true', because they provide a useful way of understanding the world. But they can also be misleading, at odds with other myths and disruptive. We are often told, and have come to believe, that culture is at the heart of civilisation, and so it is, but it is also at the heart of wars, pogroms and genocides.

A culture is many-layered. It may change and evolve but never fully discards. I have past and present memories that influence the way in which I think, although some are very faint, like the echoes from a distant star, while others are close and shine daily, like the sun. I can remember most clearly those events that have been placed in some order, like a mental filing cabinet, which might be a narrative, a religious faith or even a language, for it is hard to think of something without having a name for it. Medieval authorities called them Memory Theatres. These ordering systems belong to our culture as well, and may break apart, or even explode, so that everything that we have trusted before is hurled into doubt and chaos, which may happen on a personal or a collective level. It can happen to whole nations.[ii]

Culture is the driving force behind commerce and industry. What is money but another language, which loses its value if we play around carelessly with it and gains in value if we respect its limits and what its symbols are supposed to represent? Nor have I mentioned the so-called 'cultural industries', which have often been cited as second only to 'financial services' as the largest earner of foreign currency to the metropolitan city of London. The 'creative industries' are something different, as I hope to explain, but both contribute to what we mean by culture. If it seems that I am loading too much into one hapless, two-syllable word, I must point out that whole sections of the IT industry are devoted to analysing our likes, dislikes and websites that we visit in order to provide algorithms of our behaviour and how we think – in short, our culture.

We allow them to do so. When a website such as Google asks our permission to allow cookies on to our laptops, so that it can follow our tastes and offer suggestions about other websites, few say 'No'; and it would be inconvenient if we did, because it would probably mean that each site would require a separate password. Some are tracking cookies, which provide an overall picture of the user's likes and dislikes, so that he or she can be targeted with posts and images that stimulate predictable reactions. In 2016, Facebook went further. It promised a news-and-information service, tailor-made to the views of their consumers, so that they only saw those news stories in which they were likely to be interested, a news-feed that was 'subjective, personal and unique'.

When this principle is applied to politics, the prospect of receiving news from only one point of view runs the risk of polarising our debates still further. The Internet becomes a better tool for demagogues than democrats, for do we really think for ourselves, if the pre-selection process is done for us? We may have more sources of information, a vast number, but do we still have our own consciences? I belong to a generation that remembers what it was like to live without the Internet, cookies or algorithms, when we took decisions in which the conscience of the individual was expected to play a leading part. This is not to suggest that Millennials do not have a conscience, but that when so much of the pre-selection process can be done in advance, it may seem less essential.

Sometimes this quirky and unpredictable phenomenon, for which there is still no biological explanation, changed, or so it seemed at the time, the course of history.

In 1945, to the shock of the world, the British in a general election voted out their inspirational war leader, Winston Churchill, at the height of his fame and elected instead his second-in-command in the wartime coalition, the Labour leader Clement Attlee, with a mandate for social change. It was not just a choice of political leaders or parties but about what kind of country we hoped that Britain would become. Did we share Churchill's vision for the English-speaking peoples? Were we reformers like William Beveridge, an economist and Liberal MP for Berwick-upon-Tweed, who lost his seat in the 1945 Election and had to be elevated to the House of Lords? Or were we like Willie Gallagher, the Communist MP for West Fife, who thought of democracy as a stage in the class struggle. Tensions ran high. The firebrand Labour MP, Aneurin Bevan, called all Tories 'vermin', while the Conservativc MP, Robert Boothby, called all Labour supporters 'scum'.

Nobody in my immediate family was killed in World War II, although a family friend, Bill Blenko, a rear gunner who stayed with us in Cheltenham, died in the Battle of Britain. World War I took a greater toll. My father's brother, Harry, was blown up in the trenches; another died from gas poisoning. My mother's eldest brother, Percy, whom she adored, was killed within days of the Armistice in 1918. To the end of her life, she would murmur, 'How Percy would have loved this!' when she listened to music.

From the broad ranks of human misery scattered across Europe by the two World Wars, ours was still a fortunate family. We knew that we were. We were evacuated from the Thames estuary to be out of bombing range from the continent, but my grandparents refused to move. When my grandfather died in 1943, we returned for his funeral, passing through a gutted London and I saw an aerial dog-fight. But we lived in the upper three floors of a Regency terraced house, 3 Pittville Lawn, with friends and refugees, in a household which varied from nine to fourteen people. It was always crowded but I can remember my mother, grey-faced, standing by a window as a van passed with a loudspeaker, asking for spare rooms for those bombed out of their homes after a raid on Birmingham. She was weeping, because she could not help them.

In times of war, the worst hardship is to have nothing useful to do. She worked part-time as a hospital nurse. My father set up a factory in a garage to make rubber gloves. They were ceaselessly active, ceaselessly touching wood or keeping their fingers crossed and, when the war was over, they prayed that the spirit of common purpose should not desert them in peacetime, so that, with everyone else, they could build a better future. Above all, nothing like this, no wars, no slavery, no genocide, should ever happen again. My father quoted from his favourite play, *King Lear*: 'Never, never, never, never, never'.

(ii)

The second referendum on whether to Leave or Remain within the European Union, was held on 23 June 2016. The result was made known at 04.40 on the following morning by David Dimbleby, the BBC's senior presenter of News and Current Affairs and the eldest son of Richard Dimbleby, the BBC's official war correspondent during the Second World War. 'The British people,' he declared, 'have spoken.'

The BBC's gravitas can seem somewhat misplaced. The British people had spoken several times before on this subject, over a period of nearly 70 years, through at least ten general elections, a previous referendum, debates in parliament, on the BBC and through countless opinion polls. It remains to be seen whether the EU Referendum in 2016 was a 'momentous decision', as the Daily Mail, the voice of Middle England, said it was, or another stage in the often painful debate about our national future that the people of Britain had conducted since the end of the war. It may have been momentous but was it a decision?

The country was still deeply divided. The turnout was relatively high, 72.21 per cent, of which 51.89 per cent voted to Leave, 48.11 per cent to Remain. In a previous referendum on whether to remain within the European Economic Community (as it then was) was held on 5 June 1975, the turnout had been 64 per cent of the electorate, of which 67 per cent had voted to Remain, which suggested that, when seen as a proportion of the whole, opinion had changed little over 45 years. It remained obdurately undecided. Most European referendums require a larger majority to be considered constitutionally binding, for a narrower one risks civil disorder, but Britain has a 'first-past-the-post' tradition in politics. This is said to produce clearer results and a more decisive leadership, but not, as it happened, in this case.

Nobody quite knew what leaving the EU might mean. Did it mean leaving all of its institutions, whether they were useful or not, or only some? Did it mean breaking all trade agreements, or only some and, if so, what would replace them? Could we disentangle EU laws from British ones without causing a massive disruption and, if so, whose courts would decide over what? 'Brexit means Brexit', as the Prime Minister Theresa May kept repeating, but was that all it meant? We may have voted to take back control but control over what? Were we gaining an ounce of sovereignty but losing a ton of influence?

Over the years, very similar arguments and counter arguments have been employed, although the Cold War came and went, men landed on the moon and confidential state secrets were sprinkled across the Web. In my lifetime, there have been revolutionary changes in power and knowledge, exceeding those of any other generation in history: in nuclear physics, space exploration, climatology, genetic engineering and artificial intelligence. 'It has become appallingly obvious,' said Albert Einstein, 'that our technology has exceeded our humanity.' He may be proved right. He often has been. Nonetheless, humanity has precariously kept pace, up to a point, and managed to hold in check the forces that we have unleashed.

The European Union is one of several institutions, admittedly imperfect, designed to cope with the challenges that we have faced or lie ahead. The answers may seem to be technical, just a matter of trade deals and common law, but the real problems lie in our habits of mind, our cultures. It is very difficult to change the ways in which we think. I spent years trying to learn French at school but I still think in English and translate laboriously, word by word, with dubious results. Language is one obstacle. There are others. On my mobile, I can switch from one music station to another. I find the ones I want quickly, instant recognition: BBC Radio 3 and Classic FM offer mainly a classical European repertoire, tending to stay within the parameters of a tradition that can be traced back for centuries; BBC Radio 1 covers contemporary pop music; while BBC Radio 6 offers a compilation of 'world' music.

Different genres of music can exist side by side, appealing to their audiences, without necessarily trespassing elsewhere. There are similar differences in literature, films, fashion and marketing, and in the lifestyles that they influence and reflect. These cannot be so easily contained. Politicians are sometimes thought to be in charge of their cultures. They may have been appointed to some Ministry of Culture and hand out money to the arts, like the patrons of the past. But political leaders are more likely to be the victims of their culture rather than its benefactors. Jean Monnet, the founding father of the Common Market, admitted late in his life that if he could have started the project again, he would have begun with 'culture'. If so, he would almost certainly have failed.

The real significance of the 2016 Referendum has yet to be appreciated. It was not so much that the British agreed to leave the EU, but that they could not make up their minds. The arguments had become circular, the terms less precise, the tempers frayed, the statistics more partisan, the slogans more misleading, the funding more secretive, the parties divided, the threats alarming and the government at odds with itself. Even our special friends on the Continent protested, like the Spice Girls, 'What do they want, do they really, really want?'

A national culture should help us to sort out the differences. There are games we play and courteous ways of agreeing to differ. There used to be a classical tradition, Rhetoric,[iii] which offered instruction on how this could be done and included logic, a respect for the opponent, a moderation of language, and how to appeal in a final summary to the mind and the heart. But the rules of engagement failed. The problem may be in how our political culture has evolved: two main parties, sworn enemies, which fight during the rutting season for the chance of being in government. These tests of strength may not be appropriate for the challenges ahead. The parties may still be divided or unable to command a majority within the country.

Why should this choice of staying in or leaving the EU have been so controversial, more so than, say, arming ourselves with weapons of mass destruction? The aim of this book is to find out. This could prove, of course, an impossible task. Our national culture differs from county to county, village to village, person to person. It is an amalgam of many mini-cultures. Even Shakespeare, whom many would agree is a personification of our national culture, has so many interpreters that we may be tempted to ask: 'Which Shakespeare? Whose Shakespeare?' And yet Shakespeare should be an easy hook on which to hang national identity, when compared with all the others, such as British values, democracy and way of life. Faced by the contradictions, it is tempting to throw in the towel, admit defeat and protest that there is no such thing as a national culture, except as a rhetorical device. There are tests for those who seek to be British citizens. I would probably fail, although I was born in Britain of British parents.

Nonetheless, from a distance, by squinting to gain a better impression of the whole, we might be able to recognise that there are some habits of mind that characterise Britishness that may not be wholly exclusive but bind together a large proportion of those of us who claim to be British. We may not all regret the loss of Empire but some are still in mourning. Anglican Christianity might be another example, and cricket, and the quaint belief that there must be two sides to every question, for and against, and only two. I share many of them and sometimes have to shake myself vigorously, like a dog after a swim, to get rid of them. They always return, even when I am trying to be cosmopolitan, and I reluctantly conclude that, despite my efforts, I am not as internationally-minded as I would like to be, but rather a little Englander at heart, who lets the cat out at night, the fierce and predatory cat, the would-be British lion.

One such habit is the way in which we British tend to reason inductively, from the example to the principle, bottom-up, rather than deductively, from the principle to the example, which is the more usual approach across the Channel. Essays in French and British schools are constructed along similarly different lines. The British, it has been said, cannot see the wood for the trees and the French, the trees for the wood. While these habits should never be allowed to colour the whole picture, they help to explain why France requires a written constitution, and has had several, while Britain jogs along without one.

In the most comprehensive parliamentary debate on whether Britain should enter what was then the European Economic Community (EEC), held over six days in October 1971, the terms of entry were known and negotiations conducted, by a Heath-led Conservative government. The Commons had to decide whether the terms were acceptable. Every Member was aware that this was an historic occasion. The debates ran on well into the early hours of the morning and featured some of the best speakers of the day. There was no lack of research. Fake facts were instantly spotted. The subject cut across party lines, to the extent that it seemed strange that we should have party politics at all, and the government offered a 'free' (non-whipped) vote to its supporters, although the Labour opposition did not.

But there were blind spots, very British, or so a continental observer might complain, not a mention of Hegel! If a British opponent of the EU asked scornfully, 'What right has an eighteenth-century German intellectual to interfere in a decision about the future of the UK?', the thickly accented foreigner might retort, 'As much right as your eighteenth-century Scot, Adam Smith, has in pontificating about free trade!' Georg Wilhelm Friedrich Hegel (1770-1831) was a philosopher, whose views are still much better known in France and Germany than Britain. His explanation as to how societies evolve through a process of 'thesis, antithesis and synthesis', a 'dialectic', coloured their discussions about the future of Europe. But his voice was rarely heard in parliament or the Oxbridge debating societies. As a result, the debate in Britain might have seemed too earthbound from a mere thirty miles away, too much concerned with the details of trade, too little with the expression of a European vision.

On this occasion, the MPs decided to support the government's decision that the UK should apply to join the EEC by a majority of 356 votes to 244, which was endorsed in the House of Lords by an even more substantial majority, and confirmed four years later in a national referendum, promised and delivered by an incoming Labour government, a 'momentous decision', according to the press. But the opposition did not go away. Public opinion has remained more or less evenly divided and, although the whole world was changing around our shores, the nation still continued to worry and fret about whether we should join the European club, or keep away from it, into our current state of near paralysis.

(iii)

In July 1945, before the war was over in the Far East, the Labour Party forced a general election by withdrawing from the national government. It was a gamble. Labour was following the example of the Bolsheviks in Russia, who got rid of their government in 1917, during the final months of World War I. These were exceptional times. The wartime administrations were tired. The men conscripted into the forces knew the disciplines of war. Many wanted the whole fabric of society to change and were ready to make sacrifices to make sure that this would happen. There was a revolutionary narrative that identified the villains of the past and offered a road map, *The Communist Manifesto*, drafted in 1847 and first published in 1848. The Labour Party reprinted it in 1947 to celebrate its centenary. In its preface, Harold Laski pointed out that Marx and Engels studied the lessons of class warfare in Victorian England.

'Let Us Face the Future', the Labour manifesto, began with a bold declaration. The people had won the war; now they must win the peace. It blamed the unemployment and slump that followed World War I on 'hard-faced men' who 'controlled the banks, the mines, the big industries and largely the press and the cinema' and profited from war itself. War was capitalism's bloodthirsty expression. Labour would bring into public ownership the commanding heights of British industry – coal, steel and transport – and promised a 'radical solution for the crippling problems of land acquisition', which stopped short of full nationalisation. It was almost as revolutionary as the Bolshevik manifesto of 1917 but with one important qualification. It was meant 'for the Consideration of the Nation'. Labour was seeking a democratic mandate and the nation responded with an unprecedented swing of 12.5 per cent in its favour. Labour was elected to its first majority government in British history.

The appeal of this trenchant document can best be understood by remembering with what resolution people like my parents were determined that nothing like World War II should happen again. It was not so hard-line that it wanted to get rid of all private ownership. It promised not to interfere with 'many smaller businesses, which can be left to go on with their useful work', but 'laggards and obstructionists must be led or directed into better ways', a powerful warning shot across the bows of private industry. Nonetheless, the 'Labour Party stood for freedom', for capitalism was the enemy of freedom, although there were 'certain kinds of freedom that [it] would not tolerate', such as the 'freedom to pay poor wages and push up prices for selfish profit'.

'Mr. Churchill's Declaration of Policy to the Electors', the Conservative manifesto, chose a different theme. 'This is the time for freeing energies, not stifling them. Britain's greatness has been built on character and daring, not docility to a State machine. At all costs, we must preserve that spirit of independence.' Playing to his perceived strengths, Churchill warned that 'the conduct of foreign affairs [should not be passed] into untried hands'. Britain had 'gained the confidence of smaller nations, because, although our power has been formidable, we have tried to use it with restraint and for high purpose'.

This trustworthiness was needed in the international arena to 'prevent future wars of aggression' and his government would act in the 'closest possible concert with all parts of the British Commonwealth and Empire'. He praised the newly constituted United Nations and 'our prevailing hope is that the foundations will be laid on the indissoluble agreement of Great Britain, the United States and Soviet Russia'. He promised that there would be 'freer movement of men and women within the Empire' with additional measures to foster Imperial trade. India should be granted dominion status, further efforts would be made to educate the colonies and encourage them to achieve self-government within a reformed Commonwealth and Empire, whose Imperial pink still coloured a third of our school atlas.

Over the manifestos hung unanswered questions. In 1945, Britain had the largest national debt in its history, standing at 250 per cent of its gross domestic product (GDP). While this might be reduced in time, both parties were proposing plans for post-war reconstruction that required a great deal of extra money. Would the owners of the industries that Labour intended to nationalise be compensated – and by how much? Who would pay for the modernisation of the factories, the mass building programme and the education of the colonies? Throughout the Empire, there were rebel groups prepared to govern themselves without the help of a British education. Could Britain borrow more money to fund its colonial wars? 'All this,' as Churchill admitted, 'could not go on.'

Within the span of one lifetime, Britain had ceased to be the wealthiest nation in the world and become one in debt to its creditors in the US and the White Commonwealth. Never before had we been so reliant upon the cultural ties of the English-speaking peoples.

Both parties spoke of the Soviet Union as a friendly ally, and so during the war it was, but the crimes that had been committed under Stalinism were well known, the show trials and massacres of the *kulaks*, small-time, farm-owning gentry. Although the scale of these atrocities may not have been fully understood, there were many Russian refugees in Britain who lived to tell their tales: Arthur Koestler's allegory of Stalinist oppression, *Darkness at Noon*, was published in 1940, when he was under British detention as a potential alien spy. Some left-wingers might dismiss their testimonies as anti-Soviet propaganda or as stages in the modernisation of the Soviet Union but should anyone else? Within months of the election, Churchill was warning American audiences of an 'Iron Curtain' descending across Europe. His hope for an 'indissoluble agreement' lasted for less than a year.

In neither manifesto was much attention paid to the future of Western Europe and, in retrospect, this seems the oddest omission of them all. Our troops were stationed there in large numbers and we had fought two world wars to defend one part of Europe from another. In February 1945, Churchill, Roosevelt and Stalin had sat down together in Yalta in the Crimea, to split the continent up into spheres of influence with the declared aim of returning all its nations to self-governing independence. Britain, the United States and the Soviet Union formed the triumvirate of the principal occupying forces in Europe, the guarantors of its peace and security. But for the purpose of fighting an election at home, Yalta was not mentioned and all that amounted to a policy for Europe was that Germany should not be allowed to re-arm.

It was a kind of middle-distance blindness. Labour was preoccupied with how to get rid of the 'hard-faced' bosses, while the Conservatives were concerned with what would happen to the Empire. Across the Channel, there were historic cities that had been damaged and gutted as thoroughly as London, even more so. There were twelve million refugees, and more were expected, and there were all kinds of shortages, from coffee beans to electricity, including the threat of outright famine. Only the smaller Liberal Party argued that 'the tasks of peace, like those of war, are too vast to accomplish alone. Much patience and self-control will be called for in harmonising various national interests.' In particular, it warned that the 'threat of famine in Europe, and our own reduced capacity to pay for imports, mean that more food must be produced at home', our own version of a Common Agricultural Policy.

Between July and November 1945, Britain lost the chance to play a leadership role in Europe. It was in a prime position to do so. In September 1946, speaking in Zurich, Churchill called for a United States of Europe and expressed the hope that France and Germany should settle their ancient differences. Their aim should be to create a new grouping of nations that would uphold the high standards of their two civilisations. He did not suggest that Britain should be part of it. Decades later, this speech was cited by both sides in the EU Referendum to suggest that Churchill was in favour (or not) of a more integrated Europe in which Britain would (or not) take part; but he seems to have stood in front of an open door and hesitated to go in.

The 1945 General Election was a disaster for the Liberals, which, until the end of World War I, had been one of the two major parties of government. It was reduced to twelve MPs, starting the spell of 'born-loser-man-ship' that continues today. It comes as a surprise to many Liberals to be told that they belong to an *élite* that ruled for decades before the forces of Thatcher, Farage and Trump managed to topple them. To which Liberal Party were they referring?

And yet there is a grain of truth to this perception. Two committed Liberals, John Maynard Keynes and William Beveridge, influenced the course of post-war reconstruction as much as any other two political leaders from any other party. Both were civil servants, economists and social reformers. Both were elevated to the peerage, both were academics, both went to public school and Oxbridge, and neither was a business man: the 'liberal elite' personified. Since neither could work through a governing party of his own persuasion, each sought to influence one or other of the two main parties.

The results were an amalgam of their Liberal views and those of the host party, which might be, at different times, Conservative, Labour or an informal three-party alliance. Their influence transformed the host parties as well. Conservatives developed a Keynesian wing, which accepted state intervention in the market, while Labour became embroiled in a rivalry between those who favoured outright nationalisation and those who sought a more moderate intervention along Keynesian lines. What began as small cracks in the narratives of the two main parties developed into long-lasting ideological fault lines.

In the interwar years, Keynes was a civil servant who took part in the conference at Versailles, where the peace treaty with Germany was signed. But he did not approve of the 'astronomically high' terms of reparation that his superiors at the Treasury had negotiated. He protested that:

> the policy of reducing Germany to servitude for a whole generation, of degrading the lives of millions of human beings, and of depriving a whole nation of happiness should be abhorrent and detestable . . . even if it were possible, even if it enriched ourselves, even if it did not sow the seeds of decay of the whole civilized life of Europe.[iv]

Within a few years, the effects would be seen in the rise of Hitler's National Socialist Party.

In 1933, at the height of the Depression, Keynes published *The Means to Prosperity*, which went against orthodoxy by proposing that a government that was struggling to make ends meet was entitled to borrow more money to kick-start a sluggish economy. Once the country was back on the road to prosperity, the borrowed money should be repaid but he saw no value in austerity for its own sake. In 1936, he published his *General Theory of Unemployment, Interest and Money*, which would become a standard textbook, outweighing, in terms of Western political influence, *Das Kapital.*

He met Roosevelt, influenced the New Deal, and helped to negotiate the agreements which led to the establishment of the World Bank and the International Monetary Fund. He died in 1946 but Keynesian economics lay behind the Marshall Plan for Europe and, in 1999, *Time* magazine saluted him as one of the most important people of the twentieth century, because he had 'saved capitalism'. He was more modest about his role in history but hoped that he had contributed towards his true goal – 'the brotherhood of man'.

For many, his theories were counter-intuitive. Why should the victorious nations rebuild the economies of those that they had defeated? Was not that a reward for aggression? Was any government entitled to issue bonds or print money to tackle public works that could be undertaken in time by the private sector? Keynes' brief retort was that in time we are all dead. His detractors pointed out, however, that governments like individuals can borrow beyond their means to repay. The ghost of Keynes the Improvident would come to haunt the Western corridors of power for many years to come. Nevertheless he offered a halfway house between the 'command' and the 'free market' economies. Without him, Britain would not have enjoyed full employment in the 1950s or West Germany its *Wirtschaftswunder*, its economic miracle.

His influence spread in many directions. Keynes was married to a ballet dancer and, as a friend of the Bloomsbury literary circle, he pioneered the establishment of the Arts Council of Great Britain. He provided the theoretical basis for the economics of the programmes of welfare and social reform, for which his colleague, William Beveridge, became the leading authority. In 1942, Beveridge published his report, *Social Insurance and Allied Services,* which provided the blueprint for the Welfare State, including the National Health Service that the post-war Labour government brought into being. In 1944, he published *Full Employment in a Free Society*, promoting Labour's goal of fair shares for all without threatening wholesale nationalisation. It provided what became known as the Third Way.

Under those circumstances, why did the Liberals come out of the 1945 Election so badly and go on to lose every election since? The answer may lie in the fact that it had few significant patrons, neither from business nor the trade unions. It could, however, turn this weakness to its advantage by claiming neutrality in the class war. In 1945, its manifesto was modest, a mere six pages, with twenty bullet points. Where the other parties made bold statements, the Liberal Party offered proposals for reform, nationalisation where appropriate, equality for women *within the workplace*, environmental protection, political harmony within Europe and site-value rating, all the worthy but mind-numbing topics that became the despair of its party conferences. All that can be said of its manifesto was that it tried to offer real solutions to real problems, but where were the fanfares for Liberalism? Where were the grand narratives?

Democratic politics is, at best, one third substance, two thirds show business. Parties need colour, lights and music: they need good stories. Labour summoned up the history of the working-class movement for its benefit, from the Levellers to the Jarrow Crusade in 1936. Conservatives evoked the empire builders, the traders and missionaries whose daring allowed Britain to rule the High Seas and brought Christian values to the darkest parts of Africa. For the purposes of winning an election, it did not matter if their narratives were accurate or not, one-sided or not, useful or not.

Perhaps the most striking feature of the 1945 manifestos is how little the narratives of the three political parties have changed. Labour still sees itself as the party of the working classes, even though the pits have closed, the factories are automated and Fordism has become post-Fordism. Conservatives still see the nanny state as the enemy of freedom, praise the buccaneering entrepreneur and, in the absence of an empire, talk of the Anglosphere. Liberals still want to save the individual from the 'tyranny of the masses' and talk about the 'community' as if it were a synonym for humanity. They sing from ancient hymn sheets.

For professional politicians, the mood music matters. At the time of the 1945 election, the tunes were cheerful. God, having granted victory to the English-speaking peoples, placed upon them the duty to lead mankind towards a world without aggression. International disputes could be settled peacefully in the new United Nations building in New York, generously provided by the US government. By 1948, the circumstances had changed. In Britain, the flush of victory had faded, the Iron Curtain had descended over Europe and we were embroiled in another existential crisis. The Labour government was divided between its Keynesian and Marxist wings and the rest of the country wanted to know when butter rationing would end.

Slowly, the strains of victory became nostalgic, then merely repetitive but we could not get the tunes out of our head. The words might be forgotten, the musicians might have packed up their instruments and adjourned to the pub, but the melodies lingered on. Whenever a future British government faced a crisis, it summoned up the Dunkirk spirit. It defended the White Cliffs of Dover by evoking the Spirit of the Blitz. The BBC has replayed episodes of *Dad's Army*, Nigel Farage's favourite programme, for more than five decades.

When, during the 2016 EU Referendum, more than 70 years later, a dock worker was asked in a BBC interview why he intended to vote for Leave, he replied, 'Why should Brussels tell us what to do? We won the war, didn't we?'.

***

Chapter Two
The Dream of M. Monnet

(i)

It was a privilege to live in England after the war and to grow up at the heart of the British Empire. So I was told as a child and so, as an adult, I believe to be true. The times were hard: rationing, restrictions, austerity. None of us lived as we wanted to live but there was a spirit of renewal, which our leaders encouraged. The troops were everywhere but they were Allied troops. We saw the newsreels, heard Richard Dimbleby's description of the walking corpses in Belsen and knew what suffering we had been spared. The structure of our society was not broken. We had not been occupied. We respected authority. The heroes of our films were kindly father figures, like Robert Donat or Jack Hawkins. They knew what was best for us. The discipline at my school was Roman. We stood to attention when the teachers came in. We called out 'Adsum' at roll call.

It was hard for us to imagine what it must have been like to live in occupied Europe, the fear and the loathing. It was even more difficult to guess at the state of mind of those who had been taught that they were saving the world, and marched to popular anthems, only to discover that they had been fooled. Their battered eagles piled up in alleyways. Somewhere in that pile of rubbish was a tattered Union Jack. How did it get there?

In France, the situation was complicated. The north and west had been occupied and bore the brunt of the fighting, but the south was not so badly affected. It had lasted the war under the Vichy regime, which cooperated with the Nazis. But there was a climate of suspicion in the south, which outweighed the material benefits, for it was hard to know who might be an informer. This led to reprisals, and a sense of alienation, which persisted long into the peace.

In 1944, de Gaulle returned from exile in London to weed out the collaborators and few from the Vichy regime survived. His next step was to hold a constitutional conference, which produced a new constitution for the

Fourth Republic. It separated the presidency, representing the French nation, from the executive, which was in the hands of the President of the Council, the Prime Minister, who was given the authority to form the government. The electoral system embraced proportional representation (PR) to elect the National Assembly, which included directly elected representatives of the French colonies in Indo-China, the Caribbean, Algeria and elsewhere, and it gave the smaller left- or right-of-centre parties the opportunity to take part in what turned out to be short-lived coalition governments.

The new constitution soon came under attack from the larger parties, the Gaullists and the Communists. De Gaulle wanted a stronger presidency and blamed the 'party system'. 'How can you govern a country,' he said, 'which has 246 varieties of cheese?' The Communists were thought to receive their instructions from Moscow. After the war, however, the French public turned its back on 'command-and-control' politics and endorsed the new constitution in a referendum with a 53 per cent majority, although many voters (31 per cent) abstained. De Gaulle retired to the country and waited for his recall.

In Britain, the Fourth Republic became an object of fun, because of its rapid changes of government, 21 in twelve years. Some critics, including the teachers at my school, went further by suggesting that there was something about the French character that was inclined to argue too much, unlike the British, who had a better team spirit. It was thought to be a national trait. In post-war Britain, Paris was renowned as an intellectual centre for artists and those sorts of people, but, for the purposes of running a country, not to mention an Empire, British pragmatism (bottom up) was considered to be more effective than the theories (top-down) of those who dreamt away at the *École normale supérieure* (ENS), the *élite* academy of scientists and philosophers, which embodied the strengths of French culture.

In fact, the coalition governments of the Fourth Republic had a more impressive record. Against a background of strikes and demonstrations, they seized the opportunity, as we did in Britain, to establish a new system for social security, including a national health service. With the help of financial support from America through the Marshall Plan, they re-built the country's industrial infrastructure, and the economy grew at a steady pace. But its most ambitious proposal, promoted by the Christian Democrat leader, Robert Schuman, concerned the 'supranational' administration of the Ruhr valley.

The river Ruhr is a tributary of the Rhine, in the heart of the Rhineland, and its valley was considered to be of supreme economic importance. It spanned a region rich in coal, the primary resource of the industrial age, and was the home of the steel industries. It was of similar value to

German and French industrial productivity as the coalfields in South Wales were to the British. The valley's dams had been the target of the British Dambusters' raid of May 1943 with its bouncing bombs; and its sprawling towns, such as Essen and Dortmund, contained the munitions factories of the Third Reich. The nation that controlled the Ruhr valley was in the position to provide the industrial muscle to rebuild and mastermind the post-war peace.

It was also a region of historic importance. The Ruhr Valley was part of Germany, but since the end of World War I, it was deemed, under the Treaty of Versailles, to be a de-militarised zone. No German troops or munitions factories were allowed. In 1936, the Treaty was broken, when the Rhineland was invaded and reclaimed by Hitler's *Wehrmacht*. France appealed to Britain for support, but the British government was reluctant to intervene, due to its policy of appeasement. The Rhineland became the contaminated seedbed for World War II.

Schuman's family came from another disputed region. His father was born into French-speaking Alsace-Lorraine, but became a German citizen, when the region was seized by Germany as the result of the Franco-Prussian war of 1870-71. His mother was born in Luxembourg, where Robert received his early education, but he went on to study law, economics, political philosophy and theology from universities in Metz, Berlin, Bonn and Strasbourg, until, garnered with high degrees, he became a French citizen in 1919. He was elected as a *député* to the National Assembly, a position that he held (except during the war) until 1958. He served two terms as the French Prime Minister, 1947-48, and he was the foreign minister and finance minister in coalition governments other than his own.

His first task, as he saw it, was to secure a lasting peace in Europe by making 'war not only unthinkable but materially impossible' by pooling Franco-German production of coal and steel under a common High Authority 'within the framework of an organisation open to the participation of other countries of Europe'. This was an extraordinary gesture of faith, for France would have to relinquish her claim on the Ruhr valley and place it in the hands of a 'supranational body' that had yet to be invented. Such a proposal could only have been made in the late 1940s, when the future of Europe was still so insecure and memories of Nazi occupation so vivid. It needed the persuasive voice of someone like Schuman, who knew all the anthems by heart, not just the tunes, but the words, the allusions that lay behind the words and all the competing national narratives.

Perhaps Schuman was also being carried along by the tide of history, for there were others who were searching for peace and stability in continental Europe along similar lines. Jean Monnet, an economist and diplomat during the war, put forward an alternative plan for the Ruhr valley, which would retain political power in the hands of France, while granting easier access for German manufacturers. In Germany, the former mayor of Cologne, Konrad Adenauer, was another potential ally. He was seeking the agreement of the Allied forces in Europe to establish a Federal Republic of Germany, West Germany, democratically elected, as opposed to the puppet regime, East Germany, dominated by Moscow. Adenauer was a staunch Catholic, like Schuman, and his family also came from the Rhineland. The containment of Communism was in their eyes part of a wider struggle against state-sponsored atheism.

On the other side of the Atlantic, a former American diplomat in Moscow, George Kennan, was advising Roosevelt's successor as the President of the United States, Harry S. Truman, of the threats from Stalinist Russia. He urged that America should contain Soviet expansion by offering its European allies economic and moral support, as well as providing a military presence. His views influenced the European Recovery Programme, the Marshall Plan, which came into being in April 1948. During the next four years, the United States gave $12 billion in grants and loans to Western Europe. France was the second largest recipient ($2,296 million) after the United Kingdom ($3,297 million), but this aid did not come without strings. It required the relaxation of trade barriers, modernisation, union membership and the recognition of human rights, including *habeas corpus*, the full Keynesian package, combining investment, reconstruction and social reform. But the aid could not be spent on colonial wars.

While Kennan was persuading politicians in Washington to support the Marshall Plan, Schuman was putting forward the idea of a European Assembly to provide the administrative structure for the Ruhr valley, to settle any commercial or industrial disputes and to encourage common European practice in such matters as union representation. But his aspirations went further. His wider aim was to bring together those European countries that claimed to be democracies and subscribed to common principles of human rights into one body that could guarantee peace in Europe, a common market.

This plan excluded Spain and Portugal, which were still fascist dictatorships, and the Soviet satellite states, but could have included the United Kingdom, where the first statutes for a Council of Europe were signed at St James's Palace in London on 5 May 1949. But the Labour government under Attlee decided not to become a member. Britain was self-sufficient in coal and steel, and saw no reason why it should sacrifice part of its sovereignty for a cause from which it derived no material benefit. In a two-day debate about Europe, the then Chancellor of the

Exchequer, Sir Stafford Cripps, warned that we would be taking a 'grave risk with the economy' if we went in; but, in his maiden speech, the new Member for Bexley, Edward Heath, warned the House that we would be taking an even graver risk if we stayed out. There are echoes of this debate in the Ealing film comedy, *Passport to Pimlico* (1949), which shows Britain groaning under socialist restrictions and Burgundy revelling in wine and enterprise.

Many British politicians thought that the Council of Europe would become another talking shop, useful for sorting out the Ruhr, but of no wider significance. But Schuman had other ambitions. Speaking in Strasbourg, the newly designated capital for the Council of Europe, within ten days of the signing ceremony, he expressed his vision:

> We are carrying out a great experiment, the fulfilment of the same recurrent dream that for ten centuries has revisited the peoples of Europe: creating between them an organisation putting an end to war and guaranteeing an eternal peace. The Roman Church of the Middle Ages failed finally in its attempts that were inspired by humane and human preoccupations . . . Audacious minds, such as Dante, Erasmus, Abbé de St-Pierre, Rousseau, Kant and Proudhon, had created in the abstract the framework for systems that were both ingenious and generous. The title of one of these systems became the synonym of all that is impractical: Utopia, itself a work of genius, written by Thomas More, the Chancellor of Henry VIII, King of England.

Schuman was proposing a civilisation of semi-independent nations, which would pool some of their differences in the interests of peace and security and which would express what he called 'the European spirit' and the 'European cultural family'. His reference to Thomas More, a Catholic saint, served the double-purpose of bringing England into the debate and quietly reminding his listeners of the folly, as he believed, of the Reformation: 'Our century has witnessed the catastrophes caused by the unending clash of nationalities and nationalisms, [and we] must now attempt and succeed in reconciling nations in a supranational association.'

How many of Winston Churchill's 'English-speaking Peoples' would understand what Schuman meant by the 'European spirit' and the 'European cultural family'? Would they even have recognised all the names on his list? Churchill and Schuman both looked back to the past to find a model for the future, but the British Empire was not the Holy Roman Empire – nor was it as badly destroyed as the other European empires,

German, French, Dutch and Belgian. It could be patched up, revived, turned into a Commonwealth, which, with the help of the English-speaking peoples, might form the basis of a new world order.

It is tempting to speculate about who might have been on a list of 'audacious minds', if it had been devised by Churchill instead – fewer clerics, no doubt, and more men of action. Would Cecil Rhodes have been among them? For decades, many in Britain treated Schuman's European project as another trade deal, handicapped by the do-gooding of bureaucrats. But there were those on the continent who believed that Britain was nothing more than a nation of shopkeepers, who would do deals with the devil, if it brought them a dishonest buck. Neither view, it must be admitted, was wholly wrong.

Schuman's challenge was how to create a European civilisation from the fragments of old empires; but ours, we pragmatic British, was that we saw no need to do so.

(ii)

My father left school at the age of fourteen at the outbreak of World War I. During the post-war slump, he cycled to London twice a week from Southend to study electrical engineering at night school. After his exams, he joined Callenders' Cables, a pioneering construction company, founded in the 1880s to manufacture and install electricity cables. It expanded its trade across the world, 'lighting up', or so it claimed, 'the Empire'. During World War II, it was responsible for PLUTO, the pipeline under the ocean. Before then, in the 1930s, my father left to join a new company, Associated Contracts (AssoContra), whose intention was to harmonise the technical specifications of cable manufacturers in Europe and to prevent them from being undercut by cheaper cables from Japan.

AssoContra was a cartel, or had the makings of a cartel, against which the Labour Party railed, because it would have been a monopoly in private hands. The Conservatives disapproved of it in theory as well, because it restricted competition, but, in practice, they condoned it, because it was doing a useful job and nobody else could do it as well, not even with the help of top civil servants. After the war, AssoContra was on the front line for the reconstruction of Europe, for there could be no building programmes, no factory modernisation, no transport systems without restoring power and light to the continent, which meant harmonising the business models of the cable companies.

My father's job as Assistant General Secretary was to organise meetings that took place in London or on the Continent in opulent hotels, where the directors of cable companies from nations that had recently been at war could get to know each other again. He had never been to university and was keen 'not to let the side down' in front of all these Continental intellectuals and businessmen. He only spoke English and relied upon the AssoContra secretaries to translate German, Italian and French for him; but he took a phrase book to bed at night and, with my mother, tried to learn a new expression every day. In school holidays, the family sometimes went with him, which was why I first went to France, in the years just after the war, when the bread was black and the coffee made from roasted acorns.

We entered France in my father's 1936 Rover, black, with running boards and a spare wheel screwed to its boot, spent half a day passing through customs at Boulogne, changing our travellers' cheques and calculating the exchange rates, my schoolboy task. We followed our RAC route that led through the ruined towns and villages of Normandy down to the less materially damaged regions of the South. We drove at no more than 50 kilometres an hour with stops for picnics and to let the car cool down. It took four days to reach the Mediterranean, 'pretty good going', according to my father, where we stayed at a *pension*, while he went off to AssoContra meetings in a hotel in Nice. This gave me the chance to study my grammar and tiptoe a little deeper into the waters of French culture.

Life begins by accident. I picked up a copy of Albert Camus' *L'Étranger*, discarded in a hotel lounge, and found the language easy to read, plain and matter-of-fact, but it drew me into a world that seemed so dark and uncompromising that I wondered whether I should be reading it all. The first sentence begins, '*Aujourd'hui, Maman est morte*' ('Today, my mother died'), which led me to expect that there should follow an expression of sadness, a memory perhaps, a touch of mourning. But for the narrator, Meursault, there were no such pieties. Her death was an incident like any other. The matter-of-fact tone was a mark of his character. He felt nothing, cared for little and casually shot an Arab stranger because the sun got in his eyes. When he was arrested and faced the guillotine, he had no defence. He lived in a world without any structure, values or beliefs. It was, in Camus' word, Absurd.

As a creature of the dystopian universe that was perhaps to come, Meursault soon crossed the Channel. *L'Étranger* was published in Stuart Gilbert's translation in 1946 and influenced such British writers as Colin Wilson (*The Outsider*, 1956) and Anthony Burgess (*A Clockwork Orange*, 1962). Meursault was a French prototype of what became in the 1960s the British anti-hero, such as Bill Naughton's *Alfie*, casual, cool, without a conscience. But in these Anglo-Saxon versions there was a drift towards moralising that was missing in Camus. In Britain, we asked such bottom-up questions as, 'What is wrong with the youth of today?' instead of confronting the riddles of philosophy that seemed to preoccupy the French. The key word is 'seemed', for behind a word like 'Absurd' lay the ingrained experiences of helplessness, colonialism and occupation.

Camus was brought up in the Belcourt district of Algiers, the capital of Algeria, then a French colony. His father, a farm worker, was killed in World War I and his mother worked as a cleaner to support the two of them. He studied his way through the French academic system and entered the University of Algiers to read philosophy, gaining his *Diplôme d'études supérieures* in 1936. He became known as a left-wing activist, a writer and man of the theatre, at a provincial level, until the typescript of *L'Étranger* fell into the hands of a rising Parisian *philosophe*, Jean-Paul Sartre, eight years his senior, who wrote an essay, '*Explication de* L'Étranger', which appeared on the eve of the novel's publication. For a decade, their names were associated, two leading French-speaking intellectuals, considered to be existentialists, until their disagreement in 1952, which revealed more than a row between friends. It was like the parting of the ways between the hard, the soft and the liberal Left.

Unlike Camus, Sartre came from a socially and financially privileged background. His mother was the cousin of Albert Schweitzer, the Nobel Prize winner. His father died when he was young and he was brought up in the household of his grandfather, Charles Schweitzer. He was admitted to the *École normale supérieure* in the 1920s, becoming a *normalien*, a member of the French intellectual *élite*. Whereas Camus knew what it was like to scavenge for a crust of bread, Sartre, despite his internment during the war, did not. While one might seem to be more grounded in bitter experience than the other, both were left-wing activists, whose views were deeply stained by the rise of fascism in the 1930s and the civil war in Algeria during the post-war years. Both asked the same question: 'What would a class-less society look like? How could it be achieved?'

Sartre was anti-capitalist and anti-religious – by passion and intellectual conviction. 'Existentialism' confronts an ancient riddle: 'Which came first, essence or existence?' Was there an idea in the mind of God, before Man was created, or did human beings evolve from the primitive forms of chemical interaction into the upright mammals that exist today? European thought encouraged the idea that 'essence preceded existence', which was at the heart of most Christian teaching and the idealism of Plato. In my British school, I was taught that, although I might behave badly and harbour wicked thoughts, there was a model of how I should conduct my life, that perfect example was Jesus Christ. I was a copy of that ideal, although admittedly a very imperfect copy.

Sartre proposed the exact opposite, 'existence preceded essence', which meant that we were born without any requirement as to what we should become. I had the potential to decide what sort of person I should be. To achieve this state, I had to be 'free'. I had to rise above my childhood conditioning and see in a true light the way in which I had been moulded by living within a capitalist society. The true existentialist threw off the burden of old-fashioned morality in order to find a new freedom, which, if embraced in good faith, would lead to a truly classless and egalitarian society, communism.

Sartre went to great lengths to dissect the bourgeois society of his upbringing – in his auto-biographical writings and particularly his biography of Flaubert. He became a champion of those who flouted every law and custom of French middle-class life. He called Jean Genet a 'saint' – a homosexual prostitute with a conviction for robbery with violence, who became the playwright of the underworld. Sartre brought together strands of thought that had challenged Christian teaching for more than a hundred years. He combined Darwinism with Socialism, Marx with Freud. More than 50 years after Nietzsche declared that 'God is Dead' and that Will was paramount, he confronted the fascist version of Nietzsche's Popular Will with an account of how an individual might achieve Free Will of his or her own. This bore an uncanny resemblance to the way in which the Soul rose above the circumstances of its coming-into-being, as described by the nineteenth-century Christian philosopher, Søren Kierkegaard.

In common with many *normaliens*, he probably attended the lectures on Hegel by Alexandre Kojève, the Russian-French polymath, which influenced his whole generation; but Sartre would not allow himself to be upstaged by anyone else. He was a prolific writer, a novelist, essayist, dramatist and editor of the left-wing magazine, *Les Temps Modernes*, on whose editorial board sat his life-long colleague and partner, Simone de Beauvoir, who wrote *The Second Sex* (1949). This book, which influenced so many others, described how women were relegated to an inferior role to men in all walks of life – marriage, spinsterhood, law, business and politics. Sartre and de Beauvoir were tireless campaigners for the underdog – homosexuals, blacks, servants. Their alienation was turned into a virtue, for they were the outsiders, who witnessed the injustices behind the gauze curtains. They knew what lay behind the screens of privilege, which hid the few from the dispossessed many.

As a teenager, *Les Temps Modernes* was the one French magazine that I wanted to read. I struggled with the French, gave up, struggled with the philosophy, gave up again, was awestruck by the confidence of its politics, but went on struggling, because it was telling me something that I wanted to hear. I wanted to believe that the myths that had brought such distress to the twentieth century were, like recreational drugs, mental habits that we could give up, if we tried hard enough. For me, existentialism was a way of growing up.

I could be anything that I decided to be. I had been taught to believe that the middle-class life of a British country town was tolerant, generous and god-fearing. So it was for my family. Yet the thought that it might be intolerably oppressive for those who did not conform – and we all knew of such people – was alarming. The suspicion that I might secretly be one of them was even worse, although I had no difficulty in conforming. I still went to school, swotted for my exams, and rarely played football in the public park with the Dun Alley gang, because they were Irish and, according to my mother, used foul language.

In these years after the war, confidence in the British way of life was high. Even its class structure was reassuring. Officers – and those of the officer class – were expected to know more, speak well and behave better than those in the ranks, although snobs were ridiculed and condemned. This can be seen in the plays and films of the period, such as Noel Coward's *This Happy Breed*, which did not disguise but celebrated class differences. Working together, as in the wartime coalition, proved that the lower, middle and upper classes could live together in happy harmony. They should not be at each other's throats. We British 'could take it' and the Exhibition of 1951 proved that we could make it as well.

The radicals of France and Algeria had no such comfort. They had seen their Vichy government conspire with the enemy. Their lands had been occupied and they had lived under a repugnant regime. How could they feel confidence in their governments or in a society where it might be hard to tell who had collaborated and who had not? What seemed so subversive in British eyes, the demolition of cherished beliefs, was for the readers of *Les Tempes Modernes* the necessary first step in the creation of a new world.

Not all of Sartre's colleagues shared that vision and Camus was one of them. If a human being was 'free' in the sense of having no moral structure to hold him or her in place, he or she, according to Camus, would be driven towards testing the limits of freedom, often at the expense of others. In his play, *Caligula* (1944), the free and all-powerful Man quickly drifted towards becoming a tyrant. Sartre called him an old-fashioned pessimist and it led to their public split in 1952, in which Camus swore that he had never been an Existentialist. His life's work, he insisted, had been a struggle against nihilism; he, like Sisyphus in his essay, *The Myth of Sisyphus*, rolled an immense rock to the top of a mountain, only to see it waver and then roll back down once more. Only in that split-second of success, when the stone was precariously perched, did he feel some satisfaction. The war against Nazism was over. The next struggle had not yet begun.

I do not know whether my father would have experienced such doubts. He may have, but he concealed them. He led me to believe that Right, by which he meant God's Will, would triumph in the end, as it had done in World War II. His parents worshipped within a Protestant sect, the Christian Israelites, but my father was not an evangelical, quite the reverse. He liked to use cricketing metaphors. Honest men 'played the game', 'with a straight bat' and 'respected the umpire's decision'.

At his Memorial Service in 1964, I asked one of his business colleagues, Dr Stadler, the chairman of Swiss Railways and President of Les Cableries et Trefileries de Cossonay, why my father came to be so widely respected among the eminent businessmen who attended AssoContra meetings. 'We trusted him,' was his answer. In the circumstances of post-war Europe, I took this to be the highest compliment.

The more politically astute might have noticed that AssoContra located its offices not in any major European country, but in Liechtenstein, haven to the wealthy and bank vault to the wicked. There seemed no clearer justification for a new order in Europe than that its cabling should have been coordinated through one tiny principality, a relic of the Holy Roman Empire, sheltered by its mountains, the Three Sisters, whose army (one man) died in 1936.

(iii)

Two years before Schuman put forward his proposal for the supranational government of the Ruhr valley, his friend and colleague, Jean Monnet, expressed an even wider vision. It concerned the future of Europe, although in 1943, in the thick of the war, it seemed even less likely to be realised. He was a member (*Commissaire á l'Armement*) of the French National Liberation Committee, General de Gaulle's government-in-exile. He insisted that: 'There will be no peace in Europe, if the states are reconstituted on the basis of national sovereignty. . . . The countries of Europe are too small to guarantee their peoples the necessary prosperity and social development. (They) must constitute themselves into a federation.'

He was speaking in Algiers and his views were not confined to the future of France but extended to the French colonies as well and, by implication, all the other European empires of the pre-war years that were now on the brink of collapse. Europe's nineteenth-century wealth was largely based upon trade with its colonies in Africa, India, Indo-China and Latin

America, but could it continue to do so? If not, was there an alternative? Monnet believed that the solution lay in seeking to build an economic zone for the European nations that were democratically governed. He thought that such a zone would prove less fragile and fractious than the old League of Nations. That was, and remains, the core argument for European integration.

Monnet was a businessman rather than an academic. He was born into a family of brandy merchants, and lived in London for many years, but travelled widely. He was an adviser to the French government at the Paris Peace Conference after World War I, where he met John Maynard Keynes. Like Keynes, he disapproved of the Allied policy of heavy reparations from Germany and proposed instead a 'new economic league', based upon European cooperation. He became the Deputy Secretary General of the League of Nations and watched in despair its decline into powerlessness before the rise of fascism.

Like Keynes, Monnet understood the need to challenge communism with a free market alternative and to prove that capitalism, regulated by a benign state, could achieve the economic growth that the Soviet Union would, despite its propaganda, inevitably fail to reach. With Schuman, then the French Foreign Minister, he helped to draft the Treaty of Paris in 1951, which brought into being the European Coal and Steel Community (ECSC). This turned Schuman's Ruhr valley proposal into an official supranational entity, open to other European countries, but governed by a High Authority, of which he became its first President. He resigned from this position, when the ECSC failed to include a new source of energy, nuclear power, which also required in his view a European dimension.

'Every succeeding scientific discovery,' said Anthony Eden, Churchill's successor as Prime Minister, 'makes greater nonsense of old-time conceptions of sovereignty.' The nuclear industries were a good example. It was unthinkable that every country in Europe should develop its own atom bomb, but it was equally unthinkable that the nations should be denied the benefits of nuclear research, which ranged from cheap power to the development of isotopes for medical use. Europe needed to develop its own safe methods of disposing of nuclear waste, for one act of carelessness could endanger everyone else. The answer was to seek deeper cooperation at an international level.

In 1940, Monnet proposed a Franco-British Union to Winston Churchill and came to chair the Franco-British Economic Co-ordination Committee. According to Maynard Keynes, he shortened the length of the war by as much as a year through his diplomatic skills. He was both an idealist and a pragmatist, who understood the differences in approach between the French and the British, even when they were seeking similar goals. While pursuing his aim of a federal Europe, he was careful to proceed in slow, practical steps, not wishing to persuade any country to join against its will, but confident that the benefits of membership would convince all but the most entrenched nationalists.

He is said to have written in a private letter (April 1952) that, 'nations should be guided towards the super-state without their peoples' understanding what is happening. This can be established by successive steps, each disguised as having an economic purpose, but which will irreversibly lead to federation.' Why 'federation'? Because no country would be allowed to subsidise its industries, raise its tariff barriers or adopt oppressive labour laws, to the disadvantage of other members. Through collective action, he believed that the European Economic Community could play its part in facing the challenges of the age: disarmament, space travel and the large gap in wealth between the rich and the poor.

This may suggest that Monnet was behaving in a Machiavellian manner, hiding his true intentions from the electorates of Europe. In France, he was accused of being an agent of the Americans and, in Britain, of being a Franco-German conspirator seeking Continental dominance, gaining a reputation for devious behaviour that has sullied his name for decades. The letter's authenticity has been questioned, but its drift was in line with his thinking. Despite their proud histories, all European countries faced a challenge to their former self-governing independence, when matched beside the new superpowers, the US and the USSR. How could they keep up with events?

Supranational institutions had already been brought into being under such pressures. The North Atlantic Treaty Organisation (NATO) was a case in point. Signed in Washington, DC, in 1949 by twelve member states, the treaty declared that an armed attack against one member would be considered as an attack against them all. It was a response to the military threat from the Soviet Union and to contain what was perceived to be a worldwide communist conspiracy. As a sacrifice of sovereignty, the demands of the European Coal and Steel Community paled into insignificance.

In the early 1950s, the United States was the world's only functioning nuclear power and provided NATO with its defence umbrella. But, as a former British colony, it was opposed to all forms of European imperialism. Would NATO come to the support of the French forces in Algeria or the British in Cyprus and Malaysia? The answer was no. NATO was an alliance for defence, but the treaty held consequences for internal politics elsewhere. De Gaulle was suspicious that the war against communism, led by the

Americans, was merely an excuse for taking over regions of the world, formerly controlled by European empires, the British included. This view was shared by a young English brigadier with army experience in India, Enoch Powell, who became a British MP and a cabinet minister.

France and Britain sometimes behaved as if NATO were an interim measure to let them regain their military independence. They built their own atomic bombs, tested their ballistic missiles and tried to keep up in the arms race. Monnet was right, however. No European country on its own could compete with the technological prowess of the two great powers. The possible spread of nuclear weapons around Europe added to the most existential of all existential threats. This fear led to the establishment of the European Atomic Energy Community (Euratom) in 1957, when, after the signing of the Treaty of Rome, the ECSC was incorporated into one new organisation, the European Economic Community (EEC).

Monnet drafted the Treaty of Rome, whose correct title was the Treaty Establishing the European Community, and its Preamble expressed his vision for Europe that he persuaded six other countries (Belgium, France, West Germany, Italy, the Netherlands and Luxembourg) to share. The aim was to 'lay the foundations of an ever closer union among the peoples of Europe' by removing the barriers to trade within the EEC and 'affirming as the essential objective of their efforts the constant improvement of the living and working conditions of their peoples'. The EEC intended to contribute by its 'common commercial policy to the progressive abolition of restrictions on international trade', in accordance with the 'principles of the Charter of the United Nations'; and it resolved to seek to pool 'their resources to preserve and strengthen peace and liberty'.

The EEC required its own legal system, which became the European Court of Justice, its Executive or High Authority, its Common Assembly elected through its national parliaments, and its special Council of Ministers, the representatives of their various governments. The structure was intended to combine democratic accountability with effective executive power and to respect the national identities of its members. Britain hesitated. Only time would tell whether Monnet's assumptions were right that geo-political pressures would force nations to work more closely together. Meanwhile, Britain was content to construct its future on the known strengths of kith, kinship and the Crown. It stayed out.

Monnet offered four principles for good behaviour in this free trade area – the mobility of goods, capital, skills and labour – but this was an example of where top-down logic could come into conflict with bottom-up. 'Mobility of labour' was a founding principle in his vision for Europe, for in theory, employment levels around the region should find their own balance, like water in a tank. But what happens if the locals complain about foreigners? 'If I had to do it again,' Monnet is reputed to have said, 'I would have begun with culture!'

He may never have said this well-known remark attributed to him and, if he did,nobody knows what he really meant. It sounded like a U-turn. He had acted throughout his life as if spreading the benefits of a properly organised, level-playing-field market economy would provide the answer to the wars in Europe. National cultures were secondary obstacles. He seemed to think, as liberal economists did, that groups of people with different languages and traditions could live peacefully side by side, if no one was too badly in need. Had he suffered a death-bed conversion by promoting the cause of national identity instead?

Jacques Delors was one of those, who thought he knew exactly what Monnet meant. Europe, according to Delors, had a 'spiritual' dimension – a risky issue in some parts of Europe, such as Northern Ireland, where the Common Market was suspected of being a Roman Catholic plot. Delors became the eighth President of the European Commission and was a generation younger than Monnet. It was his Eurocentric and left-wing habits of mind that so irritated Mrs Thatcher during the 1980s. After the signing of the Maastricht Treaty in 1993, Delors called upon the leaders of the newly created European Union (EU) to 'reinforce that common cultural consciousness without which Europe would be in danger of losing its identity and become nothing more than a large, mundane market place'.

From Mrs Thatcher's point of view, the 'mundane market place' was the expression of popular choice, more legitimate in a democracy than the views of subsidised intellectuals. His remarks alarmed many intellectuals as well, for he spoke as someone who did not know much about the arts but knew what he liked. In Delors' opinion, Europe's identity reflected the diversity of its 'national mentalities': the passion of the Swedes for psychology, the Germans for ecology and the French for history.

The more cosmopolitan Monnet might have retorted that such national stereotypes were a large part of the problem. French culture in London was associated less with history than soft porn, more Folies Bergère than the Louvre. French publishers produced sexually explicit works, such as Henry Miller's *Tropic of Cancer* and James Joyce's *Ulysses*, which were banned in the UK and the US. In Anglo-American movies, the Italians were passionate lovers or priests, Germans were shaggy-haired geniuses or goose-stepping Prussians, and the Swedes went skinny-dipping at midsummer and committed suicide during the rest of the year. Multiculturalism was not the answer to such misconceptions. It was a description of them.

Monnet, however, would have agreed with Delors that the material incentives of free trade would never be enough to overcome the piled-up grievances and local narratives that had accumulated across Europe over many centuries. He would have been sceptical of top-down attempts at a cultural policy such as Cities of Culture, mere sticking plasters over the hole that should have been a European identity. Sandwiched between the East-West protagonists in the Cold War, each country was struggling to rebuild its border controls, currencies and taxation, as well as the infrastructure of roads, railways and cables. There were fragments of a common heritage in Europe, based on its classical roots in Athens and Rome, Christianity and the Enlightenment; but these had been under attack from Modernists since the start of the century. Most radical intellectuals, such as Sartre, were hell-bent on destroying the past or, at best, calling its most eloquent values into question.

Was Monnet among them? Would he have tried like a good liberal to build a bridge between the irresistible and the intractable? Was that what he meant by beginning with culture? Of course, I never met him. I never knew any members of his family, or any of his friends, or visited his brandy factory, and he may not have said these words in the first place. Yet, whether he said them or not, whoever said them for him, and whatever might have been the intention, these words were still worthy of their Delphic utterance.

***

Chapter Three
The Floating Island

(i)

We English are suspicious of intellectuals. The very word sounds pretentious. An intellectual is not an academic with specialist skills, though he or she may have plenty of degrees, nor an expert, a pundit or a guru, but someone with a range of knowledge, who can provide a quick assessment of the human condition and where we are all heading, in other words, a bluffer. As the Anglo-American poet, W.H. Auden, pointed out:

To the man in the street who, I'm sorry to say,
Is a faithful observer of life,
The word, intellectual, suggests straight away
A man who's untrue to his wife.

An intellectual is someone who thinks too much, is out of touch with his or her feelings, and may subversively blow up the status quo. Iain Macleod, a Conservative minister during the 1960s, was blamed by his colleagues for being 'too clever by half'.

In England, Sartre was thought to be an intellectual in that pejorative sense by my teachers, although Existentialism as a fashion was popular. It was the Left Bank's classless and a-moral style, free from sexual inhibitions, which attracted us so much. In contrast, Britain after the war was very strait-laced. There was censorship on sexual and religious subjects in all forms of publishing: the codes of conduct on dress and language were strict. My father was rarely seen in public without a tie or hat. Before the close of television each evening, the BBC played 'God Save the Queen', following the example set by cinemas and theatres. The virtues of ancient Rome – courage, discipline and patriotism – permeated the routines at school, which were modified during prayers by Christian love and humility. Rules were there to be obeyed; and, as in Rome, there was corporal punishment, if we as teenagers did not.

The history of the Roman Empire inspired all empire-builders everywhere. It was the inherited model for conquest and civic rule throughout Europe, including Britain. 'What did the Romans do for us?' was a question asked in Monty Python's *Life of Brian* (1979), from an anarchic comedy team, anticipating the answer from our school textbooks: 'Roads, law, language, civilization . . .' The fall of the Roman Empire constituted a warning against the degeneracy that Existentialists seemed to be advocating: free love, students up to no good at street corners, the behaviour that got Oscar Wilde into trouble.

But Existentialism did not wither in the face of moral disapproval. It was the unacknowledged poetry of Gay Pride, militant feminism and Black Power. It spread amongst the youth movements of the 1960s, anti-war, anti-white supremacy. It penetrated the Baader-Meinhof gang in Germany, and thrived among US conscripts to Vietnam. In May 1968, Sartre linked arms with the students, whose riots threatened the French economy, led to President de Gaulle's resignation and, with riots elsewhere, threatened the stability of the so-called civilized world.

Existentialism became a familiar thread in the social tapestry to come. Sartre matched middle-class values, yarn by yarn, and, where he could, unravelled them. But his political vision was less than all-embracing. It stopped with the idea that all men, acting with free will and in good faith, would embrace the classless society. He clung to the fading example of the USSR. A different approach would come from another quarter: Alexandre Kojève, the towering European proto-intellectual, whose uncle was the Russian Abstract artist Wassily Kandinsky. Kojève did have an alternative proposal and, as one of de Gaulle's advisers, was in a better position than Sartre to implement it.

Like Monnet, Kojève believed that the nations of Europe were too small, as separate sovereign states, to maintain their independence in the face of the geo-political pressures. But instead of a federal solution, he argued that like-minded states should work together in what he called 'empires'. The process had already begun. There was an Anglo-Saxon Empire, composed of the English-speaking peoples, and Kojève predicted that a denazified Germany would eventually join them. There was a Slav Empire, extending beyond the Soviet Union to the states of Central Asia and offering support to Mao Zedong's Red Army against the nationalists of Chiang Kai-Shek, the allies of the Anglo-Saxons.

Where would France be in this brave new world, a dominion of the Anglo-Saxons? In a paper submitted in 1945 to de Gaulle's interim government, he proposed that the aim of French foreign policy should be to create a 'Latin' empire, consisting of France, Spain and Italy and extending across the Mediterranean to North Africa to include Algeria, Tunisia,

Morocco and the Islamic states. Kojève believed that the future of the rebuilt Europe lay with 'culture'. The nations of the three Empires spoke different languages: Anglo-Saxon, Slav and Latin. They had adopted three different forms of Christianity – Protestant, Orthodox and Catholic – on which were based their various laws, customs and sense of natural justice.

The economic policies of the Anglo-Saxon and the Slav Empires were almost equally 'flawed'. Kojève, a Russian by birth, denounced the 'barbaric statism' of the Soviet system, but he was also critical of the 'unregulated cartels and mass unemployment' of the Anglo-Saxons' Free World of capitalism. A Latin Empire would be different. Unlike the Anglo-Saxons and Slavs, whose habits of mind were threatening and imperialist, the Latin Empire would not be aggressive. It would deploy its military might only to protect its borders and its sphere of influence, the nations of the Mediterranean. Their 'spiritual kinship' would be based upon 'liberty, equality, fraternity', the cornerstones of the French Republic.

The Latin temperament cultivated the 'art of leisure', which was 'the source of art in general' and its temperament pursued the 'aristocratic sweetness of living'. The Latin Empire should aspire towards the harmonious society, where the internal contradictions that bedevilled previous social structures, would be progressively removed, leading to, in his phrase, 'the end of history'.[i] He proposed to de-Italianise the Vatican and to seek a rapprochement between the Catholic Church and Islam, and called for a new French political party, led by de Gaulle, as the figurehead of the France that had fought for its freedom.

Kojève joined the Department of Economic Affairs. He was part of the French team, which delivered the General Agreement on Tariffs and Trade (1947), the forerunner of the World Trade Organisation. He negotiated a trade deal between the EEC and the US in 1963. But his background was not that of an economist, but of a philosopher, who became a bureaucrat, according to his friend, Raymond Aron, to discover 'how history worked'. His presence at the heart of the French political establishment is worth noting in itself. Would Churchill have asked Bertrand Russell to sit in on cabinet discussions?

The Latin Empire never became a political reality, but Kojève provided a persuasive vision of the role that France might play in the post-war years. In 1945, the newly formed United Nations was offered the home that became its headquarters in New York, at the heart of the Anglo-Saxon 'empire'. But in the same year, a treaty was signed to establish UNESCO, the United Nations Educational, Scientific and Cultural Organisation. It was offered its first offices in a hotel in Paris, where it moved in 1946, and the French government built its headquarters at the

Place de Fontenoy in Paris, which opened in 1958. France thus became the landlord of a large, global, cultural headquarters, which embraced thousands of other governmental and non-governmental agencies, which it indirectly helped to support.

Kojève's vision shaped the Gaullist vision of the new Europe, which was not just that of an economic zone, but as a phase in the unrolling of history. As an authority on Hegel, he subscribed to the view that, while reality was indivisible, mind and body united, the human understanding of reality progressed through many apparent contradictions, the 'dialectic', towards a harmonious resolution. That was the evolutionary process in action. Hegel, whose thought was steeped in Protestantism, became the bridge between the idealism of the German Enlightenment and such non-Christian philosophers as Marx, Nietzsche and Heidegger. Kojève was the historian, interpreter and curator-in-chief of a long European tradition of thought that only crossed the Channel in a much diluted form.

Kojève challenged the idea that the Cold War was between the freedom-loving democracies of the West, led by the US, and the Marxist-Leninist tyrannies of the East, led by the USSR. He was once accused of being a Soviet spy but, if so, he must qualify as the least undercover of any undercover agent, for his views were well known across the Continent. But he could be seen as a treacherous friend, for he did not support the views of either side. For those in central Europe who were trying to defend their borders against Soviet expansion, he was a dangerous bear in sheep's clothing, an intellectual who was 'too clever by half'.

In contrast, George Kennan, the relatively non-intellectual US diplomat who first advocated the policy of the 'containment', complained that there was something about the American mentality that always went to extremes. Having been persuaded that communism was a threat to world stability, his countrymen were seeing Reds everywhere, behind every insurgency in the post-imperial world, in Hollywood, the media and under the bed.

This hardening of opinion came with the start of the war in the Korean peninsula in 1950, when the North Koreans, supported by communist China, invaded South Korea and made rapid progress. The United States called for a response from the UN's Security Council, which in the absence of the Soviet Union passed a resolution that demanded North Korea's immediate withdrawal. An army was assembled, led by the US, but including large contingents from Britain and the Commonwealth, and a much smaller one from France. Four years later, a formal ceasefire was declared but with no peace settlement.

In 1954, the US President, Dwight D. Eisenhower, expressed his belief that the loss of South Korea would have led to the 'domino' effect of other countries in South-East Asia falling to the forces of international communism, Cambodia, Malaya and French Indo-China. The sheer scale of the Cold War became apparent. It penetrated such remote islands in Micronesia as the Bikini Atoll where the Americans tested their nuclear weapons, and into the heart of Europe, Berlin, a divided city. There was always the threat of a Third World War, which was only averted, many thought, by the prospect of nuclear annihilation.

Those who believed in the principles of the Free World – free speech, free elections and duly elected governments that were not above the law – looked across to the practices of the Soviet Union and its satellites and shuddered. For them, the Cold War was a struggle between freedom and tyranny, good and evil; but, for a top-down Hegelian like Kojève, it held a different message. In the fullness of time, these 'contradictions' would be resolved, but the Cold War lasted for 40 years when history seemed more likely to end in a nuclear accident. The Cold War illustrated his analysis of two Empires, held together by their 'cultures', squaring up to each other across the globe. But where was the third Latin Empire? Nowhere, except in his mind and that of General de Gaulle.

(ii)

The governments of the Fourth Republic were in no position to build the Latin Empire, even if they wanted to do so. They were struggling to retain their dependent territories in North Africa and Indo-China. They had more in common with the British, who were facing similar problems in Kenya, the Gold Coast and Malaya. Both countries were trying to regain their strength against left-wing rebels on one hand and ultra-nationalists on the other. Neither was in control of events.

In 1956, the French, British and Israelis found a common cause. An army-led coup in Egypt deposed King Farouk, an ally of the British, and established an Arab republic, 'neutral' in the Cold War. The new military leaders revoked a 1936 treaty between the UK and Egypt, which gave the British government the right to maintain a military garrison with 80,000 men to defend the Suez Canal. This army was considered vital to the defence of British interests (including oil) in the Middle East and east of Suez. The Egyptian army could not directly challenge this stronghold, but its size provoked resentment. Instead of threatening what it dared not attack, the Egyptian government looked for support from both sides in the Cold War, taunting the British and Americans by negotiating with the Russians, in what was seen as a battle for the largest Islamic nation in the Middle East.

When this attempt at Cold War power politics failed, the Egyptian president, Gamal Abdel Nasser, nationalised the Suez Canal. This was owned by the Anglo-French Suez Canal company, which had built the canal and operated it for more than 70 years. Nasser may have wanted to seize the leadership of the Arab world; but the British, French and Israeli governments, sensing danger, invaded Egypt in October, hoping to depose Nasser and to restore the canal as an international waterway, controlled by the Western allies.

The Tripartite Aggression, as it became known in Arab circles, won the battle, but not the war. Nasser sunk tankers to blockade the canal and the US government under Eisenhower refused to intervene in what it regarded as another colonial adventure. The invasion lasted for nine days before a UN peacekeeping mission came in to restore order, but the damage to Anglo-French colonial interests had already been done. The blockade of the Suez Canal added about 5,000 miles to the sea route between Europe and the Far East. At a time when the only way to transport large amounts of goods, equipment and soldiers was by sea, it turned the defence of French Indo-China from being a difficult campaign into an impossible one. The British faced a similarly demanding task with their dependencies, their oil interests in the Gulf and their trade with the Commonwealth and Empire.

Before Suez, it was possible to believe that the glories of Britain's Edwardian empire could be restored. Great container ships and passenger liners still manoeuvred their way up the Thames estuary to the Port of London. The sun had not set on the Union Jacks, fluttering over colonial offices from Salisbury in Southern Rhodesia to Hong Kong, Rangoon to Grenada, Ceylon to the Falkland Isles. After Suez, the remains of what was still the British Empire was in a twilight zone, where the light was rapidly fading.

For many in Britain and throughout its Commonwealth and Empire, the Suez debacle represented an immense shock to their pride. They had been put in their place by their cousins across the pond, worse than an embarrassment, a shameful humiliation, which was hard to forgive and harder still to forget. They had been defeated by their post-war poverty, an untrustworthy ally and the shadow of the distant mushroom cloud that placed the future of mankind at risk. A large door on their past had closed.

Nothing is wholly lost. Nothing is forgotten, however much we may try to suppress it. Behind every documented event, there lie the shadows, alternative versions of what might have happened or even (according to dissidents) really did. There are newsreels of the resignation speech of Sir Anthony Eden, the British Prime Minister at the time of the Suez invasion, a tall handsome man with a clipped moustache, strained with worry and sickness, going down like a naval commander with his ship Britannia. Only a hardened cynic would doubt his word when he stated at the time that Nasser was another Hitler, funded and armed by the Soviet Union and on the enemy front line in the war against communism. Why did the US government not back him up, as the British had supported them in Korea?

There were many explanations, then as now. Was there distrust for historical reasons? Did the Americans, the anti-imperialists, think that Eden was trying to revive the Empire? Or was it more personal? President Eisenhower's Secretary of State, John Foster Dulles, was a staunch anti-communist, a dour son of a Presbyterian minister, who distrusted the Edwardian elegance of someone like Eden. They never liked each other. Both were physically ill and Dulles would soon die. Or was this the moment when Eisenhower realised that there could be only one leader of the Free World and, in the age of nuclear weapons, it was time for the most powerful nation on earth to exercise its authority? Did he remember his own struggle for leadership with General Montgomery, an elegant Anglo-Irishman, who favoured a quick strike against the Axis forces in the last months of the war, as opposed to his Broad Front?

Or had the Americans acquired imperial ambitions of their own, slyly taking over the countries that they offered to protect? Did they intend to cut down to size those Europeans, who wanted to act on their own? History is a hall of mirrors. At every step, the angles change and another perspective comes into view. Before Suez, the British were often thought to be the diplomats of the English-speaking peoples, the ones with international experience, latter-day Greeks, bringing civilised values to the strength of the Americans, latter-day Romans. After Suez, the glass cracked and the image fractured. Side by side with the cool English gentleman, nonchalant before danger, stood his counterpart, the decadent supremacist, not to be trusted, the Oxbridge traitor of spy movies. Both return, like the BBC's Dr Who, in time-bending disguises – a Scarlet Pimpernel into a James Bond, a Sheriff of Nottingham into a Goldfinger – and both contribute to the Britishness of being British.

A national identity, if such a thing exists, is composed of many contradictions. I was brought up to believe that the British Empire was, with qualifications, a Good Thing. It carried the benefits of Christian civilisation to regions of the world which existed, or so we were told, in 'savage ignorance'. It was superior to other European empires. I still glow with pride when I hear that Afghanistan, of all places, has taken up cricket as its national game and when the Caribbean poet, the late E.A. Markham, told me to 'play with a straight bat', I heard the voice of my father.

For 20 years after the war, there was a Secretary of State for the Colonies and a Secretary of State for Commonwealth Relations, and both were kept apart from the Foreign Office, which only dealt with foreigners. Lives were devoted to good works in the colonies. Almost every family had its pioneering cousins. We knew that there were rebel fighters. We called them terrorists. Our children's books, not comics, were full of adventure stories set in Africa, India or China, where there was little doubt as to who was on the right side. We were.

But for more than 60 years, since the very height of the British Raj, there were those who denounced the empire and called it a folly or gross exploitation. There were writers and philosophers, such as J.B. Priestley and Bertrand Russell, who wanted Britain to become more like Sweden, small but civilised. Which was the more 'British', Rudyard Kipling or E.M. Forster? Both were writers of the Raj, patriots with different points of view, conservative and liberal. Before Suez, most would have chosen Kipling, who died in 1934, who always backed the Empire to the hilt, but was not an entrenched white supremacist. He conceded that Gunga Din was the better man. After Suez, many might have chosen Forster, whose use of racial and class nuances exposed the cracks in the imperial walls that storms would open and cause to come crashing down. 'Two Cheers for Democracy', he wrote, worried that the Free World would collapse from its sense of self importance.

The retreat from Suez shocked the whole country, but for some it was a humiliation and for others it was an overdue lesson in realism. There were those whose suspicions were confirmed that the Empire had been betrayed. In 1954, the League of Empire Loyalists (LEL) was formed as a far-right pressure group within the Conservative Party. Its membership rose from 300 in 1955, before Suez, to 3,000 in 1958, with influential names, such as Lord Ironside, once Chief of the Imperial General Staff. Its core team was brought together by A.K. Chesterton, cousin of the writer G.K. Chesterton, from members of the pre-war British Union of Fascists (BUF), led by Sir Oswald Mosley.

The LEL's interpretation of the Suez adventure was that the Soviet Union and the United States, 'bolshevism' and 'capitalism', masterminded by a secret Jewish conspiracy, joined forces against the Empire to cause its downfall. The LEL collapsed in the early 1960s, shunned by mainstream Conservatives, but many of its members joined other anti-immigration, pro-Empire and far-right parties. These were brought together at Chesterton's invitation to meet at his Croydon apartment in 1966, where they formed the National Front.

Some were merely thugs. They marched in the constituency, Ealing North, where I was the parliamentary candidate for the Liberal Party, one of Jo Grimond's recruits. At one rally, the Labour activist, Blair Peach, was killed. Surrounding this Nazi-like core were those who mourned the loss of Empire and felt that some terrible injustice had been done. They could not understand why Britain, having won the war, should now be so poor. They must have been betrayed – if not by the Jews, then by a capitalist-Bolshevik conspiracy; if not by them, then by the liberals, who let in the immigrants from the colonies; and if not by the liberals, then by the members of the EEC, which had swallowed up Marshall Aid and was now on a federalising mission of its own.

At one level, the Conservatives restored confidence with great skill after suffering such a humiliation at Suez. After Eden's resignation, the new Prime Minister was appointed through the secret processes of consultation that then characterised the party. By appearance, Harold Macmillan was an Edwardian gentleman of the old school, reassuring to the shires, but he was an Anglo-American by birth. He had fought in two world wars. He was on the liberal wing of the party and related to a well-known and reformist Liberal family. He had represented a northern constituency in the 1930s, Stockton-upon-Tees, where there was a high level of unemployment. It transformed his political outlook. He was the living epitome of a 'One-Nation' Tory.

Macmillan had supported the Suez invasion. He was Foreign Minister under Eden, one of its architects. He was under the impression that the US would not intervene. But he was a pragmatist, 'unflappable', capable of taking the steps to repair the Anglo-American Special Relationship. As Minister for Housing in the early 1950s, he fulfilled an election pledge to build 300,000 new homes, using the Keynesian method of borrowing money to stimulate the economy. He was one who, with his Conservative colleague R.A. Butler, helped to mastermind the reconstruction of Britain. The cartoonist, Vicky, labelled him Supermac, but his willingness to adapt to the circumstances of the times ran counter to those who hankered after Empire, particularly when in 1962 he sought British membership of the EEC.

Another consequence of the embarrassment at Suez, more slow-burning but equally explosive, was the loss of confidence in authority. Before Suez, a BBC reporter, Franklin Englemann, asked Eden politely whether he had a message for the nation. He duly provided one, in clipped formality that brooked no dissent. In 1958, one interview transformed television journalism. It was conducted by a newcomer, Robin Day, who had trained as a barrister. He subjected Macmillan to what was described in the Daily Express as 'the most vigorous cross-examination that a Prime Minister had been subjected to in public'. It made Day's reputation, but did no harm to Macmillan, who emerged as a thoughtful politician, even a statesman, with his image improved. It helped him to win the general election in 1959, in which Day stood as the Liberal candidate. Real politics had come to the living room screen.

The hierarchies of power within British society were subjected to a critical re-examination – within the Church, education and the army. Before Suez, the school stories of Frank Richards were vastly popular. They featured Billy Bunter and the fiercely cane-wielding Mr Quelch in public (fee-paying) schools, where boys were sent to learn the rules of life. Girls came later. Now the trend was towards 'comprehensive' education in classless, co-educational schools, of which Holland Park, which opened in 1958, was a trail-blazing example. Was this social engineering? 'Yes,' said the liberal-left, proudly.

The upper classes were having a bad time. After Suez, they were bundled in with the 'Establishment', a 1950s word, which brought together politicians, lawyers, generals, arch-bishops and the House of Lords, into one sitting target for humorists. Not since the days of Gillray and Richardson had they been treated with such contempt. On the fringes of this arena were the revolutionary hyenas, sniffing the blood and cackling. A new route opened up for Oxbridge graduates, who saw their chances in the Foreign and Colonial Offices declining. Satire became a well-paid profession, which led through college revues, the Edinburgh Fringe and the West End, to late-night shows on black-and-white television.

Nothing was exempt, not even the atom bomb. In *Beyond the Fringe* (1960), Peter Cook, imitating Macmillan, read out the Home Office instructions about what to do in the event of a nuclear attack: 'There will be a four-minute warning. Let me remind you,' he added unflappably, 'that there are some men in Britain who can run a mile in four minutes.' Cook, with Richard Ingrams, was the owner of the magazine, *Private Eye* (founded in 1960), whose mixture of satire and investigative journalism took over from *Punch*, as the nation's leading humorous magazine. *Punch* closed in 1992 after 161 years of publication.

But there was another kind of reaction to Suez, the super-abundance of war movies. Before Suez, most British war films were based on best-selling memoirs, such as *The Wooden Horse* (1950) and *The Dam Busters* (1955). They had a stamp of authenticity. After Suez, the mood changed. They became very glossy.[ii] They were action-packed, minimally based on real events and star-studded. They had big budgets. They boosted the morale.

For more than 60 years since 1956, the British public has been provided with daily screen reminders of how we won the war, which seamlessly merged into the war against communism, and finally ditched such political labels to become a war against all sinister foreign conspiracies, like SPECTRE in the James Bond movies, which were similar to the Jewish conspiracies of the LELs' direst warnings. They trumpeted the Special Relationship. But for those who were more sceptical, this habit of glamorising the Anglo-American track record of winning wars seemed obsessive, big boys gloating in the playground.

'There are no good, brave causes left!' cried out the first of the angry young men, Jimmy Porter, in a new play by an unknown actor, John Osborne, *Look Back in Anger* (1956) at the Royal Court Theatre in London.

'Disrupt the spectacle!'[iii] cried out the far left and far right in unison.

(iii)

'Since 6 August 1945,' declared the author and philosopher, Arthur Koestler, in his Preface to *Janus: A Summing Up* (1978), 'our species has been on borrowed time'.

'From the dawn of consciousness . . . man has had to live with the prospect of his death as an *individual*; since the day when the first atomic bomb outshone the sun over Hiroshima, mankind as a whole has had to live with the prospect of his extinction as a *species*.' In other works, Koestler went further. He characterised his generation as the first with the capacity to destroy humanity and perhaps the planet. Few disagreed with him. 'I do not know with what superior weapons World War III will be conducted,' said Albert Einstein, 'but World War IV will be fought with sticks and stones.'

Koestler had fled from the havoc in central Europe in 1939 to settle in Britain as a liberal country, where it was still possible to write, publish and meet other intellectuals, without running the risk of a knock on the door at midnight. Other immigrants included the philosopher, Karl Popper, the artist, Feliks Topolski, the gallery owner, Anneli Juda and the theatre historian, Martin Esslin, who became the BBC's Head of Drama. As an unofficial group, they added another dimension to the Britishness of being British.

Topolski came from an aristocratic family in Poland, who studied as a painter in Warsaw and Paris, and came to London to record King George V's Silver Jubilee, attracted by 'its exotic charm'. Koestler and Esslin were born in Budapest and were Jewish by birth, but not by religion. They became British citizens and fiercely defended what they considered to be its values, the respect for democracy and human rights. Popper was raised in Vienna and belonged to an influential Jewish family. He took up Marxism at university and joined the Communist Party; but he became sceptical of

Hegel, Marx and 'historicism', the belief that humans were inevitably the product of their historical circumstances. Following a study visit to Britain in 1936, he applied for and secured a teaching post in New Zealand. Popper returned to Britain after the war.

Koestler was a Communist Party member until 1938, when he resigned in disgust and wrote *Darkness at Noon*, a thinly disguised fictional account of the Stalinist show trials. It was published in 1941, when he was under detention in Britain as a refugee without an entry permit, but his personal knowledge of totalitarian regimes made an immediate impact upon those in Britain (like Bernard Shaw) who during the 1930s were inclined to place their trust in Stalin and Hitler as great patriotic leaders. 'Nothing is more sad,' he wrote, 'than the death of an illusion.'

In Britain, he met Eric Blair (George Orwell), a fellow journalist, who became a close friend and wrote two allegorical novels, *Animal Farm* (1945) and *1984* (1949). Shortly after he was granted British nationality, Koestler bought a farm in the Welsh hills, near Bertrand Russell's country home, where he discussed the future of mankind with those who shared his fears for it, famous Liberal and Labour family names, the Foots, the Huxleys, the Laskis, the Stracheys and Russell himself. Top of the list of tough questions was that of nuclear warfare, where the answers led on to more riddles, like a cunningly constructed maze.

The world was full of conferences for world peace, too many. In 1948, Julian Huxley and Topolski visited the Congress of Intellectuals for World Peace in Wroclaw, Poland. It was supposed to be neutral, but, in reality, it was secretly funded by the USSR, which also financed the World Peace Council. All resolutions condemned capitalism, the West and the United States. When Huxley and Topolski tabled a motion to the effect that 'it was the first duty of intellectuals to be intelligent', it was soundly defeated. In June 1950, Koestler and Russell attended the first Congress for Cultural Freedom in West Berlin, funded secretly by the CIA. Words like peace and freedom were nuanced by the money behind them. Whose peace? Whose freedom?

Without such a global agreement, what were the choices in a nuclear age? Would it be voluntary disarmament? Which would be the first country to put up its hand? After Suez, Britain became the third nuclear power to explode a hydrogen bomb, a thousand times more powerful than the bomb that destroyed Hiroshima. The author, J.B. Priestley, wrote that: 'Now that Britain has told the world she has the H-bomb, she should announce that she has done with it, that she proposes to reject in all circumstances nuclear warfare.' In February 1958, the Campaign for Nuclear Disarmament (CND) held its first meeting at Central Hall, Westminster, attracting an audience of 5,000, which elected Russell as its first president.

In 1959, the Labour Party included nuclear disarmament in its election manifesto, which was thought to be one reason why it lost the election. After a fierce fight within the party which was never resolved, this commitment was reversed. It was a nagging conundrum. To give up the bomb unilaterally might turn out to be little more than a pious gesture, sending British negotiators 'naked into the conference chamber', but to retain it, would encourage others to build their own nuclear arsenals.

While unilateralism lingered as a seductive tune in the music of the left, other voices were raised to stop the spread of nuclear weapons – 'non-proliferation', whereby the nuclear powers would share some of their secrets with those that had none, on condition that they did not make such weapons themselves. The first 'non-proliferation' treaty took some thirteen years to negotiate, and some thirty more before China and Russia could be persuaded to join, but there were still other countries, such as North Korea, which refused to join and had their own reasons for not doing so. The English-speaking peoples, led by the United States, were determined that the best bombs and delivery systems should be held in their hands, as the global guarantors of their responsible non-usage in what became known as the arms race.

There had been serious talks between Britain and the United States about sharing their nuclear secrets since 1942, when such weapons were turning from theory into manufacture. But they had been hampered by mutual suspicion. After Suez, in March 1957, Macmillan met Eisenhower for the first time as the leaders of their respective nations in Bermuda, a British colony. They had been comrades in arms in North Africa. Both were keen to mend the cracks in the Special Relationship and nuclear co-operation seemed a promising way to start. By the end of the year, such a partnership seemed vital. In October 1957, the Soviet Union launched its first space satellite, Sputnik, which suggested that their technical prowess with intercontinental rockets outstripped that of America.

To maintain the balance of power with the USSR, the US needed to find some place closer to the European continent as a safe haven for its rockets and bombers. Britain was its first-choice launch-pad. In return, Macmillan negotiated a Mutual Defence Agreement (MDA), signed in July 1958, a bilateral pact on nuclear arms cooperation, which transformed the Special Relationship into the most powerful military alliance in the second half of the twentieth century. Macmillan described it as 'the great prize'. It was more than an agreement to exchange information, but rather to share (or not to duplicate) US and UK research. When in 1960 the British government decided not to continue with its Blue Streak rocket programme, it turned to the US for its near-equivalent, to be built under licence in Britain. It also participated as a junior partner in the construction of submarines to fire ballistic missiles, the ultimate deterrent, so that, by 1980, Britain could claim to be 'invulnerable to a pre-emptive attack'.

Elsewhere, the MDA aroused unease and suspicion. From Moscow's perspective, the decision to base US planes and missiles on British soil brought the threat of a nuclear attack across the Atlantic, some 3,000 miles closer. In 1963, the Soviets sought a similar facility in Fidel Castro's Cuba, in what became known as the Cuban missile crisis.

From the French point of view, the MDA was an example of how the Anglo-Saxons might be seeking to turn France into a vassal state by providing the main force within NATO. In 1958, after the collapse of the Fourth Republic, de Gaulle became the French President under the newly constituted Fifth Republic and ordered the development of an independent nuclear arms programme. The French hydrogen bomb was detonated in 1966. With de Gaulle determined to pursue a French defence policy, there could be no non-proliferation treaty within the EEC; but progress was made on an independent nuclear research programme with the formation of Euratom, incorporated into the Treaty of Rome in 1957.

Its aims were modest, no bombs or ballistic missiles, but offered an EEC monitoring system for the nuclear industry. In 1957, when a fire broke out in the nuclear processing plant at Windscale and spread radioactive material into the Irish Sea, Euratom worked with the British Atomic Energy Authority to learn from this accident. As research started to include radioactive materials in other industries, Euratom became an indispensable way of reassuring the electorates that the nuclear industry was not only concerned with building bigger bombs but had higher ambitions for mankind.

Britain became a member of Euratom in 1973, after successfully negotiating to join the EEC. Perhaps such monitoring should have been carried out by the United Nations, but in a less than perfect world, still diplomatically frozen by the Cold War, Euratom was intended to bring the threat of nuclear devastation under some measure of regional control. But neither the awesome terror of Polaris missiles, held responsibly in Western hands, nor the monitoring and research of Euratom went far to calm the fears of those like Koestler and Russell, who prophesied the annihilation of mankind.

This threat permeated the public imagination during the 1960s. It occurred and recurred in books, films and plays. It was rarely far away. Nuclear missiles might be part of a global conspiracy, foiled by Bond. The actions of a rogue general, as in Stanley Kubrick's *Dr Strangelove* (1964), might set off a Doomsday Machine. The Swiss playwright, Friedrich

Dürrenmatt, wrote a play, *The Physicists* (1961), in which an atomic scientist took refuge in an asylum: it was his duty to ensure that his work was never known to the outside world. Above the politics of the daily world, above all the resolutions for peace and harmony, above all the manifestos and economic plans, hung the mushroom cloud.

Might human evolution come to the rescue? Koestler was not a Hegelian, like Kojève, who believed that these contradictions would be resolved in harmony over time. He developed his own theories. His later books, *The Ghost in the Machine* (1967) and *Janus: A Summing Up* (1978), put forward the idea that the mind, like all living creation, was a 'holarchy', which contained 'holons', particles of being that, like the two-headed god Janus, aspired towards the future and looked back towards the past, simultaneously. The balance was all. The balance between them determined our destiny.

Were we as a species capable of handling the powers that science had unlocked? Our history suggested otherwise, but nothing was inevitable, not even disaster. We had to adapt. We had to learn how to use the tools that science had placed in our hands. Karl Popper's seminal work, *The Open Society and its Enemies* (1945), a defence of liberal democracy, pointed the way. This, according to Koestler, should be the primary mission of politicians and economists, artists and scientists alike, and of every institution, including the EEC and NATO. Trade was not enough. It was only a beginning. A common court of justice was not enough. It was only a legal framework. What was required was a transformation of our habits of mind, which took into account the advances of science and sought a flexible social framework to meet the challenges ahead. Mere sovereignty was not good enough. We needed to change our very minds. What was at stake was human survival.

***

Chapter Four
The Wind of Change

(i)

On 3 February 1960, addressing the South African parliament in Cape Town, the British Prime Minister, Harold Macmillan, said:

> As a fellow member of the Commonwealth it is our earnest wish and desire to give South Africa our support and encouragement, but I hope that you won't mind my saying frankly that there are some aspects of your policies which make it impossible for us to do this without being false to our deep convictions about the political destinies of free men to which in our own territories we are trying to give effect.

Those 'aspects' were the policies of 'apartheid' or racial separation, introduced by the all-white Nationalist government in South Africa after World War II. Apartheid was another expression of racial theories that had been in circulation for more than half a century. In Nazi Germany, the Aryan races or those of German stock were considered to be *Übermenschen*, superior humans, as opposed to the *Untermenschen*, inferior beings, which ranged from creatures that were barely above apes to those, like the Slavs, who were destined to serve rather than to command. This hierarchy was thought to reflect their different stages in the evolutionary process and, as a scientific theory, it was upheld by some respected biologists as well as racist bigots. It conferred upon the higher orders of mankind, the duty to protect and nurture the lower ones, 'the white man's burden'.

This was known to the Edwardians as Social Darwinism and was once the scientific orthodoxy. It justified white supremacy and even, broadly speaking, class distinctions, so that like racehorses, human beings could be assessed by their pedigree. Careful breeding from superior stock produced stronger and faster animals, which was why Social Darwinists considered it advisable to deter marriage with lesser breeds and to keep them apart, to avoid genetic contamination. Under its Nationalist government, the South Africans, who had sent soldiers to fight for the Allies in war and for the Free World against communism in peace, developed an all-embracing system, in which whites, blacks and coloureds lived in separate districts, were forbidden to marry outside their race or even sit with a person of another race in the park. Only the whites could vote.

Macmillan was on a tour of the British dependent territories and dominions in Africa. It was the intention of his government to bring as much of the former Empire as possible into an informal club, the Commonwealth, by granting them self-governing independence but trying to retain their trading links and kinship with the Mother Country. It was intended to be the model for the association of friendly nations that British governments would propose for Europe as well. But there were two issues that might threaten its future: apartheid in South Africa and possible British entry into the Common Market.

Two Commonwealth conferences were held in London in May 1960 and March 1961 to thrash out these vexatious issues. Malaya, newly independent in 1958, objected to South Africa's inclusion in the Commonwealth, if it retained apartheid. What was the point of having a club, if its membership rules were so lax? Malaya was supported by other non-white countries, but the white dominions, with the exception of Canada, favoured keeping South Africa within the Commonwealth. Their declared aim was to assist a process of peaceful democratic change but also because they may have thought perhaps that apartheid was a good idea.

When in doubt, Supermac favoured the Big Picture. In his speech to the South African parliament, he likened their situation to the last years of the Roman Empire, when, as a consequence of the very values that the Romans introduced, smaller nations were seeking to govern themselves. He reminded his sullen listeners that the world was split between the Free World, which believed in democracy and human rights, and the Communist countries, which delivered nothing but servitude. But there was a third group of uncommitted nations, which should be encouraged to stay within the Commonwealth by supporting its true values. He ended: 'The wind of change is blowing throughout the continent. Whether we like it or not, the growth of national consciousness is a political fact.'

Decolonisation in Africa was as much a feature of the post-Suez Conservative government, as the independence of India had been to post-war Labour. In 1960, Ghana, formerly the British Gold Coast, became an independent country within the Commonwealth, with institutions based upon Westminster models, even down to the courtroom wigs. Zambia (Northern Rhodesia) and Kenya were to follow in 1964. The British government had a serious choice to make. Should it foster its links with the white Commonwealth at the expense of the non-white countries, a global apartheid, or should it embrace the principle of non-discrimination, fair treatment for all within a colour-blind community of nations?

This was not a speech that Macmillan was compelled to make. He was on an official visit. It might have been more diplomatic to voice his misgivings in private. The Americans were not instructing him. They had problems of white supremacy of their own. Politically, it caused him trouble. South Africa was a prosperous and strategically placed ally but, because of his intervention, as the South Africans saw it, in their internal affairs, it left the Commonwealth in 1961, having declared itself an independent republic. Within weeks of speaking these words in Cape Town, Macmillan's fears were proved right. The South African police opened fire on demonstrators in the black township of Sharpeville, killing seventy-nine people, a massacre.

In the UK, the League of Empire Loyalists split from the Conservatives, leaving a vocal minority of sympathisers within his own party, and joined with the British National Party, eventually to set up the National Front. Some army chiefs complained that the Prime Minister was giving too much encouragement to terrorists, such as the Mau Mau in Kenya. Perhaps, as some suspected, he had decided to abandon the Commonwealth in favour of the Common Market and was clearing the way of troublesome allies.

But it is hard to resist a different conclusion. He was seeking the moral high ground. He chose to make a statement of principle in a hostile arena, knowing that his words would be heard not only in South Africa but throughout the world. They were heard in Alabama, where, in 1962, a Democrat, George Wallace Jnr, ran for the office of Governor on a policy of racial segregation and made a bid for the presidency. They were heard in the White House, by the young President John F. Kennedy. Three years before Martin Luther King called upon his thousands of supporters to march on Washington, DC, Macmillan announced that he too had a dream – that racial segregation would have no place in the friendly club of civilised nations that he hoped of that the Commonwealth would become.

In the context of the Cold War, he was countering left-wing egalitarianism with its liberal alternative: equal treatment under the law, equal respect for human dignity and equal right to seek happiness. But it was no less revolutionary for being liberal, for there were very few countries in the world where some kind of racial segregation did not apply, not least in the black African colonies to which his government was seeking to bring independence. In some places, the Civil Rights movement amounted to a cultural revolution, for it replaced a class of white civil servants and administrators with their indigenous alternatives. Nowhere was social justice achieved overnight.

Nor was Britain exempt. The Roman Empire maintained as a matter of principle that free citizens, as opposed to slaves, should be allowed to visit Rome freely, the Imperial City. Britain followed its example, as in so many ways, and her post-war governments encouraged mobility of labour throughout its Commonwealth and Empire. London was the great attraction, the mother city. This served two purposes. The government offered a haven to those who felt that they might be under threat or dispossessed after national independence. It calmed their fears. But Britain was suffering from a shortage of labour. It needed to recruit from its citizens overseas. In 1948, HMT *Empire Windrush* landed at Tilbury in Essex from Jamaica with 500 families from across the Caribbean.

From 1948 until 1971, boatloads of immigrants arrived from the Caribbean to fill vacancies in the NHS and on the railways, while small traders from the Indian sub-continent and Asian-African communities opened corner shops and restaurants throughout the UK. There was some emigration from the Mother Country to the white dominions as well, but the demographic picture of towns and cities in Britain started rapidly to change, prompting fears of racial clashes.

'A sizeable part of the entire population of the earth,' warned the Home Secretary, R.A. Butler, 'is at present legally entitled to come and stay in this already overpopulated country.' He was presenting a new Commonwealth Immigrants Bill to parliament in November 1961, shortly after Macmillan had introduced a bill which allowed his government to open negotiations to join the Common Market.

These two debates were linked in the minds of every member of the House of Commons. If Britain were to sign up to the EEC's rules on 'mobility of labour', the free movement of peoples from its dominions might prove to be a serious obstacle. Would British citizens from the Commonwealth and Empire have equal rights in the EEC? One might have to be sacrificed for the other, a choice that few wanted to make.

Butler emphasized that the government did not want to stop Commonwealth immigration, merely to 'control' it. The numbers had risen from 60,000 in 1960 to 113,000 in the first ten months of 1961, of which 54,000 came from the West Indies and 19,000 came from the Asian sub-continent. White families moved freely from one part of the Empire to another, as they always had done. Nobody wanted to restrict their movement.

But black and coloured immigrants were moving into ghetto-like districts, where they were resented by the locals and exploited by slum landlords. Was it possible to control one group and not the other without making the distinction between black and white, poor and rich? Would this not be apartheid? If not, was there some kind of filtering process, based upon non-racial qualifications, such as education, wealth or even a points system?

Within the Commons, there were two prevailing sentiments. The first, and the most dominant, was the fear of returning to the race hatred of the 1930s. The memories of the Holocaust were too vivid. But the second was that immigration might lower the living standards of the working classes. In South Africa, the dramatist, Athol Fugard, wrote about the plight of blacks[i] under the Pass Laws But he also described the struggles of the poor white farmers to hold their own against the invaders from the north. It was similar in Britain.

In 1961, some MPs passionately defended the Commonwealth; according to the Labour MP, Sydney Silverman, it was 'almost the only and quite the best free association of free peoples acting together for peace throughout the world'. In his view, the EEC was a threat to the multicultural character of the Commonwealth, substituting narrowly European values for the wider range of beliefs that the old Empire represented. Outside Parliament, on the far left were those who wanted the workers of the world to unite, to get rid of the Commonwealth and the Common Market altogether; while on the far right, the British National Party (BNP) was on the march, demanding a white Britain. But the centre ground, reflecting the views of was held by the liberal-left and the liberal-right, championeding a society where all races were treated equally under the law.

In Ealing North, the constituency where I stood as the Liberal candidate at the 1966 General Election, my impression was that the process of assimilation went relatively smoothly. We had a good number of immigrants, but I knew of no slum landlords, like Peter Rachman, who dominated the nearby terrace blocks in Notting Hill. We had BNP marches, but no major riots. While canvassing, I heard some complaints about the smell of curry and the noise of reggae, but they were mainly good humoured. We were helped by the Commonwealth game, cricket. These were the great days of West Indian cricket, with the three Ws (Worrell, Walcott and Weekes) and Garfield Sobers. They gave a sense of pride to the Windrush community and inspired every boy who loved cricket. The team that terrified our local side in Ealing were the Brixton Beehives, no hiding of ethnic identity there.

Ealing North was a mainly middle-class constituency with little unemployment. Elsewhere in the country, there were larger anti-immigrant marches, which warned of further troubles ahead. In 1964, in the suburb of Birmingham, Smethwick, a Conservative, Peter Griffiths, unseated the former Labour cabinet minister, Patrick Gordon Walker, using the slogan, reportedly borrowed from the BNP, 'If you want a nigger for a neighbour, vote Liberal or Labour.' Griffiths denied that he was racist, but supported apartheid and South Africa.

There were others who claimed not to be exactly racist either, but who felt that the arrival of immigrants had been imposed upon them by a 'ruling elite'. It may have had the highest principles in mind, but it had not considered the effect of sending children to schools where a dozen different languages were spoken It failed to understand how the differences in culture and religion might undermine the social conventions that held families together, the very structure of any British society.

Nor did the government foresee how a spirit of alienation could build up over time and start to influence other decisions that it might have to make, such as whether or not to join the EEC. If this happened, it would be another jolt to the British way of life.

(ii)

Civil Rights was the great liberal cause of the second half of the twentieth century. It transcended all others, from Northern Ireland to the Australian outback, from the defence of the Inuit in Canada to the bussing of school children in Alabama. As a political movement, it may have started as the rejection of apartheid in South Africa and segregation in the Deep South; but it spread to include those who were treated as second-class citizens for other reasons, or worse, as outcasts and pariahs. Wherever there was thought to be unfair treatment, a Civil Rights lobby could often be found to speak up on behalf of the victims, until it was sometimes hard to distinguish the genuine ones from the born troublemakers.

In 1965, under a Labour government, the first Race Relations Act was passed, whose purpose as to prevent 'racial discrimination in public places' and to ban all expressions of hate 'on the grounds of colour, race, ethnic or national origins'. But this was hard to define or monitor. In 1968, the Act was amended to cover 'housing, employment and public services', but it had to be revised again in 1973. A Community Relations Commission was established (with a Liberal MP as its first chair) to promote 'harmonious community relations'. Assisted by the vagueness of its definition, Civil Rights merged into political correctness and descended through layers of committee rooms into the nooks and crannies of daily life.

During the 1960s, the mood in the country changed, or so it seemed at the time. It became more tolerant and open to influences from abroad. London, always a cosmopolitan city, 'swung', according to *Time* magazine. Nobody knew how long this liberal progressive mood would last, but it seemed irreversible. And yet, across the Western world, wherever Civil Rights triumphed, there could be found pockets of resistance, like Confederate enclaves, where a seemingly irrational anger could erupt and reveal the passions beneath.

The French have a useful word, *la structuration*, which sounds clumsy to English ears. It refers to the way in which we seek or are given roles in life, which form part of a wider, inter-locking pattern of work, family life and beliefs, a social structure. It can be applied in a Marxist sense to the roles that we play in the production, distribution and exchange of goods. It can apply to the British class and the Indian caste systems, and to the customs that surround social institutions, like marriage and inheritance. Nations can sometimes be defined by their structure, so that the UK might require a monarchy, an unwritten constitution, an elected 'first-past-the-post' parliament and a legal system based upon precedence to be what it claimed to be, an independent sovereign state.

These institutions evolved over time, as the British (like any other nation) learnt more about themselves and adapted to circumstances. Modern Britain was different from, but also an extension of, the Imperial Britain of its past, retaining its identity through its 'structuration'.[ii] The Civil Rights movement accelerated the momentum for change so that, for many, it was not so much an evolutionary process as the wholesale demolition of cherished beliefs. It embraced other movements: Gay Pride, Black Power, feminism and, for street philosophers, Sartre's Existentialism. The Catholics in Londonderry marched against the Crown.

In Britain, the Sexual Offences Act was passed in 1967, which brought into law the recommendations of the Wolfenden Report (1957) that 'homosexual acts between consenting adults in private should no longer be a criminal offence'. It repealed what had been described as the blackmailers' charter. But few in authority had expected the arrival of gay bars, gay pride marches or AIDS. The Church of England finally endorsed contraception and acknowledged that sexual pleasure within marriage should no longer be regarded as a sin. But when theatre censorship was abolished and private strip clubs flaunted themselves in the West End, many Christians felt that the floodgates had opened. There was no shortage of examples of bad behaviour, epitomised by the downfall of the then Secretary of State for War, John Profumo, who lied to the House of Commons over his affair with a girl who was also sleeping with a Soviet Naval Attaché.

Each liberalising measure was greeted with horror by the socially conservative. One of their targets was the new-look BBC whose Director General during the 1960s was Hugh Carleton-Greene, the brother of the novelist Graham Greene. He sought to transform the BBC from a middle-brow institution to one which reflected the post-Suez mood of scepticism and generational change. Following Robin Day's example, political interviews became more challenging, documentaries more incisive and the first topical satire came on air, *That Was the Week that Was* (*TW3*). There was some relaxation of the BBC's language codes. Within the appropriate context, such words as 'masturbation' were allowed, and the subject could be discussed, although 'fuck' and 'cunt' were not.

These changes were not always popular with the BBC's political masters and *TW3* lasted for just a year, from November 1962 to December 1963, gathering huge audiences, before it was taken off air before the 1964 Election, never to be seen again. But its success was noted and repeated across the Atlantic, with David Frost, its British presenter, pioneering a trend towards late-night political satire. Carleton-Greene's loudest critics, however, came from Moral Rearmament, a Christian revivalist movement. One member, Mary Whitehouse, started the Clean Up TV Campaign in 1964 and became the first president of the National Viewers and Listeners Association (NVLA), which she founded.

Whitehouse denounced Carleton Greene as 'the devil incarnate . . . who more than anyone else . . . was responsible for the moral decline of the country'. She gathered support from the Lords Longford and Hailsham, the journalist Malcolm Muggeridge, the pop star Cliff Richard and an up-and-coming Conservative MP, Margaret Thatcher. They started to exert much pressure on the BBC, until Carleton-Greene, while not naming Whitehouse, complained of 'a dangerous form of censorship' that came in the wake of their campaigning.

Even the film censor, John Trevelyan, was liberally inclined. He declared that his main qualification for his job was that he did not believe in censorship.[iii] It was his view that a government should not impose moral standards upon the country but intervene only where there was obvious social harm. This could be hard to prove, but those who campaigned for Moral Rearmament did not require such proof, 'Would you allow your own daughter to wear mini-skirts in public?' To which the liberal might reply, 'How would you stop her?'

For those that swung with swinging London, Mary Whitehouse was a figure of fun, a provincial schoolmistress with an eye for misbehaviour. She had a low opinion of television, 'a medium for entertainment that should not be allowed to meddle frivolously with such matters as politics and religion', a view shared, according to her *Memoirs*, by Mrs Thatcher. In September 1971, the revolt against a 'permissive' society that seemed to permit too much reached its climax. The Festival of Light rally in Hyde Park was attended by 100,000 people with more than seventy similar rallies around the country.

'This is an age,' stated Bob Danvers-Walker, voice of Pathé News, 'when men with dirty minds and tongues flourish because up until now there has been no militancy against those degenerates who befoul every form of art.' He may have had in mind the Royal Shakespeare Company's season in 1964, condemned by a member of its own board as 'dirty', or Edward Bond's *Saved* at the Royal Court in which a baby in a pram was stoned to death. But these were celebrated as 'breakthrough events' by critics in the British liberal press. They revealed a pioneering spirit to match the examples from the World Theatre Seasons at the Aldwych. The West End opened up to great companies from abroad, Brecht's Berliner Ensemble among them, which confounded those who much preferred Agatha Christie.

A divide opened between those who regarded themselves as the enlightened few and those who claimed to belong to the moral majority, both seeking the high ground. All liberals believed that they were fighting against an old Establishment, whose hypocrisy was matched by its naivety. One example of the double standards was the BBC programme,'s *Jim'll Fix It*, which raised money for charity and answered requests from children for wonderful things to happen. The series ran for 20 years from 1975 to 1994. The NVLA gave it an award and Mrs Thatcher liked it as well. She invited Savile to Chequers, the country residence of the British Prime Minister, and awarded him a knighthood.

This gave him a position of an almost untouchable privilege within the BBC and in the hospitals and care homes that he visited which he, as a serial paedophile, freely abused. The extent was not widely known until after his death; but what turned out to be as shocking as the activities themselves was the licence that he was given to pursue them.

There were other dark corners into which Mary Whitehouse's Festival of Light failed to penetrate. Beneath the soft porn of London's strip clubs, which she freely attacked, there was a substratum of dungeon and S&M clubs, which specialised in 'the English vice', caning, sometimes on minors.

These clubs she ignored. Perhaps she had never heard of them. They were usually overlooked by the police as well, because corporal punishment was still legal and openly practised in private schools and the training centres that Whitehouse applauded. Her barrister, John Smyth, ran Christian camps for young men, where he freely flogged them. There was a Roman tradition of stoical obedience and the respectful fear of authority that developed a brotherhood useful to the officer classes. Decades later, however, the legions of the abused complained about how they were treated as children. Headmasters resigned in disgrace, with bishops and football coaches, and the full scale of the activities became known.

But the let-it-all-hang-out liberals and the uptight conservatives held one overriding concern in common. What sort of nation would post-Imperial Britain become? How should we conduct ourselves in a nuclear age? Were we still a Christian country? The anxiety could be felt as much in the bravado of the Bond movies as in the seminars on parenthood. Did a wedding ring indicate nuptial slavery? Germaine Greer's *The Female Eunuch* (1970) feared so, but was soon attacked by her counterblast, Arianna Stassinopoulos' *The Female Woman* (1973). There was no certainty anywhere. Politicians were derided, clergymen were mocked and after the last screening, audiences streamed out of cinemas with indecent haste, instead of waiting for the National Anthem to be played.

The battle for Civil Rights sometimes had the effect of undermining the social structures upon which men and women had come to rely. The 1968 sewing machinists' strike of the women working in the Ford factories at Dagenham and Halewood was a case in point. Their demands were for no more than fair play, equal pay for equal work, and it led to the first Equal Pay Act in 1970, a long-overdue piece of legislation. What was meant by 'equal work'? In most British households, the man was the breadwinner and the woman the homemaker, a division of labour to which my parents did not object. Equal pay for women, however, challenged the status quo. A man did not have to be one who brought the money home, the forager or warrior ant. He might have a rival within the family. Some men felt that they were losing their family authority.

Social changes require mental preparation. They need debate, modelling, trying things out in less dangerous circumstances than real life. When Nora walked out of her family home in Ibsen's *A Doll's House* (1879), she inspired a Continent-wide debate about the rights and wrongs of marriage. In London, *A Doll's House* was parodied in a play, written by *The Times* theatre critic, entitled *Breaking a Butterfly*: she should have stood by her man, however loathsome he was.

The theatre has been the licenced game area for Western civilisation since the days of the ancient Greeks. This primary function for the theatre was well understood by the then head of BBC Drama, Martin Esslin, and the Finance Director of the Arts Council of Great Britain (ACGB), Anthony Field, who was appointed in 1958. Field advised the incoming Chairman, Arnold Goodman, under the new Labour government, elected in 1965. Field, Goodman and Jennie Lee MP, Aneurin Bevan's widow, transformed the prospects of the ACGB.

Its government grant was tripled and was spent, with the help of the local authorities in the creation of a new chain of repertory theatres – in Liverpool, Manchester, Birmingham, Coventry and Stoke, whose public role was similar to that of the German city and state theatres and the French *maisons de la culture*. The ACGB may still have been a contentious institution, pioneered by Keynes, but its higher public funding led to an increased authority among artists and gained cross-party support. In 1964, Britain, which had previously had no national theatre, suddenly found itself with two, the Royal Shakespeare Company (RSC) and the National Theatre, temporarily housed at the Old Vic Theatre in London, under its star actor-director, Laurence Olivier.

These developments did not bridge the gap between those who welcomed such changes and those who found them threatening, between those who swung and those who dangled, and the gulf widened between the cosmopolitan baby boomers in cities like London and those who felt that they were missing out. 'Sex began in 1963,' mourned the poet Philip Larkin, 'rather too late for me.' This mixture of optimism and disapproval also coloured the debate between those who wanted to enter the EEC and those who wanted to stay outside.

There were those who, since the days of the 1945 election, had favoured the idea of sacrificing some sovereignty for participation in a wider European community. The Common Market was an economic success. It would soon become the largest trading bloc in the world. But those who hankered after lost imperial glory saw signs of betrayal. Pride in our past was strong. To abandon the Commonwealth in favour of an economic arrangement with those countries on the Continent which had recently been our enemies was hard to accept. Only a nation in decline, insisted the League of Empire Loyalists, would even contemplate such a prospect.

(iii)

'There are some,' Macmillan admitted, 'to whom the whole concept of Britain working closely with other European countries is instinctively disagreeable.' He who had fought in two World Wars could understand how they felt, but he urged them to think differently. Isolationism was not the answer. Britain should join, while the EEC's institutions were still being developed, and use 'what influence we have for the free development of the life and thought in Europe'.

He was speaking in the Commons on 2 August 1961, to move that 'this House supports the decision of Her Majesty's Government to make formal application to initiate negotiations to join the European Economic Community'. It was 'one of the gravest decisions' that Britain could take, for the 'underlying issues – European unity, the future of the Commonwealth, the strength of the Free World – [were] all of capital importance'. The motion was carefully worded. It did not ask for the permission to negotiate, but only to 'initiate negotiations', for the government had other interests to consider.

Foremost among them were those of the Commonwealth. Although it was agreed that this far-flung collection of nations could never provide an alternative to the Common Market, there were areas where they might come into conflict. These included 'mobility of labour' and 'Imperial Preference' in trade. There had been two conferences of Commonwealth prime ministers to discuss these issues. There were the national interests of the farming and fishing industries to consider, the coal and steel industries, and those of manufacturing, and the universities. Throughout the summer, MPs, knowing that this crucial debate lay ahead, had consulted with their constituents as to what joining the EEC might mean.

Finally, there were the interests of Britain's colleagues in the European Free Trade Area (EFTA) to bear in mind, the 'outer seven' member states which included Norway and Liechtenstein. Britain had formed an association with them in 1960 to meet the growing strength of the EEC. How many of them would wish to add their signatures to the Treaty of Rome? But as Macmillan went through the list of potential pitfalls, it was clear that his mind was made up. Britain should join the EEC. Failure would be 'a tragedy'.

What were his reasons? Some were economic. Since Suez, the British economy had performed better than expected, with full employment and rising standards of living, but it was still fragile, living on borrowed money and losing its share of Commonwealth trade. Like every other European country, Britain was unable to compete in the space race and enjoy all the political, economic and military opportunities that this implied. As Nigel Birch MP, pointed out during the debate, the 'United States spent £2,600 million on space research or £1,000 million more than Britain on its whole defence system'.

Space research and nuclear energy, however, were only two of the many fields that science was opening up for the benefit of mankind. The choice presented was whether Britain should turn its back upon a thousand years of history, as the Labour leader, Hugh Gaitskell, warned, or whether to gamble on a technological future that offered incalculable gains and risks. Was it not better to be a second-class country with its freedom intact, rather than to sit at the high table of another world power, having sacrificed one's independence to do so?

At the top of the motives of those who wanted to join the Common Market, and also for those who did not want to do so, were the memories, still fresh, of the Second World War. Macmillan's memories were as vivid as anyone's, spanning both world wars, but his primary concern was with the security of the Free World. If Britain joined the Common Market, with her Commonwealth ties intact, she would bring together the major forces for democratic freedom into one grand alliance. Britain in Europe was the last remaining piece in a jigsaw that would include the Special Relationship with America, the English-speaking peoples of the British Commonwealth and Empire, and the post-war democracies in Western Europe.

That was his grand vision, expressed with tact and modesty, for he knew that many would disagree with him, and it was endorsed in the Commons by a substantial majority. But from President de Gaulle's point of view, the British application to join the EEC represented an Anglo-Saxon intrusion into its affairs at a time when, as Macmillan said, the very institutions were being formed. 'What is the point of Europe?' de Gaulle asked his Minister of Information, Alain Peyrefitte, in 1962, 'It must be to prevent domination either by the Americans or Russians.'

Britain was a 'maritime country'. It looked overseas to its old colonies for cheap food and labour. Its economy was fragile, the pound was weak and its defence was tied into the US nuclear programme, a dependency that de Gaulle wanted to avoid for France. De Gaulle was himself at odds with other members of the EEC, the Belgians and the Dutch, who favoured British entry, and his vision for a Europe of sovereign states, '*l'Europe des patries*', in which the glory and independence of France would shine brightly, was not shared by them. 'The Europe of tomorrow,' insisted Paul-Henri Spaak, the Foreign Minister of Belgium, 'must be a supranational Europe.'

France was a founding member of the EEC and retained a veto on its decisions, which it could use in an emergency. When Britain first applied to join in 1962, de Gaulle replied with a short answer, 'Non', during a news conference at the Elysée Palace on 14 January 1963. That three-letter word echoed around the world's media as the supreme rebuff, no further talk, no negotiation, and in Britain, it strengthened the hand of those who had argued that entry into the EEC was a bad idea. France, without leaving NATO, decided that it would pursue its own independent defence policy with its own hydrogen bomb, which it would use for exclusively peaceful purposes.

Macmillan was faced by anti-Europe rebels, harassed by the unnecessary Profumo sex scandal, and lost his ascendancy over his own party, according to the cartoonist Vicky, like a rocket that failed to lift off from the runway. In October 1963, dogged by ill-health, he resigned, handing over to a new leader, Sir Alec Douglas-Home (who called a general election in 1964, which the Conservatives narrowly lost).

In the following month, November 1963, his ally in the White House, whom he had fully supported during the nerve-wracking days of the Cuban missile crisis, John F. Kennedy, was assassinated in Dallas by a lone gunman, Lee Harvey Oswald. There was an abundance of conspiracy theories, but one conclusion was obvious. The US leadership of the Free World had changed hands, with many key questions unanswered, among them how to contain the rebels, the Viet Minh and the Viet Cong, in French Indo-China.

During World War II, the French colonial holdings in south-east Asia, consisting of Vietnam, Cambodia and Laos, were conquered by the Japanese forces. After the war, they were returned to French administration which ruled through friendly Vietnamese leaders. But there were rebel forces in North Vietnam, led by a charismatic general, Ho Chi Minh, which were being supplied with arms by the Chinese and the Russians. The Allied powers, led by the Americans, responded by helping to fund the Franco-Vietnamese government in Saigon to contain what was seen as another threat from worldwide communist aggression.

When Kennedy died, his successor, the Vice President, Lyndon Baines Johnson, made clear his intention to defeat the Viet Cong by military means alone, without the help of the French or even the British. The Viet Cong proved stubborn enemies, however, well used to the jungle battleground, and the war in Vietnam escalated, claiming more lives and growing more unpopular by the weeks and months in the United States, until in 1968, a presidential election year, Johnson announced that he would not stand again.

In Gaullist France, the Vietnam War was especially unpopular. There had been family and trading links with the country, a French-speaking culture and a historical narrative that dated back to the Jesuit missionaries in the seventeenth century. In the eyes of some French patriots, the war in Vietnam was another act of Anglo-Saxon piracy.

Although Britain had not sent any troops to Vietnam, only a Commonwealth peace-keeping mission which failed to keep the peace, it was still seen by the French as part of the Anglo-Saxon Empire. In 1967, the Labour government under Harold Wilson decided to apply again to join the Common Market. It was supported by a larger majority in the Commons, including the 12 Liberal MPs who were solidly in favour, with the anti-EEC rebels split evenly between the Conservatives and Labour. Although Wilson had promised the re-birth of Britain through the 'white-heat' of its industry, this had not yet happened. It was still burdened by its unreformed nineteenth-century infrastructure and its economy was suffering as a result. Britain was losing its share of overseas markets, including those of its Commonwealth.

De Gaulle was not convinced. The tone of his reply was very sympathetic, patronising, but firm. It was his 'dearest wish' to welcome the UK into the European family, but there were still 'formidable obstacles'. Britain was not European enough. It was too tied to its transatlantic Big Brother, whose secrets it shared, without sharing them with France. Britain was the launch pad for the US bombers. Had France (or NATO) been consulted?

The second application was rejected, leaving Britain more isolated than before. These were febrile times. The perilous balance of power that had kept the Cold War from getting too hot was losing its hold on global affairs. In the United States, the anti-war movement was gaining strength and Moscow was losing its iron grip over its puppet regimes in Poland and Czechoslovakia. Across the world, a new generation was taking over.

The tipping point was 1968, a US presidential election year. It began with the *Tet* Offensive, *Tet* being the word for New Year. The Viet Cong, the communist movement in South Vietnam, which was assumed to be a spent force, launched an attack on twelve cities and blew a hole in the US Embassy in Saigon. No battle was actually lost, but the episode was a reminder to US voters that the war was by no means over. In February, 48,000 new recruits had to be conscripted and yet more families dreaded the arrival by post of the draft card. In April, the Civil Rights leader, Martin Luther King, was gunned down, while in June the former President's brother, Senator Robert Kennedy, a presidential candidate, was shot by a Palestinian, Sirhan Sirhan, under mysterious circumstances.

At the Democratic Convention in Chicago in August, Civil Rights campaigners from across the United States staged mass rallies to back the antiwar candidate, Eugene McCarthy, and were roughly treated by the city police force, which was accused of Gestapo-like tactics. Nor were the disturbances confined to America. They spread across Europe. In West Germany, the offices of the right-wing Axel Springer newspaper group, which supported the Vietnam War, were attacked by student revolutionaries. Their leader, Rudi Dutschke, was murdered in a copy-cat killing of Martin Luther King.

In France, the *événements de mai* began with demonstrations against the war, mainly by students, which were taken up by the trade unions and turned into a general strike. Sartre was among them, linking arms, but the main organising force was the French Communist Party, whose aim was to bring down de Gaulle and the French government. But they had to fight against the news from the other side of the Iron Curtain, which told the story of how the Prague Spring failed to materialise into a summer. The liberally inclined Czech leader, Alexander Dubček, was summoned to Moscow, and peremptorily sacked.

De Gaulle responded to the demonstrations by calling a general election in June, which he won, and followed this with a referendum to provide a new constitution for France, which would have given the President, himself, greatly increased powers. But this was a step too far for the left, led by the socialist leader, François Mitterand, who declared after a broadcast by de Gaulle that 'what we have heard is the voice of dictatorship'. De Gaulle lost the Referendum and retired to the country to write his *Memoirs*, which he never completed. He died in 1970. His staunch ally in the formation of the Common Market, Konrad Adenauer, died in the previous year. The leading political figures of the Western world, once all-powerful, had died, retired or were turned out of office within the space of four years.

Throughout the turmoil of 1968, another revolution was taking place, television by satellite. It influenced the climate of opinion towards the Vietnam War. In 1966, US public opinion was in favour of the war. Few commentators opposed it, except Walter Cronkite. War photos were a twentieth-century art form, but they were of yesterday's events. The satellite images were immediate. We could see an army general shooting an unarmed suspect or a naked child fleeing against a haze of napalm. There was less control over was what was being screened. An incident might occur that no military spokesperson could defend.

Slowly, the military lost control over the war narrative. No general could proclaim a glorious victory, when with the help of satellites we could all watch the messy undergrowth of war. This had an impact upon US public opinion. Polls revealed a large swing from 28 per cent of the population who opposed the Vietnam War in 1966 to 50 per cent against in 1968. This was a foretaste of what was to come. The immediacy of satellite television made it more difficult for the government to offer an official narrative that daily events could contradict.

During the 1960s, the space race was between the two major powers, the US and the USSR. No European nation had the capacity to send up its own satellite, although France and Germany did so together in 1974. Britain had to rely upon the Special Relationship to provide the facilities for its own space research. Communication satellites were only the start of what could be achieved. In 1961 and 1963, respectively, the first man, Yuri Gagarin, and the first woman, Valentina Tereshkova were sent into space by the USSR. In December 1968, the US Apollo 8 spacecraft splashed down in the Atlantic, having spent six days circling the moon. The first moon landings took place six months later. There could be no turning back. We were forced to look at our planet differently. The rock upon which we had built our homes was merely an object in space.

Globalisation in the mind began in the dark regions beyond the orbit of our earth. It came to represent a future for mankind to which all Western European countries could merely aspire. Only as a group of nations could they effectively contribute. There was another lesson to learn. The view from space nagged us to recall that our first obligation was to protect our planet, a duty that transcended sovereignty, politics and all other human endeavours.

***

Chapter Five
Acid Rain

(i)

In 1952, 4,000 people died in London from smog, the mixture of smoke and fog that accumulated in the Thames valley over four cold and windless days of winter. 8,000 more died in the following weeks. These statistics were compiled by the Ministry of Health from evidence supplied by the new National Health Service; and they elevated what had been considered an infernal nuisance, the Victorian 'pea-souper', into a spur for political action.

The first Clean Air Act was passed in 1956, but it was followed by others, each more extensive than the one before, affecting more daily lives, until, like Civil Rights, it joined with similar causes and became a mission to protect, and even save, the planet from global warming. As its aims became more ambitious, disruptive and speculative, they were harder to confirm from personal experience. The melting of the Arctic ice cap may be a bigger menace to mankind, but it did not send a person to a hospital bed, heaving to breathe.

The aim in 1956 was to persuade householders who were still burning coal in their grates to turn to its smokeless derivative, coke, and then to oil or electricity. The problem was also caused by coal-burning factories. The legal height of their chimneys was raised to prevent their smoke from lingering in the blackened streets. As the emissions entered the higher wind streams, the sulphur dioxide and nitrogen dioxide from their furnaces mixed with the water particles in the atmosphere to cause what was known as acid rain. This turned what was thought to be a local problem into a regional one. Acid rain damaged crops, harvests and trees, and spread across the North Sea from Britain to scorch the forests in Scandinavia.

There was much denial. It was very hard to prove that a car plant in Dagenham could curl the tulip fields of Holland or that, as the winds changed, factories in the Ruhr valley might not cause similar damage elsewhere. Questions of liability were involved, as with oil spillage at sea. Which government could impose what penalties? At first, this seemed to be wishful thinking, since nothing could be proved, but, as images of the earth from satellites became available, the effects of wind-driven pollution could be observed in detail. Whole industries could be held to account. Some supra-national body, with its own courts, judiciary and means of settling disputes, had to be constructed that all countries would respect for the protection of the environment was, or should be, in everybody's interest.

Once more, the independent sovereignty of European nations was brought into doubt not by the US or the USSR, but by the scientific information that the Cold War and the space race brought in their wake. One trigger for change came from the lateral thinking of a maverick scientist, James Lovelock, who was working within the National Aeronautics and Space Agency (NASA) in the United States. Lovelock was born in 1919 into a British working-class Quaker family, passionate about education. He studied at night school before being admitted to the University of Manchester to read chemistry under Alexander Todd, a Nobel Prize winner. He joined the Medical Research Council to study the effects of heat and radiation in war, and became part of a team seeking to discover solutions to problems that were partly medical, partly environmental, and might require political or military intervention.

In 1961, he was seconded to NASA under the umbrella of the Mutual Defence Agreement (MDA), negotiated between Eisenhower, who founded the space agency, and Macmillan. His first task was to develop instruments to analyse the atmosphere of other planets to discover whether they, like Earth, had the capacity to sustain life. Mars, he decided, offered little chance – too little oxygen, too much carbon dioxide – but this did not stop NASA from sending up a space probe to discover that he was right. This research led him to speculate about the atmosphere surrounding the earth, the combination of gases that allowed us to breathe and protected us from the full force of sun's rays, so that our planet could enjoy a relatively stable environment.

He came to the view that our atmosphere was self-sustaining in the sense that biological activity on Earth absorbed the harmful chemicals and heat from the sun and transformed them into the energy necessary for its survival, thus creating a benevolent circle, in which life itself created the circumstances conducive to living. The forests in the Congo and Amazon basins, the vast expanse of the oceans, the changing seasons, biodiversity and the activities of man all contributed to the sustainability of a living planet, which he named, borrowing the term from his friend, the author William Golding, Gaia. In the legends of ancient Greece, 'Gaia' was a primordial deity, the ancestral mother of all life, and the very use of the word was transformative. It changed the way in which many people thought of the planet. Instead of being an inanimate rock upon which life had mysteriously appeared, it became the living partner in human survival.

But this terrestrial equilibrium could be damaged or destroyed. Cutting down rainforests or polluting rivers might lead to a chain reaction in which human activity damaged the capacity of the planet to adapt and regenerate, and cause something like acid rain on a global scale. Lovelock undertook research that demonstrated how this might occur and had already done so. He developed the electron capture detector that analysed the presence of chlorofluorocarbons (CFCs) in the atmosphere, which caused damage to the ozone layer surrounding the earth. This filtered the sun's rays to prevent the planet from overheating. CFCs were widely in use within industry as a propellant in aerosol products and refrigerators, but as a result, holes in the ozone layer were gradually getting larger, admitting more of the sun's rays and thus causing skin cancers, climate change and global warming.

The consequences were not hard to predict: rising sea levels, changing weather patterns, destruction of habitats and, if left unchecked, the baking of the planet. Lovelock's research was confirmed by other scientists, but often opposed by the industries concerned. In 1974, a paper was published by two academics, Sherwood Roland and Mario Molina, which led to an investigation by a US Congressional Committee. It concluded that there was enough evidence to justify international action and over the next fifteen years, concerted lobbying produced a very rare treaty, the Montreal Protocol, to be signed by all the 197 countries in the United Nations. Its aim was to phase out the 'substances that deplete the ozone layer', pollutants that now ranged beyond CFCs to include fossil fuels.

In as much as there could be general agreement among climate scientists, global warming became their common concern. Opinions differed, however, as to how much was caused by human activity or was part of a cycle of natural geophysical events, in which ice ages were followed by heat waves, and so on. Although it was possible to measure many effects of global warming, the total picture was, and always would be, beyond the range of the most powerful computers to analyse, the data too abundant to collate and always changing, due to factors of which some were known, others unknown, and might always be unknowable. Gaia was a compelling idea, not a proven fact, and nor could it ever be, but this reflected more upon the limitations of the scientific method than of Lovelock's thesis. At a certain point, all factual knowledge broadens out towards faith or speculation.

Those who were committed environmentalists, such as Friends of the Earth and Greenpeace, leapt upon Lovelock's theories with delight, while other scientists were more cautious, pointing out the seeming inconsistencies or errors. In the UK, Lovelock found powerful advocates, including Jonathan Porritt and HRH Prince Charles, and across Europe, the Greens grew as a political force, often on the fringe, but occasionally finding a place in government. As with Civil Rights, undeniably good causes mingled with doubtful, harmful or silly ones; and it was sometimes hard to tell the difference between them.

Lovelock was not an easy leader to follow, a rebel and an iconoclast, who could turn on those who respected him most and deride them for naivety. 'Equality' in his view was a denial of evolution. He championed nuclear power, poured scorn on renewable sources of energy and was apocalyptic about global warming, forecasting that mankind was already reaching the point of no return.

He despaired that governments in the free world could ever summon up the political will to face the challenge. Lovelock was not the first prophet to despair of democracy. What was the alternative? Decisions have to be taken, structures that can command public support have to be built and political processes have to be found whereby a convincing case can be converted into effective action. Like Churchill, another natural rebel, Lovelock was not one to suppress his visionary energy to 'the docility of a State machine'. The consequences of his theories, however, have spread far and wide into the details of working lives.

Coal and steel, the main drivers of the Industrial Revolution, which built the war machines and were in the process of being retooled for peace, became pantomime villains in Green eyes. The power stations on the Thames at Battersea and Southwark were phased down and closed in the 1980s, one to be turned (irony of ironies) into a gallery for modern art, the Tate Modern. The other was useless for thirty years.

The physical resources that enabled Britain to become the first industrialised nation and created the wealth that built the railways were no longer essential to its survival as a country. Mining villages fell into decline and their populations scattered in search of other work. Although the Greens were not responsible for the decline, the fact that many seemed to welcome it, did not endear them to those who had become surplus to requirement.

As Britain evolved from a post-Imperial nation to becoming almost a post-industrial one, so its structure changed. It was not only the cotton workers in Bolton or the miners in Wales that risked losing their ways of life, but the classics graduates as well, backbone of the ruling classes. Within the

Establishment, there was a certain impatience with the technocrats, who warned of disaster, but did not seem to know on which side their bread was buttered, particularly when their evidence came from extra-terrestrial sources.

Perhaps too we all had mixed feelings about abrasive individuals, like Lovelock, the rebels who proved the majority wrong, and wanted them in almost equal measure to fail or to succeed. In the 1960s, there were still pockets of contented living in Britain, where nothing seemed to have changed very much, and the moon was still far off and romantic, and a third of the world stood up for the Queen, and cricket was still played on village greens, where the women of the parish made cucumber sandwiches for the tea intervals.

And it was still possible to believe that what had happened over the previous 50 years was an enormous aberration, an unnatural catastrophe, from which, with God's will, we would eventually escape. But in the heart of London, at the Aldwych Theatre, an actor on stage released a cloud of butterflies into the auditorium, but held one caught by its wings, and, flicking a cigarette lighter, set it ablaze.

A stage metaphor, but which were we? The actor, the burning butterfly or among those that miraculously escaped?

(ii)

This shocking theatrical moment came from a partly improvised drama documentary about the war in Vietnam, staged in 1966 by the Royal Shakespeare Company (RSC) and directed by the *enfant terrible* of British theatre, Peter Brook. The incident had a Jacobean intensity, similar to the tearing out of Gloucester's eyes in *King Lear*, which forced you to watch, while shuddering at its brutality. The butterfly represented a Buddhist monk, who set fire to himself on the steps of the US Embassy in Saigon, as a protest against the war. This was Brook's way of trying to shake the British public out of its attachment to the Special Relationship, illustrated by the play's ambiguous title, *US*.

Elsewhere, the actress, Glenda Jackson, called for napalm in Hampstead to bring home the horrors of Vietnam, almost a terrorist threat, and the fact that it was made on a public stage by a company subsidised by the Arts Council of Great Britain demonstrated the rebellious boldness of a new theatre generation, led by Peter Hall, the RSC's charismatic young director. Hall was appointed to run the Shakespeare Memorial Theatre at Stratford-upon-Avon at the age of twenty-nine; and transformed what had previously been a summer theatre. It dated back to the times of the eighteenth-century actor,

David Garrick, but Hall turned it into an all-year-round repertoire theatre, with a semi-permanent company, along the lines of German state theatres, whose scale and ambitiousness had long been the envy of British directors.

The Shakespeare Memorial Company was the wealthiest regional theatre in Britain, supported by the Flowers family of local brewers. The chair of its board was Sir Fordham Flower, who raked together the assets to create what was meant to be the first British national theatre. The intended National Theatre in London was still in the planning stage after a century of planning. Not only was the RSC's management structure influenced by continental models, but its repertoire as well, its casting and intellectual aspirations. Kenneth Tynan, the theatre critic and one-time literary manager of the National Theatre (NT) once described the RSC as a theatre for university thespians, unlike the real NT under its first director, Laurence Olivier, which was good, old-fashioned showbusiness. He might have added that it was the first German-style 'state' theatre in Britain, the home for 'high seriousness'.

More than any other art form, the theatre reflected the gulf between the Continental ways of thinking and the British. The popular and boulevard theatres in Paris and London had much in common and regularly exchanged hit productions. But Britain had nothing to equal the stylistic excellence of the Comédie Française in Paris, the intellectual rigour of the Deutsches Theater or the Berliner Ensemble from the divided city, Berlin, the romantic passion of the Stary Theatre in Cracow or the psychological insights of Dramaten (the Royal Dramatic Theatre) in Stockholm, where Ingmar Bergman held sway. From 1964 to 1973, these great companies, and others, could be seen at the Aldwych, the London home of the RSC, in the World Theatre seasons, brought together by the actor-impresario, Peter Daubeny.

Major theatre companies were usually subsidised more generously on the Continent than in Britain, which reflected their higher social status. Some were court theatres, taken over by the state when their patrons could no longer support them. Others were national theatres, republican and democratic. They were expected to provide intellectual leadership, to maintain the vitality of their traditions and to have their world views, seriously expressed. Their directors held news conferences to which editors sent their leader writers; and even in Eastern Europe, political theatre could be as cuttingly edged as in Britain. In Moscow, the Taganka under Yuri Lyubimov could be almost as critical of state bureaucracy as, in London, the Royal Court Theatre was of the British Establishment.

But the negative side to the Continental system was what Brook described as the curse of the 'stately' theatres, slow-moving productions of well-worn classics with famous actors on long-term contracts, playing Romeo at the age of 60, besides which a good American or British musical could seem like pure joy. Whereas London audiences seemed to demand nothing more than a 'good night out', those on the Continent expected a deeper response to the challenges of the times, an 'engaged' theatre (after the French word, *engagé*) of which the RSC's *US* was a rare but trail-blazing British example.

An 'engaged' theatre was not necessarily the same as a politically committed theatre. It might have nothing to do with conventional politics at all. It was a way of considering how we might cope with the uncertainties of life within a make-believe situation, modelling our responses in advance. There were two broad approaches within the classical tradition. One was to invite audiences to identify or 'empathise' with the central character, the 'protagonist', so that they went through his or her feelings during the course of the play. The other was to distance the audience from the feelings of any one character, so that they could adopt a more critical stance.

These are the main technical distinctions between tragedy and comedy, which were derived from the analysis of classical Greek theatre by the philosopher, Aristotle, whose *Poetics* was required reading for all students of drama. Brook was born into a Jewish family from Latvia, who emigrated to England after the First World War. He spoke Russian and French, and was one of a handful of directors, including Joan Littlewood, George Devine and Peter Hall, who absorbed the influences from the other side of the English Channel as freely as he did those from Broadway. Others included the American director, Charles Marowitz, and the producer, Oscar Lewenstein, and this happy few infiltrated the system, took on and outmanoeuvred the showbusiness barons, known as the Group. With a little help from the state, the rebels changed the British theatrical scene.

At a time when British entertainment industries were basking in the glow of winning the war, continental theatres were undergoing a painful self-examination. They were striving to examine the causes of war, all wars, and why the revolution of the people was so hard to achieve and so close to tyranny, once it had taken place. Because the emotions were too raw and the gangsters, who had caused the mayhem, still alive, the stories might be dressed up in the metaphors of the Absurd or in the cool detachment of Bertolt Brecht's Epic theatre, his answer to Aristotle. But there was little room for evasion. Dramatists from both sides of the Iron Curtain in Europe understood all too well how their Continent had become civilisation's charnel house for much of the twentieth century.

They had witnessed at first hand the rise of Nazism (Brecht's *Arturo Ui*, Ionesco's *Rhinocéros*), watched the decline of the upper classes, (Mrozek's *Tango* and *Operetta*), endured the insolence of the new order (Bulgakov's *Heart of a Dog*), suffered from Anti-Semitism (Frisch's *Andorra*), experienced the hairline gap between power and madness (Weiss's *The Marat/Sade*, Genet's *The Balcony*), witnessed the horrors of the labour camps (Szajna's *Replica*) and lived in the limbo of those who were adrift in a meaningless world (Beckett's *Waiting for Godot*).

Emboldened by the evident seriousness of what was happening in Continental theatres, British theatre experienced a remarkable transformation. Assisted by grants from the ACGB and the local authorities, a chain of about 50 regional repertory theatres was developed. They may not have been as grand as the German civic theatres, or as well-financed, but they understood that their role was not merely to reflect public opinion, as expressed through the box office, but to educate as well and provide models for the ways in which we could remember the past, examine today's challenges and rehearse for the future.

There were casualties as well as success stories. The three touring circuits of the London-based commercial chains suffered. Many of the old music halls went, together with the domestic comedies and dramas that were once the mainstay of the West End. In London, Agatha Christie's *The Mousetrap* obstinately clung on. Elsewhere the little theatres, '99 seaters', which were used as try-outs for the West End, became more ambitious, following the examples of *die freie Bühne* (free stages) in Germany or *les tréteaux libres* in France. For about fifteen years, 1964 to 1979, British theatre could claim to be the most exciting and ambitious in the world. It had the best writers, the most influential directors and set designers, who won awards even at the Prague Biennale.

Its high reputation was supported upon one Herculean pillar, William Shakespeare, physically dead for 450 years, who provided both the Continent and the English-speaking peoples with the language of myths through which so much could be expressed. Hamlet was Germany, lacking the will to get rid of its dictators; Richard III was Stalin or any Mafia boss; while *Titus Andronicus* was the Soviet Union under Stalinism. At a time when many politically contentious writers were kept in check, if not in prison, Shakespeare was above the battle, an honoured name throughout Europe, and his plays could be so flexibly interpreted that they could serve many causes.

In Nazi Germany, *The Merchant of Venice* was his most popular play, with Shylock as the pantomime Jew, but, after the war, it was played to attack anti-Semitism as well, with Shylock as a victim of prejudice. The eighteenth-century critic, Gottfried Lessing, the world's first *dramaturg*, said after one performance, 'My God, the fellow has been wronged!'[i]

In 1964, a collection of critical essays, *Shakespeare Our Contemporary*, was published in English by the Polish critic, Jan Kott, which explored the ways in which Shakespeare anticipated the modern world, not only in its politics and jostling for power, but also its psychoanalysis and existentialism. Kott, who defected from Communist Poland in 1965, was one who had been through the fires of the century, a Jew who escaped transportation to Hitler's death camps, a Communist in the 1930s, an exponent of Socialist Realism, who underwent a painful journey from his youthful optimism to a mid-century realism, with Aeschylus, Shakespeare and Lydia, his wife, as his only reliable companions.

Kott influenced Brook and the generation of younger British directors, who rescued the reputation of Shakespeare from the swamp of sub-Elizabethan extravaganzas, 'doublet-and-hosiery', into which the Bard was in danger of sinking. His presence as a witness to the worst excesses of the twentieth century contributed a new voice to a rapidly changing theatrical outlook, which was becoming quick to challenge and less willing to accept, aspiring towards (in Hall's phrase) 'the nation's debate with itself – at flashpoint'.

This transformation could be felt up and down the country, in Nottingham at its new Playhouse where Peter Barnes' *The Ruling Class* (1968) failed to cure an ordinary member of the House of Lords of insanity, a British *Marat/Sade*, and at the little Bush Theatre in London, where Edward Bond's play, *The Pope's Wedding*, was first produced. It could be felt at the Edinburgh Festival, the World Theatre seasons and a host of smaller festivals.

It was appreciated abroad. The comedies of Tom Stoppard, Michael Frayn and Alan Ayckbourn were popular across the Continent, while Bond's *Saved* was named as the Play of the Year (1967) by Germany's leading theatre magazine, *Theater Heute*. It could be felt as far afield as the site of the ancient city of Persepolis, where Ted Hughes' play, *Orghast* (1970) was staged by Brook's new Centre for International Theatre Research (CIRT), on a mountain top in Iran (Persia).

For a brief period, fostered by the British Council, the Arts Council and her artists, Britain led the world in 'soft' diplomacy. In 1965, the visit of Laurence Olivier in the new National Theatre's *Othello* was triumphantly received in Moscow, the first sign of what was felt to be a thaw in the Cold War. The British boy bands – the Beatles, the Rolling Stones – were heading the international charts. Their pirated albums were played even in Siberia.

The successes of soft diplomacy are always hard to measure, but at a time when the war in Vietnam was provoking riots across Europe and the Special Relationship was in doubt, the vitality of British arts may have played its part in restoring a friendlier balance. When in 1968, a new Conservative Prime Minister, Edward Heath, approached the EEC for the third time to apply for EEC membership, he was met with a cordial welcome, not a rebuff. President Pompidou welcomed him as a true European.

The two opponents of British entry, Adenauer and de Gaulle, were dead or retired, and no longer around to block the way, but the soft diplomacy may have helped as well. Britain seemed a more exciting place. London's streets bustled with tourists. Carnaby Street fashions were sold in Florence. The British were no longer complacent but pleasant to know, the right sort of people to be invited to join the club.

There was another sign of the times. In 1976, after 20 years of planning, frustrated by British and French politicians alike, the world's first supersonic airplane, Concorde, flew from Paris to New York in two and a half hours. It was built by Aérospatiale, a French company, working in partnership with the British Aircraft Corporation (BAC). It demonstrated that the new Europe could produce technical achievements to match those of the US and USSR. Only the Soviet Union managed to build another supersonic passenger plane, but it was far, far, less beautiful than Concorde.

(iii)

The Clean Air Act was introduced to the Commons in 1952 via through a Private Member's Bill, proposed by Gerald Nabarro MP, one of a younger generation of Conservatives, who entered parliament in 1950, after the unexpected surge in his party's fortunes under its ageing leader, Winston Churchill. He was supported by another new member, Enoch Powell, and together they shepherded the proposal through its various stages until it became law in 1956. By such means, they quickly established their reputations as effective backbench MPs, who might in due course expect promotion to the government.

They shared other causes. Both were opposed to smoking and Nabarro introduced the legislation, which required health warnings on cigarette packets. They supported Sir John Wolfendon's proposal to decriminalise homosexual behaviour. Powell, but not Nabarro, was opposed to the death penalty and welcomed its abolition under a Labour government in 1965. Both opposed the Race Relations Act, were against mass immigration and, when Powell was sacked from Heath's shadow cabinet in 1968, Nabarro became his booming champion.

Neither was quite what he seemed. Nabarro, with his huge handlebar moustache and his fleet of Daimlers with personalised number plates, seemed to be the embodiment of a Shire Tory. He represented a constituency in Worcestershire, Kidderminster. In reality, he came from a poor Jewish family in London, ran away to sea at fourteen, was largely self-educated, entered the army and was honourably discharged. He became a prosperous timber merchant. Sometimes, his patriotism seemed ostentatious, as if proving his right to belong to a club to which he just been invited; and when, late in his life, he faced a summons for a traffic offence, he could afford the fine but not the blow to his reputation. He felt deeply ashamed.

Powell was a distinguished classical scholar, with a double first at Cambridge, who became a full professor at the age of twenty-five, a year older, as he ironically pointed out, than Nietzsche. At a time when the study of ancient Greece and Rome was considered to be the education for Imperial government, Powell was an acknowledged expert. Although the master of his subject, he might also be said to be its victim, by imitating its *mores* too literally. He 'wanted to be killed on the battlefield' – 'pro patria mori'. He likened those who were enlisting for war to 'bridegrooms going to meet their brides', a Latin tag with a Middle Eastern history. Fighters for the Islamic State are cheered into battle with a similar motto. But it still sounded a little out of touch in an age of nuclear warfare.

His speeches were constructed with the rhetorical skill of someone who had studied Cicero, proceeding point by point to its unanswerable climax, which often came in the form of a Latin example, so that if the listener accepted the first premise, which sounded plausible, and the second, which seemed reasonable as well, he or she would be trapped in an ascending spiral of logic, from which there seemed to be no escape. In debate, his opponent had to challenge his first assumption at the risk of sounding pernickety. He was no populist speaker, like Nabarro, but he was considered by some to be the finest orator of his age, who combined the nationalistic fervour of Sir Oswald Mosley, the British fascist leader of the 1930s, with an eloquence born in the battlefield. He had studied Nietzsche and in his younger days as an atheist, elevated the Will above Duty, and Duty above Compliance.

He was a linguist with a command of modern European languages, French, German and Italian, and a poet, whose iambic quatrains echoed A.E. Housman and the Metaphysical poets, such as George Herbert. Shakespeare was close to his heart. Although he, like Nabarro, was a passionate opponent to the EEC, he could never be described as a 'Little Englander'. His views on sovereignty were close to de Gaulle's, as the inviolable essence of identity, without which the nation would float in a limitless sea of compromise and indifference.

In March 1959, de Gaulle described how to be French and quintessentially European. 'We are,' he asserted, 'above all a white race with a culture from Greek and Latin, and with a common Christian religion.'[ii] It sounded self-evidently true, except that, even in France, the white was never so white, her culture a melting pot and her Christianity controversial. So it was with Powell's Britishness. It seemed self-evident, except to those who did not share it.

Like de Gaulle, Powell distrusted the United States; and advised Wilson not to send troops to the war in Vietnam. He abhorred the idea of being the junior partner in the Special Relationship. Either as a province in a new European empire or as the vassal of the Americans, the country would cease to be British in all but name – and maybe even in name. When the powers-that-be in the Foreign Office suggested that in these post-colonial days, it would be better to drop the 'British' from the 'British Commonwealth', Powell objected. Without acknowledging its imperial history, the Commonwealth would be meaningless, a random collection of would-be nations in an international club, as impotent as the United Nations and almost as bad as the Common Market.

Nabarro and Powell were opposed to the drift towards the liberal centre under the leadership of Macmillan and Heath, all forms of 'Butskellism' with its Keynesian economics, and were prepared to sacrifice their chances of advancement to speak their minds. Indirectly, Nabarro assisted with the rise of the UK Independence Party, UKIP, in the 1990s. Nabarro's political assistant was the PR consultant, Christine Holman, who married the Conservative MP, Neil Hamilton. Hamilton left the party to join UKIP in 2002 and became a member in the Welsh Assembly, the leader of UKIP in Wales. It felt like the start of a new political dynasty.

Powell resisted invitations to join the National Front, when he left the Conservatives in 1974, preferring to share his fate with the Ulster Unionists in the Antrim Hills, and when UKIP came into being, he chose not to become a member and refused to support the cause. The course of political history was much influenced by the choices that he did not take. If, as once seemed possible, he had embraced the Gaullist vision of Europe as the union of sovereign states and not dismissed the Commonwealth as a collapsed British Empire, he might have found a broader body of support within his party. He challenged Heath for the leadership in 1965, but only received the support of 15 per cent of the MPs who could vote for him. He was considered to be 'too clever by half' and, according to Sir Maurice Palliser from the Foreign Office, 'brilliant but mad'.

Nigel Farage, a founding member of UKIP and for many years its party leader and principal spokesman, was an admirer of Powell. He even volunteered on one occasion to drive for him. After the Treaty of Maastricht in 1992, Farage left the Conservative Party and campaigned in local and general elections as a UKIP candidate, before being elected to the European Parliament in 1998. Like Nabarro, he is a bluff populist with a booming voice, a cheerful, opinionated, pub politician; but his arguments owe more to Powell than Nabarro.

Although Powell, who died in 1998, was never a member, his thinking permeated the politics of UKIP, not only in its attacks on the EEC and immigration, but also in its views on sovereignty, identity and the Britishness of being British. Powell contributed to *The Salisbury Review*, edited by Roger Scruton, which articulated the philosophy of the new right wing. It was opposed to liberalism in all forms, including Keynesian economics and the sharing of sovereignty. Scruton denounced the Modern World – its aesthetics, its lax and godless morals and its globalism. But he did not persuade the modern world to go away.

At the heart of this philosophy lay the notion of national identity. It was not so much a matter of what you thought but of who you were, your gut instincts as well as your opinions. It was, according to Norman Tebbit MP, Margaret Thatcher's loyal supporter, the team you cheered for in cricket. When Powell was told that the West Indians in his constituency felt 'alienated', he replied: 'Well, they are aliens.' It was partly a matter of race and of culture, and partly of feeling comfortably at home within those institutions that had grown up over centuries within the British Isles, which would not have applied to the BBC, definitely not. It would have included cricket but not baseball, Vaughan Williams but not Aaron Copland, Dickens and Thackeray but not Norman Mailer. Britain was a constitutional monarchy, not a republic.

Above all, identity, at a personal or national level, meant taking responsibility for those decisions that were within your power to control. It was the way in which, according to Hegel, the Self could assist in its own fulfilment, the very goal of its being. When the institutions of the EEC intruded upon those of the UK, in pursuit of what might seem to be better trading relations, it was attacking the identity of Britain. Control of Britain's borders was not just a question of keeping immigrants out: it was a matter of defining who you were. Mobility of labour, one of the four founding principles of the Treaty of Rome, was an assault on national sovereignty, no different from and no better than, the threat from the Luftwaffe during World War II.

From this point of view, the defence of national identity was not prejudice: it was more a question of survival. When Powell was accused of being a white supremacist, he replied by making a distinction between racialism and racism. The former recognised the differences that distinguished one race from another, skin colour, the mores or customs, which were self-evidently there. But the latter, the racist, asserted the superiority of his or her tribe above the others, which was a different matter. A patriot did not have to be an imperialist, only the defender of his race.

Powell spoke in favour of apartheid, which he did not regard as racism. He championed the cause of a white Rhodesia. He believed in separate development and the repatriation of those West Indians who had come over to help with the rebuilding of Britain in the 1950s, the Windrush generation. He opposed the Race Relations Act, but this did not mean that he was prejudiced against black people. He quoted from Virgil's *Aeneid*: 'As I look ahead, I am filled with foreboding. Like the Roman, I seem to see "the River Tiber, foaming with much blood".' Powell became one of the most popular, but also the most divisive, politicians in Britain. The National Front marched and shouted his name.

For one who was merely acknowledging the differences, Enoch Powell did so in very intemperate language, but this in itself, or so he might argue, was a sign of identity. Naturally, the Englishman would reject an alien soul. Sir Gerald Nabarro got into trouble with the BBC for asking on Radio 4's *Any Questions* (5 April 1963): 'How would you feel if your daughter wanted to marry a big buck nigger with the prospect of coffee-coloured grandchildren?' The BBC removed this remark from the repeat, which the right wing regarded as liberal censorship, typical of the BBC. Natural instincts were not to be confused with prejudice and, according to some polls, 60 per cent of the public agreed with him.

From the distance of 40 years, Powell's distinction between racialism and racism seems like chop logic. He may not have wanted to put those who were black into a concentration camp; he did, however, want to get rid of them through repatriation and tighter immigration controls. This may have been less extreme than the Final Solution, but it belonged within a similar Romantic tradition, which sought to preserve the purity of the race from the invasion of alien beings. This was the story of many blood-curdling sci-fi movies. Racialism forced the believer to interpret the outside world from one angle of vision only.

But it was also an attack upon the artistic freedom and liberalism of the 1960s. Powell was not exactly a Philistine but his tastes were so conservative that his verses might have been written before World War I. After his 'Rivers of Blood' speech, he never regained his position on the Conservative front bench, but his influence spread, assisted by the belief that he expressed the views of the British public. Almost the worst that can be said about him was that he made racial intolerance more respectable, but the very worst was that, for some of his supporters, he turned it into a moral imperative.

***

Chapter Six
Untune that String

(i)

Edward Heath and Margaret Thatcher held some things in common, although they became bitter enemies, and the animosity between them, particularly over Europe, came to symbolise the divisions within the Conservative Party that last until today.

Heath was nine years older than Thatcher, born in 1916, but they represented a post-war generation of Conservative 'meritocrats', who were not 'toffs' and sought to distance the party from being too associated with those that were. Both rose from modest backgrounds and worked hard to go to university at Oxford (Balliol and Somerville), where they joined the university's debating society, and discovered their political ambitions. Both wanted to be professional politicians, studied the facts and figures, and mastered their briefs, unlike some MPs who treated Parliament as a part-time activity. Both had problems with their voices, Heath's too plummy, Thatcher's too shrill, as they both tried to match the nonchalant authority with which Harold Macmillan addressed the House.

Both were proud of their families and more attached to one parent than to the other, Heath to his mother and Thatcher to her father. But here the comparisons turn into contrasts, for Heath's father was a self-employed carpenter, often out of work. During the 1920s, his family was sometimes very poor; whereas Thatcher's father, Alfred Roberts, was a prosperous grocer, who became Mayor of Grantham.

But the outstanding difference between them, overriding temperament, gender and family life, arose from when they were born. Heath grew up in the interwar years and witnessed the origins of war – the poverty, class resentment and the rise of nationalism – and was determined, like his mentor Macmillan, to prevent anything like those circumstances from happening again. Thatcher was a teenager when the war began, when nothing mattered but the winning of it, and at the age of twenty, savoured the exuberance of victory. These memories must have been formative and influenced their future lives.

Heath financed his university career, where he studied Philosophy, Politics and Economics, by winning, firstly, a county scholarship and, then, while at Balliol, an organ scholarship, for his mother had encouraged his lifetime's passion for music. By scrimping and saving, he went to see what was happening on the Continent, attended a Nuremberg Rally as an appalled onlooker and, on his return, spoke out passionately against the government's policy of seeking a peaceful accommodation with Hitler, 'appeasement'. When war broke out, he was on a debating tour in the United States, arguing this cause. By 1941 he had been called up and given an emergency commission to join the Royal Artillery. He spent the early months of the war, manning the heavy artillery to protect Liverpool's dockyards.

His warnings attracted the attention of those who were on the anti-appeasement wing of the party, including Macmillan, which stood him in good stead in the years after the war. In 1950 he was given the chance to stand in the Labour-held seat of Bexley, which he managed to win and held for 51 years. He became the first leader of his party to be elected by his parliamentary colleagues, the youngest at the age of 49 and the model for the new Conservative meritocrats, whose claim to office depended on their worldly experience rather than their family backgrounds. This was part of his appeal, his gaucheness, his shyness, his will to succeed without the airs and graces of his self-assured predecessors. What he sacrificed in eloquence, he compensated by his clarity of mind.

But one did not have to travel widely within the home counties and the shires to find out that the toff appeal of the Conservative Party was a powerful factor in local politics. In some constituencies, there were gentry, whose influence stretched back over many generations and from whose ranks the local MPs were expected to come. They were groomed for office and the way in which they spoke, dressed and were educated, and attached to other notable families within their neighbourhoods, gave them an entitlement to govern that businessmen and entrepreneurs could never seem to match. They were the governing class. Heath always had to battle within the party against the impression that he was not quite a gentleman.

Worse, this was a self-image that he sometimes seemed to share, for he could display the hauteur of a Duchess and the nit-picking of a junior civil servant within the same speech; but this touch-me-not exterior concealed many of his strengths: his international vision, his compassion and willingness to listen to others, drawing them towards a collective decision.

While Macmillan often seemed to apologise for the EEC and looked for plausible excuses to explain its teething troubles, Heath sought ways to strengthen it, which was another reason why the French President, Georges Pompidou, called him a good European.

In the lengthy talks that preceded Macmillan's first failed application in 1962 and the negotiations that led to an agreement on the terms of entry some ten years later, Heath was the one who grappled with the internal logic of the EEC, its tariffs for each sector, its social conscience and how it handled the touchy questions of sovereignty. But for those anti-Europeans, like Enoch Powell, whom he brought into his cabinet, this friendliness smacked of collaboration. Through Geoffrey Rippon MP, who was in charge of the British application, when Heath was Prime Minister, an entry fee was agreed, which (at £100 million for the first year) was thought to be on the high side. As the Labour Shadow Chancellor, Denis Healey, pointed out, it would also rise incrementally in the following years.

Being too friendly with the French over the entry fee was the least of the charges that the right wing of the Conservative Party brought against their young and somewhat un-clubbable Prime Minister. Wider concerns were immigration and the drift towards the liberal centre, called Butskellism, a conflation of the names of Rab Butler, Macmillan's Chancellor of the Exchequer, and Hugh Gaitskell, the Labour leader who died in 1963. A Butskell administration might be expected to follow Keynesian economic practices, borrowing to invest, maintaining full employment, giving priority to the social services and reducing the gap in advantage between the rich and the poor, all causes which brought electoral success as well. But the right complained that, in the longer run, Butskellism brought more power to the state, inflation, higher taxes, lower investment and the decline in the value of the pound. These frustrated the hopes of businessmen and gentry alike and, or so it was argued, of the working classes, most of all.

Heath became Prime Minister at a time when the warnings of the right were starting to be heard. His Labour predecessor and main rival, Harold Wilson, had devalued the pound to boost sales abroad, a move which was then (but not now) within the government's control. The country was gripped within an inflationary spiral, in which higher prices were followed by demands for higher wages from the all-powerful trade unions. This led to even higher prices and even higher wage demands. The balance of payments, even with Commonwealth trade, was falling more deeply into the red.

Both Wilson and Heath tried to introduce prices and incomes policies, in consultation with unions and managements, but these were criticised by right-wing Conservatives as constituting a large extension of state power. It amounted to socialism by the back door, in which the monetary values that were placed upon someone's work were imposed top-down either by the party in power or by those, like union leaders, who held power but not the national responsibility. The trouble with modernisation, which, as all agreed, was necessary for industry and the country, was that it required more than the application of facts and figures. It also involved the trickier question of 'values'. At what point should the corporate values of the modernised state take over from the private values of those who wanted to live in a more settled and traditional way?

Democracy in Britain grew out of the shires and burghs of thirteen-century England, when representatives were called to London to form a parliament. This is why Members of Parliament today are still elected through their constituencies, physical places, rather than via their party lists, their professions or any other kind of selection. A constituency was, and still is, more than just a place on the map. It had its own identity, local narratives and ways of earning its living. Britain was said to be the victim of its class system, but there could be reasons why members of a well-known family held their privileged status. They could be benefactors, employers or significant players within a powerful local history.

In a constituency, 'class' was never a trustworthy way of finding out who might vote for you, who might not, and why. Electors frequently voted against what might seem to be their class interests. In rural districts, a farm hand might support a candidate from the gentry, because his family had once fought in the Napoleonic Wars. In times of war, the gentry led the drive for recruitment; in times of peace, they built the new town halls. If elected to Parliament, a gentleman Conservative MP would often seem to represent their districts as a natural party of government in a way that no upwardly mobile meritocrat, imposed upon the constituency from Central Office, could hope to equal.

Similarly, many Labour MPs had deep family roots within their constituencies, and in the trade unions that defended the rights of the workers. They had a local credibility that a left-wing intellectual with an impressive academic record would usually lack. To that extent, the political system always tended to be more bottom-up than top-down, which slowed down its willingness to adapt to the times. British politics may have had the reputation of being the playground of the *élite*, because of the Etonians and Oxbridge graduates who sat round the cabinet table. But they too had to respect the views of the electorate, which might be more unwilling to change its ways than the modernisers would have wanted it to be.

Yet the political climate was becoming more volatile, as the unexpected gains by the Liberal Party and other smaller parties in the by-elections revealed. Sections of the population were being compelled to change, whether they wanted to do so or not. This was not only for demographic reasons, with the coming of Commonwealth immigrants, but because it was necessary to move around the country in search of work.

The rise of the meritocrat was a sign of this wider mobility. This stemmed partly from the 1944 Education Act to ensure free education for all until the age of 15, Butskellism at its best. But a more flexible workforce was required to meet the demands for skilled labour, as old-fashioned workshops closed, industries retooled and no one knew what would happen next. The door to a more prosperous Europe was still temptingly ajar.

The supreme example of an upwardly-mobile meritocrat was Margaret Thatcher. She faced many of the obstacles that Heath had to overcome, with the mixed dis/advantage of being an attractive woman in a male-dominated House of Commons. She was 34 years old, when she first entered Parliament in 1959, who had studied chemistry at university and gathered a law degree. But she carried no unhappy memories of pre-war years, no war experiences, none of the uncertainty, only the satisfaction of belonging to a country that had won the war. She saw no need to apologise for winning.

Heath appointed her as the Secretary of State for Education and Science in his first cabinet in 1970, more than, as some critics complained, a 'token woman', but as a member of his team, who did not stray far from Butskellism. She opened more comprehensive schools than any other education minister, demanded more money for nursery schools from the cash-strapped Treasury and made token savings, such as the withdrawing of free school milk, which earned her the reputation of being a hard woman, 'Margaret Thatcher, Milk-Snatcher'.

There was no sign of the full-scale attack on Butskellism that characterised her time as Prime Minister and, in the debate which paved the way for Britain to enter the Common Market, she voted with the government. Over the next 20 years, however, a very long time in politics, the Iron Lady, who became famous for not taking a U-turn, did so in a spectacular fashion. She turned away from a Common Market that was supposed to be above national self-interest, away from the mixed economy of public and private ownership, and towards a free market economy where winners were allowed – and encouraged – to be winners.

She explained her philosophy in an interview given to *Woman's Own* in 1987:

> Too many children and people have been given to understand [that] 'I have a problem. It is the government's job to cope with it.' . . . They are casting their problems upon society, and who is 'society'? There are individual men and women and there are

> families . . . and no government can do anything except through people . . . it is our duty to look after ourselves and then after our neighbour. . . . There is no such thing as society.

(ii)

On 21 October 1971, parliamentary proceedings began for what was described in the press as the 'Debate of the Century'. The decision would have to be taken that would determine Britain's future for the rest of the twentieth century and beyond, 'without doubt', according to one MP, 'the gravest constitutional issue of all time'. The Speaker begged members to be brief. Two hundred had put down their names to be heard and it was inevitable that more would be added during the days ahead. Six days had been allocated to debate the European Communities Bill, which would approve the government's decision to join the Common Market on 'the basis of the arrangements that have been negotiated'. The terms of entry were known, most MPs had spent the summer months discussing the issues with their constituents and every leader writer had given his or her opinion, often many times.

On the first day, proceedings began at 4.00 pm and were scheduled to run until 10.00 pm, but they were extended by general consent until midnight. Over the next few days, they ran even later into the night, until the not-so-early morning, 7.00 am, but still there were members to be heard, and heated discussions continued in the corridors, and behind the benches, until one MP complained that he did not mind being heckled, but not from someone else's fringe meeting. Every speaker promised to be brief, and tried to be so, usually without managing it, and the historic importance of the occasion engulfed the whole House. Were they about to exchange their constitutional birthright for a mess of Continental potage?

There should have been more of a consensus. The Conservatives in 1962 and Labour in 1967 had applied for membership, and been rejected, while the Liberal MPs were the most pro-European of all the parties. Now the Conservatives under their new leader, Edward Heath, had successfully negotiated terms of entry, which the Foreign Secretary and former Prime Minister, Sir Alec Douglas- Home, commended to the House. After fifteen years of talk about the pros and cons of membership, the principle was agreed, the terms were known and the opportunity might not come again. The House had to make up its mind.

The issue was still highly controversial; some believed that the heart should rule the head, and others, the head the heart, which was another way of suggesting that the normal rules of debate did not apply. This was not an issue of class. The Conservative bosses were not laying down the terms of entry to Labour, representing the workers. Both parties were divided but, while the Conservative government offered a free (unwhipped) vote in the House for its members, allowing them to make up their own minds, Labour opposition MPs were instructed to vote against, although they should have been among its supporters. It was not so different from the terms that they had tried before – and failed – to negotiate.

In party terms, it was a mess. Some Labour MPs spoke in favour of the government, some Tory MPs opposed it, and they all had their reasons for doing so, which took up parliamentary time until today merged into tomorrow, and a week passed, before the still divided House came to its conclusion, which in another few years would be put before the People in a referendum. If the parties had not been so divided, there would have been no need for a referendum. A decision could have been reached in Parliament. Heath and Wilson both faced rebels within their ranks, which was why Wilson, when he was re-elected as Prime Minister in 1974, appealed directly to the country. It was more to silence the sceptics in his own party than to find out what the British wanted.

In his opening speech, Sir Alec Douglas-Home quoted from the Treaty of Rome that its purpose was 'to ensure . . . the economic and social progress of their countries by eliminating the barriers which divide Europe', a high aim, but Denis Healey, the Shadow Chancellor of the Exchequer, immediately turned to the matter of money. Britain, he insisted, was getting a bad deal. They would be paying 25 per cent of the Community's income and receiving only 6 per cent in return. It was paying too much for entry and we ran the risk of paying more in the future. It would jeopardise Britain's tottery balance of payments, the amount that the country earned from overseas trade and the amount that it had to pay out. The economic weakness of Britain demanded more protectionist measures, to prevent the patient dying from the shock of entry. We might not be able to afford to join on these terms – but could we afford to stay out?

The villain of the piece, from the British point of view, was the Common Agricultural Policy (CAP), which accounted for nearly half of the Community's spending and benefited those countries, like France, with antiquated farming interests, and penalised those, like West Germany and Britain, which had a stronger industrial base and had taken steps to modernise agricultural production. This policy was not part of the Treaty of Rome. Michael Foot, MP for Ebbw Vale, asserted that there was a backroom deal between de Gaulle and Adenauer, in which the French president, always pursuing his country's interests, refused to sign the Treaty without securing a bribe. But he gave no evidence that this was so.

The talk was of extravagantly subsidised butter mountains that melted away or were dumped on the Third World, to the detriment of farming interests elsewhere, including those of the Commonwealth. West Germany prospered from the Common Market, because under the post-war peace settlement, they were prevented from spending their resources upon war, whereas the British with their cousins across the Atlantic carried the defence burden of the Free World. This should have been taken into account. Under the terms that had been negotiated, Britain would be trebly penalised: by the CAP, the loss of Commonwealth trade and increased competition from West Germany.

Thus, voices against the Common Market were raised. On the second day, the first modest defence of the CAP was heard in the speech from John McKie, MP for Enfield. He pointed out that in the mid-1950s, there were 22 million farms within the boundaries of the Community, stretching from Normandy to the toe of Italy, small, chronically poor and family-run, but these had been reduced in number to about ten million more prosperous enterprises which could afford to buy their own tractors. The aim was to spread the wealth of the Community, so that the industrialised North could help to support the regeneration of the South and other rural regions, which might include the highlands of Scotland or farmers in the Lake District, whose incomes also depended on what the land could provide.

The Common Agricultural Policy was the largest and most ambitious attempt at social engineering west of the Iron Curtain and, in Cold War terms, it contrasted the Keynesian approach of state intervention with the Soviet Union's collective farms under state control. It had a Green agenda. Many ecologically harmful insecticides and fertilisers were banned. In Britain, during the 1950s, hedgerows were cut down to produce larger fields, but this was discouraged on the Continent. There were restrictions to protect the environment, to conserve fish stocks, to ensure the cleanliness of the abattoirs and many other matters.

In Britain, there were often similar rules, which had grown up over a longer period of time. That was the trouble with the building of a new civilisation from the fragments of the old. It all had to happen too quickly.

For some members, the Common Market was merely an economic zone, which had proved to be marginally more successful than similar trading pacts, such as NAFTA (the North Atlantic Free Trade Agreement) and EFTA (the European Free Trade Area). The politics of the EEC were considered to be of secondary importance, speculative and even dangerous, while the vision for Europe that inspired so many on the Continent was mere 'pie-in-the-sky'. The idea that the vision itself might help to explain the Community's relative prosperity was understood and welcomed by some, including Heath, but dismissed by others. They were more concerned with practical matters, such as the balance of payments. If the EEC could help to dig Britain out of its poverty, it would be welcomed, but not otherwise.

The UK was badly in need of such help. Britain, once the industrial heart of the Empire, was rapidly losing ground to its own former dominions, which were building their own factories. Having recently experienced 'over-full' employment, Britain now had one million unemployed. Our labour relations were notoriously bad and the pound had been de-valued. There was a brain drain, as men and women left their universities to seek their fortunes in other parts of the world, primarily to the dominions, but also to the Continent. The largest free trade area in the world, nearly 300 million customers, was on Britain's doorstep. It would be madness not to join.

But was Britain 'European' enough'? So the French President, Georges Pompidou, de Gaulle's successor, asked Heath, to which his answer was: 'Could Europe be Europe without including Britain?' Some suggested that this was still being somewhat evasive. The British Isles and the Continent were entwined by history; they could not be separated. But the modern, sovereign UK had a Mutual Defence Agreement with its cousins across the Atlantic, which it did not share with France and other Community members. Heath, as Pompidou knew, was a convinced European, but what about some of his colleagues? Did they believe in Churchill's remark that, faced with a choice between the Continent and the Open Sea, the UK would always follow the Open Sea?

In Parliament, Peter Blaker, MP for Blackpool South, dismissed this sentiment as 'pretty woolly'. Were the British an island race? No longer in London, whose docklands were bombed during the war and closed in the 1960s. Nor in the rest of the country, where public opinion seemed to be changing rapidly, socially, politically and sexually, and becoming more cosmopolitan. The local curry house was taking over from the fish'n'chip shop. 'Fings Ain't Wot they Used t'Be' was the title song from one British musical; 'Stop the World, I Want to Get Off' came from another. The debate straddled those who were impatient for a future of greater modernity and those who wanted to delay it for as long as possible.

'The rate and the pace of change,' confessed Ernest Marples, MP for Wallasey, a future Transport Minister, 'is becoming so great that it will become difficult for human beings to adjust to it.' Within fewer than 30 years, mankind had witnessed the destruction of Hiroshima and Nagasaki, the carnage of a million people from two now old-fashioned bombs and the start of the nuclear age, a new source of power which could take us who knew where. It had intimately witnessed the war in Vietnam and watched the moon landings on television delivered by satellite, which had transformed the way in which we saw ourselves and our planet. Civil Rights had challenged white supremacy in the former Empire; and men could no longer consider themselves to be the breadwinners in a marriage. 'Change,' Marples insisted, 'is resisted by the majority of people', but it happened nonetheless.

To take part in these technological achievements, or even to stay modestly in touch, required resources beyond those of Britain or any other European sovereign state, which was why he commended the motion to the House. But, as other Members protested, were we not discussing how to join a rich man's club with its array of rich men's toys? Would it not be better to stay poor but honest and close to our friends in the Commonwealth? Emlyn Hooson, MP, the only Liberal to vote against, quoted from Einstein: 'The dropping of the first atom bomb changed everything, but our modes of thought.'

'By some strange permutation of history,' concluded Heath as the Prime Minister, 'all these changes have come together within this very short span. Our decision tonight will vitally affect the balance of forces in the modern world for many years to come.' He pointed out that the relationship with the United States was 'not unique' and that, outside the Community, Britain would be vulnerable to 'protectionist pressures', including those from our friends across the pond. It would have little influence over any of the major trading blocs, including China and the Far East, and no prime minister could 'accept a situation in which vital decisions affecting us all were taken in circumstances over which we have no control'.

He commended the Motion to the House, which was duly passed by a majority of 356 Ayes to 244 Noes, substantial but not overwhelming. In the House of Lords, where the Conservatives held what was termed a 'natural' majority, there was a more conclusive result, 451 to 58. Thus, Parliament decided that the United Kingdom should apply to enter the Common Market on the terms agreed, a momentous decision, which was welcomed or deplored (according to the opinion polls) by nearly half the population on either side.

But Enoch Powell remained opposed and, when Heath called a snap general election in February 1974 and another in November, Powell urged Tory supporters to vote Labour, because Wilson was proposing to hold a referendum, which gave those who wanted to leave a second chance. When the referendum resulted in a win for those in favour of remaining in the EEC, he swore to fight against it in Commons, forsaking his party's whip to do so. The politics of confrontation revealed the flaws in the system. It was always claimed that electing MPs through a 'first-past-the-post' system led to decisive results, but not in this case. It was even more muddled than the coalition governments of the French Fourth Republic.

Neither side could form a stable government. The adversarial nature of British party politics meant that neither side was prepared to compromise with its main rival. The small Liberal Party was wooed by both sides. There was eventually a Lib-Lab pact, but without proportional representation, it was impossible to tell whether this represented the views of the electorate, or not. The two main parties found it impossible to decide on the most important issue of the day. The signs of political paralysis set in.

(iii)

Arthur Koestler once remarked that good government was like a well-made suit. It fitted so perfectly that you hardly noticed it was there. It allowed freedom of movement without losing its shape; but this description could be applied more accurately to the gentry who ruled the Shires than to the classless and fair-minded meritocrats in Parliament, who tried to find a one-size-fits-all solution for complicated matters.

Both Harold Wilson's first Labour governments (1964-70) and Heath's Conservative government (1970-74) faced similar challenges: how to modernise the British economy and its industrial infrastructure against a background of pay disputes, strikes and labour unrest. 'The seeds of eighteen years of [Labour] opposition,' wrote the future Prime Minister, Tony Blair, 'were sown not in 1979 [with the victory of the Conservatives, led by Margaret Thatcher] but in the 1960s, when great challenges came upon us and instead of understanding that we were being tested by the forces of change, we lived through a sad episode of betrayal, questioning integrity and motive.' A similar verdict would be passed upon his spell in office.

For the left wing of the Labour Party, modernisation meant the strict application of Clause 4 in its 1918 Constitution, which stated that one of its key political aims was to bring into 'common ownership' the means of production, distribution and exchange [of goods and services]. In 1944, the word 'common' was changed to 'public' – or 'nationalised'. It was printed on every Labour membership card. Labour's aim was the fairer distribution of wealth and to get rid of the wasteful (as the Party saw it) competition between many private companies operating within each sector of British industry. In 1936, London's bus, trolley and underground services were brought into common ownership by the Labour London County Council, led by Herbert Morrison, who became Attlee's deputy after World War II and was placed in charge of its nationalisation programme.

Labour's approach to the reconstruction of post-war Britain was to apply the principle of nationalisation to many kinds of industry – the Bank of England (1946), civil aviation (1946), communications (1947), coal (1947), health

(1948), railways, canals, road haulage and electricity (1948) and iron, steel and gas (1951), a vast political programme, which involved compensating the shareholders, creating new ministries, imposing new management structures and persuading the trade unions to give them all a fair chance. The intention may have been to spread wealth, but the effect was to concentrate power in the hands of the civil servants in Whitehall and the unions through the Trades Union Congress (TUC), which made them reluctant to adapt their normal practices. The stakes were too high, the rewards too slight and too easily blown away by a change in political fortune.

Wilson's first governments had a proud record of liberal reform. It abolished the death penalty, introduced the first Race Relations Act, decriminalised homosexual acts between consenting adults, abolished stage censorship and established the Open University. But he had often to struggle against public opinion and the mood music within his party to do so. The Common Market was a case in point. Labour was split on this issue, as were the Conservatives for different reasons, and when Wilson applied to join, like Macmillan before him, he discovered that his main opposition came as much from within his own party as from outside it. His caution towards Europe, prompted by his problems at home, was interpreted as anti-European by his partners across the Channel.

But the disputes over the Common Market were as much a symptom as a cause, for Labour was split on many other issues as well, including nuclear disarmament. It was supposed to be the party of the working classes, but as industry restructured and modernised, its loyalties seemed outdated and even anarchic. In some parts of Britain, it was still possible to separate the owners from the owned and make fun of the class distinctions between them. The film, *I'm All Right, Jack* (1959), gave such a portrait, with the bumptious trade unionist and the board of toffs. In real life, such comic book companies found it hard to survive. Union leaders were starting to behave more like responsible managers, claiming to defend the public interest before taking industrial action, while the boards of directors would boast of sports fields, pension schemes and health and safety regulations to demonstrate that their companies took great care of their workforce, 'parental' capitalism.

The General Secretary of the TUC from 1960 to 1969 was George Woodcock, who came from a family of cotton workers, but won a scholarship to Ruskin College, Oxford. He was an economist, who studied Keynes, and on the reformist, rather than revolutionary, wing of the party. He once said that the Labour movement owed more to Methodism than to Marx; but Keynes and the Common Market did not fit easily into the narrative of the further left, which interpreted history in terms of the class struggle, where compromise was betrayal.

The real battles were not between Labour and Conservative, but between the extremes of both parties and their Keynesian centres. To adapt Koestler, the two parties with prospects for governing Britain were like ill-fitting suits made in an old-fashioned style for tribes that were nearly extinct. The Conservative Party was no longer a party of toffs, Labour could no longer rely on their battalions of cloth-capped manual workers, and the Keynesian centre was split between three parties, of which only one, the smallest, called itself the Liberal Party.

This made it difficult for either government party to tackle the mounting problems that faced the country: inflation, unemployment, the rising national debt and wildcat strikes. Both Labour and the Conservatives tried to introduce a prices and incomes policy. Wilson liked to invite trade union and management leaders around to 10 Downing Street for 'beer and sandwiches'. It became a political joke. His Secretary of State for Trade and Industry, Barbara Castle, prepared a White Paper, *In Place of Strife*, in 1969, which proposed that an arbitration procedure should always be undertaken by law before a strike could be declared 'official'. This proposal divided the Cabinet, disrupted the party membership, never went to the Commons as a formal bill and probably led to Wilson's electoral defeat in 1970.

The incoming Conservatives under Edward Heath brought in the Industrial Relations Act 1971, whose aims were similar to *In Place of Strife*. It sought to enforce by legal means the collective agreements struck between unions and managements in industry. It was part of the Conservative election manifesto and duly received a democratic mandate. But it led to the miners' strike, the loss of power supplies, the three-day working week and the downfall of Heath's government in 1974, when he went to the country with the slogan, 'Who Governs Britain?' He was told brusquely by the British voters that he did not.

The Industrial Relations Act was repealed by Labour, when it returned to office, and replaced by the Trades Union and Labour Relations Act 1974, which was very similar, although some of its 'offensive' provisions had been removed. These amounted to the suggestion that the workers were to blame for the industrial disruptions, rather than the management, which was thought to be provocative. But the strikes continued, the balance of payments got worse, the rate of inflation increased, Wilson resigned and, after the Winter of Discontent of 1978-79, his successor, James Callaghan, called a general election to decide who governed the country. He was also told by the voters that he did not.

The moral was that no party could win an election by offering a sensible prices and incomes policy. It stirred no gut instincts. Under first-past-the-post, the winning side took all. There was too little room for shades of opinion. This did not lead to decisive government. The victories might be marginal. Governments might be kept in office by pacts with smaller parties. The winners did not win for ever and soon had to face another election, which might turn the tables. At a time when the country faced bankruptcy, it was polarised by its ill-fitting politics, which reflected the divisions of a nostalgically recalled Edwardian Britain.

There was always the 'elephant in the room', coal. At a time when many disputes seemed to be about the minutiae of management, 'who does what', most union and management officials realised that major changes were coming their way, inevitably so, and the battles between them were as much about a jockeying for the position ahead as solving the problems. The coal industry was an example. No British workers had contributed more to victory in war or prosperity in peace than the miners. Coal was Britain's primary source of power. Without coal, trains could not run, cities would not be lit and homes would be left without heating. The towns and villages that depended upon coal as their main source of income stretched across the country, from Wales to the north of England, and into Scotland.

These were settled communities. They had their traditions, their historical narratives and political clout. They had their choirs and brass bands, their poets and novelists, their sports clubs and showbusiness circuits. The mining communities were almost a nation within a nation; they had brought down one government and seemed ready to bring down another, if their demands were not met. The heyday of coal, however, was coming to an end. It was a wasteful and polluting source of energy. Since the mid-1960s, it was known that there were huge resources of gas and oil in the North Sea, but the discovery of the vast Forties Oil Field in 1970 transformed the prospects of the oil companies, particularly British Petroleum (BP). It was generally understood that oil and gas would soon rival and overtake coal as a main source of power for the country, although it would take some time before the fields could be developed. But somebody still had to tell the coal miners.

There were other potential sources of energy, nuclear power, and the 'renewables', such as wind farms and tides. If its economy were to be modernised, Britain had to bring to an end its dependence on coal, a nationalised industry, but its trade unions, representing not only the miners but, effectively, the mining towns as well, would be certain to resist. Under any circumstances, this would be a test of political leadership. The fact that the two major parties were wedded to the rhetoric of class warfare, management versus labour, made the situation worse. The mood was inevitably confrontational. While the leaders pleaded for calm and fair play, the sounds from the ranks increased in bitterness. Every pit threatened by closure became a new battleground.

The ten years that separated *In Place of Strife* in 1969 from the Winter of Discontent in 1978-79, when rubbish was left lying around in the streets and even the gravediggers went on strike, were ones of intense political activity in which little seemed to change, except to deteriorate. Britain was the sick man of Europe and, even as a new member of the EEC, it could not decide whether it wanted to be there. Both parties were divided. When Wilson's Labour Party defeated Heath's Conservatives in 1974, his cabinet contained three members, who were passionately against the EEC, Tony Benn, Michael Foot and Peter Shore. It was a sign of the dysfunctional political system that, on such a crucial matter, neither party could be sure of the loyalty of its members. The 1975 Referendum was supposed to settle the matter

In daily life, when difficult decisions have to be taken and the outcomes are uncertain, the doubts seem to spread and take over control in places where there should be no problems at all. In that respect, a nation is no different from an individual. There were delays in building the National Theatre on the South Bank. Inflation made nonsense of the estimates. In Northern Ireland, young Republicans took their cue from the US Civil Rights movement and marched against discrimination in employment and housing. They were joined by members of the new Provisional Irish Republican Army (PIRA), more deadly than their Dublin-based IRA leaders. It was as if all the enemies of Britain could sense its weakness.

Britain, it was said, was becoming ungovernable. 'Unhappy is the land that has no heroes,' mourned the assistant in Brecht's *Galileo*, seeing his master crushed by the threats of the Inquisition. 'No,' replied Galileo, 'Unhappy is the land that has the need of heroes.'

***

Chapter Seven
The Smack of Firm Government

(i)

During the 1960s, I had three part-time jobs. None was well-paid or likely to lead on to fame and fortune. All were time-consuming. At university I married a concert pianist, Sally Mays, who (like me) was self-employed and irregularly paid, and we had two sons. Common sense should have told me, as other people did, that it was time to settle down, find some steady employment with prospects and behave like a respectable family man.

I tried. Heaven knows, I tried. But I now realise that I was looking for positions at a level above what I could expect from my impressively typed, but fundamentally shaky, CV or asked for skills and experience that I had yet to acquire. Nobody headhunted me. Nobody even seemed to think that I had a head to hunt. And yet, with every failed attempt to climb up the social ladder, I would feel a pang of outrage that lasted for at least thirty seconds before a comforting calm descended. Frankly, the BBC was not good enough for me. Why should I want to teach at a university outside London? I would open my copy of Herbert Marcuse's *One-Dimensional Man* (1964) and realise how lucky I was to be out of it all.

Marcuse was the 'Father of the New Left', the philosopher of the drop-out generation and for those like me who failed fully to drop in. He was born in Berlin in 1898 and emigrated to America in 1934, where he worked for the Office of Strategic Services (OSS) during the war, the forerunner of the Central Intelligence Agency (CIA). His role was to analyse the rise of fascism in Europe and the culture of Nazi Germany, for which, as a member of the Frankfurt School of Critical Theory, he was eminently well qualified. Like Kojève and Popper, he was an authority on Hegel, Marx and Freud. Like Sartre, he associated political freedom (but only on the left) with the emancipation of the libido, the sexual wellspring of all human activity. His seminal work, *Eros and Civilization* (1955), held a re-assuring message for someone like me who liked to think that by climbing into bed with someone I fancied I was contributing in some small way to the liberation of mankind.

Marcuse blamed communism and capitalism alike for turning human beings into mere economic factors within the cycle of the production, distribution and exchange of goods. They became like the goods they produced, in that their purpose in life was to get up in the morning, go to work, take part in a process that manufactured and sold washing machines, cars or something similar, go home in the Morris on which they spent much of their income, turn on the dishwasher that they were buying on hire purchase, and so to bed, exhausted. They were slaves to the consumer society, which did not make their lives richer, happier or longer, but controlled almost every second of their time on earth, even when magnanimously the bosses gave them a day off. What did they do with this 'freedom'? Watch war movies, soap operas and game shows. The whole entertainment industry was designed to shut down their critical curiosity with sentimental propaganda.

That was the typical life story of the one-dimensional man, whose mind, imagination and natural instincts were constrained within a system whose purpose was not to bring wealth to the many but power to the few. In order to sustain this unhealthy lifestyle, there had to be not only continuity of consumption, but overconsumption and planned obsolescence, which helped to destroy the environment as well. Obesity, pollution and life-killing frustration were all by-products of the consumer society. They imposed an artificial structure on the ways in which we lived and were as full of barriers to true freedom as in any communist bureaucracy.

Marcuse was not a lone voice. He left the services of the US government in 1951 to research and teach at Columbia University, and then Harvard, where he found a generation of receptive students. He had younger colleagues who thought along similar lines and published sociological studies which became best-sellers. William Whyte's *The Organisation Man* (1956) described how a company could dominate the lives of its employees even beyond their retirements. Vance Packard's *The Hidden Persuaders* (1957) gave details of how the ad men manipulated consumer demand, capitalist brain-washing, and in *The Waste Makers* (1960) he outlined the ways in which products were made to break down or need updating, 'planned obsolescence', to maintain the continuity of public demand.

These books sold in millions of copies. But Marcuse was the father figure, who placed all their critical views of the West into a wider philosophical framework that looked back to Hegel and Marx and forward to a future in which the drop-outs inherited the earth, because they had not lost their humanity in pursuit of what the economist, John Kenneth Galbraith, called *The Affluent Society* (1958), another best-seller. Marcuse looked towards those who seemed to be marginal and of no political influence – the blacks, the gays and the unemployed – to save humanity from the consequences of its irresponsible behaviour.

Nobody could call me an organisation man. I liked being self-employed and my three part-time jobs may not have brought much money, but they were engrossing in every other way. I was a talent scout[i] for a film company, Paramount British Pictures, which was taken over by its American parent company, Paramount Pictures, and, finally, by Gulf Oil within its consumer products division, after which I thankfully quit. I read scripts, saw new plays and wrote lengthy reports, which mostly never saw the light of day.

But my experience as a tiny cog in a great show business machine gave me an insight into how the entertainment industry worked, where its priorities lay and how it interpreted public demand. It brought me into contact with the British theatrical scene at a time when it was enjoying a remarkable renaissance. There was a feast of new playwrights (Osborne, Pinter, Stoppard, Ayckbourn, Bond and many more), new actors, directors and theatres, of which the proposed new National Theatre in London was the most exciting prospect. It helped with my second part-time job, on which I hoped to base my career, as an all-purpose freelance writer, and contributor of reviews for the splendidly stylish *London Magazine*, then edited by the poet and cricketer, Alan Ross.

My third part-time job was the most reliable and in many respects the most rewarding. I taught classes in theatre and creative writing in the non-vocational adult education institutes that were run by the Inner London Education Authority (ILEA). The best known was the City Literary Institute in Holborn, founded in 1919, which flourished in the interwar years and helped to compensate for the shortcomings of public secondary education. The entrance fees were minimal, the range of subjects was hyper-eclectic and the place was open from nine o'clock in the morning until eleven o'clock at night.

The downside of being 'non-vocational' was that some students joined simply to find out what the fuss was about and left after a couple of classes, but those who stayed did so for other reasons than gaining a qualification or any other kind of material advancement. They wanted to explore the subject, their own ideas and aptitudes and, in some cases, to discover aspects of themselves that their daily lives seemed to suppress. The City Lit was the British institutional answer to Marcuse's 'one-dimensional man'. For those who wanted to be multidimensional, the City Lit had workshops for them all.

The place buzzed and hummed with different languages. The Creative Writing classes attracted anecdotal memories from across Europe. One of my first students was a Polish Jew, who had escaped as a child from the Nazi occupying forces in Lwow[ii] by hiding under the legs of a man who was dying from typhoid. The soldiers did not want to get too near him. Miraculously, she was reunited with her parents after the war, but the experience left deep scars that her hours under psychoanalysis were seeking to heal. She wrote a play, *The Scaffolding*, about her life under internment. She became devoted to her first analyst, which bordered upon a sexual dependency, of which she herself was well aware. Was he a saviour, a seducer or another control freak? I wanted to know.

When she left my class, I wrote the outline of a play for my small ILEA drama group, *The Well-Intentioned Builder*,[iii] based on an anecdote from a French writer and jazz musician, Boris Vian. It told the story of a builder who was asked to investigate a patch of damp in a family home and went on to knock the house down. Was he a builder or a demolition expert? Was her analyst a doctor or a kind of rapist? These were the questions that I put to my students, not knowing the answer myself, and they responded by interpreting this Absurdist metaphor with examples from their own lives. One attempted to give up smoking but divorced his wife instead, while another tried to change his job but decided to emigrate. The final script was enriched by the experiences of the group and we called it, misleadingly, 'collective' writing.

In another part of London, Peter Brook was going through a similar process with the group of actors, whom he had brought together for the RSC's production of Peter Weiss's *Marat/Sade*,[iv] set in the asylum of Charenton. They were asked to explore their own internal forms of madness, so that there would be no clichéd imitations of insanity, but rather their own nightmares, brought to the surface to blink vacantly under the spotlights. Two members of my group took part in his rehearsal processes and there were rumours of nervous breakdowns and of actors collapsing under the strain, but the final stage effect was startling, original and forced the audience, of which I was a member, to think again about the close relationship between sanity, madness and politics.

The man from Hampstead who influenced us all was the voice teacher and actor, Roy Hart, who came to Britain from South Africa on a scholarship to the Royal Academy of Dramatic Art (RADA), but gave up his career in mainstream theatre to study at the Alfred Wolfsohn Research Centre. Wolfsohn had been haunted by the cries and agonised screams of soldiers on the battlefields in World War I and came to realise that the voice had a range and expressivity that normal speech and singing failed to reflect. The constricted voice was the exact metaphor for Marcuse's one-dimensional man: we spoke one-dimensionally.

The release of the voice was thought to stimulate other forms of release, the discovery of the body and its emotional resources as well. When Hart took over the Round House in Camden Town to stage, with his company, the Roy Hart Theatre, a powerful Greek legend like *The Bacchae*, the audience wandered into a jungle of sound and movement, with little order but the celebration of being alive. The process took over from the performance, and harked back to earlier religious rituals, and looked forward to such events as the Scratch *Messiahs* at the Albert Hall, organised by a chemistry don, Gavin Parks, where anyone could come to sing along with the well-trained soloists in Handel's oratorio, if he or she knew the tunes.

The results should have been clumsy and cacophonous, and sometimes they were, but they could be inspirational as well. They influenced other artists and directors, who became better known than Hart himself. The Polish director, Jerzy Grotowski, employed his methods in *The Constant Prince* (1967), which was hailed at the *Théâtre des Nations* as a major event, the voice of the new Europe. Grotowski's book, *Towards a Poor Theatre* (1968), transformed the reputation of small companies. His influence could be felt in the tribal rock musical, *Hair* (1967), and even on the slopes of the Mountain of Mercy in modern-day Iran, overlooking the ruins of Persepolis, where Brook and Ted Hughes staged *Orghast* (1971), a ritual chant, partly inspired by Hart.

The composer, Peter Maxwell Davies, wrote *Eight Songs for a Mad King* (1969), based on the writings of George III, for Hart's company. When, at the Theatre Royal, Lincoln, the company ran out of time for a dress rehearsal, the artistic director, Philip Hedley, asked them to hum Hart-like through *Romeo and Juliet*, the play's emotional progression, without using any of Shakespeare's actual words. In the case of my ILEA group, what began as vocal exercises, inspired by Hart, became a factor in drawing the group together and helping them to express the heart of the story, which could be shaped into a formal public performance.[v]

My aim was not to extend their vocal range, but to encourage them individually to seek those notes within the very centre of their voices with which they felt most at ease and to remove all signs of strain and awkwardness, so that their 'median tone', as we called it, felt purified and simple. They were then blindfolded and asked to recognise each other's voices and respond to one another, in little improvisational phrases, like jazz. These fragments grew into the choruses of *The Well-Intentioned Builder*, for the house that was to be knocked down was played by the actors themselves. Memories were contained within those walls that so oppressed the solitary woman, who was trying to live within its cold and friendless rooms.

The play ended on an optimistic note. The house was knocked down, its memories blown away, and the woman looked calmly at the empty site. 'How bare the earth looks,' she said, to which the builder replied, 'Now we can begin to build.' As a national metaphor, there were those in my group who wanted this to happen to Britain and those who did not. We were more or less evenly divided. But none of us could decide, as we listened to the strangled vowels of the meritocrats in Westminster and all the other harsh intemperate voices, whether our political builders were well-intentioned or not.

And Britain was still a floating island in a very turbulent sea. We were in the middle of the Cold War, where the nuclear missiles of one side were playing 'Who's chicken?' with the missiles of the other side. There were anti-government demonstrations across the Western world, which was bad enough, but there were very few demonstrations on the other side of the Iron Curtain against anything at all, which was even worse. Political leaders were changing places with bewildering regularity and we still did not know whether or not we would get into the Common Market – or even wanted to do so. We were groping in the dark.

Our consciences were plucked in this direction or that – by the fate of the malformed thalidomide children or the mass shooting in Sharpeville, by napalm in Vietnam or the under-funding of the NHS, by the poverty in the streets or the jetsetting of the celebrity classes. According to the supporters of Moral Rearmament, we were losing the resilience that at one time, during that still unforgettable World War II, was offered by Anglican Christianity and the belief that, if we behaved well and obeyed the Ten Commandments, God would be on our side and we would eventually win.

All that remained of that simple faith was the slogan on student banners: 'Make Love, Not War'. But the banners were everywhere.

(ii)

The answer to inflation, according to the American economist, Milton Friedman, was simple. It was to control the supply of money. The classic definition of inflation was of 'too much money chasing too few goods' and so, if more money came into the system than was justified by the provision of goods and services, prices would rise, the currency would lose its value and those who would suffer most would be those on the bottom end of the scale, with small fixed incomes and with no leverage to extract more from their employers.

Inflation was caused by governments, by nobody else. Greedy trade unionists should not be blamed: they were only doing their job for their members. Grasping owners and bosses were not at fault: they were only seeking the best deal for their shareholders. But workers and bosses always had to work within whatever amount of money was available within the system. While too little money constricted growth, as happened before the Great Depression, too much money created artificial booms, 'stagflation', in which a stagnant economy was disguised by rising prices and incomes, all sound and fury that, like Shakespeare's idiot, signified nothing.

But why should governments risk the stability of their societies by causing inflation? Friedman blamed Keynesian economics and, broadly, the honourable motives of those who went into politics to make the world a better place, only to find that the situation was more complicated than they had thought, the post-war generation of do-gooders. By printing too much money, governments reduced the value of the currency in circulation, 'taxation without legislation', which allowed them to indulge in the pursuit of worthy causes, which turned out to be better in the intention than the result. Friedman gave Doing Good a bad name.

'When a government . . . tries to rearrange the economy, legislate morality or help special interests, the costs come in inefficiency, lack of motivation and the loss of freedom.' While there may seem to be some immediate benefits, the overall effect was harmful, because there was no increase in the wealth of that society and thus in its ability to adapt and evolve. 'The most important single fact about a free market is that no exchange takes place unless both parties benefit.' Governments cannot take such decisions. Only individuals could decide whether particular deals were to their advantage or not, but through the accumulation of such choices, mankind slowly progressed.

Friedman was born in New York in 1912, to a Jewish family of refugees, who had escaped to America from Ruthenia, once a sovereign state in the heart of war-torn Europe, now forgotten as a district of Ukraine. In all his writings, for he was a journalist, as well as an author and a Nobel-prize-winning economist, the spirit of the buoyant immigrant to the New World could still be felt. It was an infectious optimism, the relief at leaving the old Europe of pass laws, racial prejudice and hostile police, to enter through Staten Island, to gaze at the Statue of Liberty and set foot in the land of opportunity, the United States, as twelve million immigrants had done before. When Friedman wrote about freedom, it was not with the messy uncertainty of the rough sleeper but with the glow of the young man, ready to roll up his sleeves and build a home for his family. That kind of freedom was where civil society began.

Even the sound of his name, 'freed man', had a symbolic ring. It eerily contained the message that the Free World had previously lacked. The Cold War was not between the Anglo-Saxon and Slav 'Empires', but between those who believed that the evolution of mankind lay in releasing the spirit of independence that characterised the US Constitution and those that did not. The free market represented a wider freedom than mere consumerism. It provided the transactional basis for a free society, and was thus the best guarantor of 'life, liberty and the pursuit of happiness,' the principles upon which the US had been founded.

'Underlying most arguments against the free market,' Friedman wrote in *Capitalism and Freedom* (1962), 'is a lack of belief in freedom itself', which sounded at the time self-evidently true. It fitted in so neatly with the narrative of the English-speaking peoples, where even the British Empire was built not upon conquest, or so it was said, but upon free trade. It echoed Churchill's remarks in his post-war manifesto where he asserted that this was the time for 'freeing energies, not stifling them', and that Britain's greatness was built upon 'character and daring, not the docility to a state machine'.

It suited the Hollywood movies of happy families in a free society, where *Mr Blandings Builds His Dream House* (1948) and *Mr Smith Goes to Washington* (1939). His aphorisms resonated and lingered. It should come as no surprise that the two political leaders who came to embody his ways of thinking were those whose appeal included an element of nostalgia, Ronald Reagan, a film star from the 1940s, and Margaret Thatcher, the super-efficient housewife, never seen without her handbag, with two children and a financially successful husband in her shade. Her disapproval was like Mrs Miniver, pursing her lips against the doodlebugs.

But you had to go a long way back into human history before finding that bare-earth freedom that Friedman seemed to be advocating, to the Garden of Eden perhaps. Civilisations are built upon one another, like layers of coral, and each level provides the circumstances that constrict the foundations of the next. There may be, as Friedman said, 'no such thing as a free lunch', but it is also hard to find such a thing as 'a level playing field'. There are always shifts in the exchange rates, added transport costs, someone who knows someone who knows someone. 'Free trade' is usually more of an aspiration than a fact.

The Britain that Thatcher inherited might have served as an illustration for a Friedman textbook. It was a model of how not to run an economy, teetering on the brink of bankruptcy, a country of disgruntled workers, who had suffered under waves of altruistic governments. They had all tried to legislate for a better world to come – and failed. Was that an accurate description of Britain during the 1970s? Of course not! It vastly oversimplified the picture, but it was plausible enough to convince those who felt that Britain had followed the wrong road since the war. They mourned the loss of empire and were convinced that now was time to take back control, and privately relished the smack of firm government.

'This is not a confrontation between right and left,' said Thatcher in 1975, when she took over from Heath as the leader of the Conservative Party, 'I am trying to represent the deep feelings of those many rank-and-file Tories in the country, who feel let down by their party and find themselves unrepresented in a political vacuum.' She was speaking in her constituency, Finchley, but, at the time, 'vacuum' seemed an odd word to describe the frantic to-ings and fro-ings as various ministers tried to reconcile the demands of the unions with the economic crisis in the country. The vacuum was one of conviction, rather than politics, which Thatcher, inspired by Friedman, brought to her analysis of the nation's problems and her solution to them. After two decades of 'Butskellism', Thatcher stood up for those who believed in freedom, morality and the British way of life.

'Where there is doubt,' she said on the steps of 10 Downing Street, when she became Prime Minister in 1979, 'may we bring faith. Where there is despair, may we bring hope.' She used the words of St Francis to express her strong conviction that the tonic to revive the sick man of Europe lay not in more government but in less. She hoped to lift the burden of the state from the shoulders of those who were doing all the work, the businessmen, the industrialists and the traders, like her father, who created the nation's wealth. 'The trouble with socialism,' she declared, 'is that it runs out of other people's money.'

But, paradoxically, it required a single-minded and determined government to reverse the bad habits that had led to too much government. Her first step was to control the supply of money, and thus inflation. She raised interest rates and limited the subsidies that kept the nationalised industries afloat. This led, at a time of already high unemployment, to even more job losses, as managements tried to keep within their newly restricted budgets. Unemployment rose from one million to over three million in her first three years in office; and in 1981, she was the most unpopular prime minister in British history, with an approval rating in the polls of only 23 per cent.

But her popularity improved when the monetarist arguments became better known. She curbed the power of the trade unions, not by one Industrial Relations Act, as had previously been tried, but in a series of smaller Employment Acts, which whittled away at wildcat strikes and the 'closed shops' imposed by the unions. When the confrontation came over the future of the coal industry, Thatcher made sure that she would win it with the police and the army at full stretch. A Soviet newspaper gave her the nickname of the 'Iron Lady', who proved her mettle more in confrontation than compromise.

The next step was to return the previously nationalised industries into private hands, 'privatisation', a policy that marked her years in office and transformed the British economy. It began with the sale of Britoil in 1982, continued with British Telecom in 1984, and entered its full flush with the disposition into private hands of such national assets as British Aerospace, British Gas, Rolls-Royce, British Leyland, British Steel, the water authorities and public housing. Finally, council houses were sold to their sitting tenants.

To handle this massive transfer of power and money from public into private hands required the services of an enlarged, deregulated and more flexible City of London. The Big Bang took place on Monday, 27 October 1986, when the British Stock Exchange, following an agreement with the government dramatically modernised itself and opened its doors to digital trading from across the whole world. In retrospect, this could be seen the high point of her ministry, exceeding even her three election victories. It demonstrated that Britain was once more a global power, at least in financial services, a hub for international trading, which, according to Friedman, was at the heart of the Free World and of civilised society.

It produced a worldwide investment boom and turned the mantra of socialism inside-out by asserting that private ownership was good, even when it led to vast inequalities of wealth and influence. Competition would redress the balance in time. But Big Bang Monday might never have happened – nor all her other measures to reform the economy – if it had not been for one quixotic gesture that transformed her reputation and that of her government.

The restoration of British rule to the Falkland Islands, after the Argentinian invasion, made no economic sense. It was by almost any standards a risky gamble. At a time when the rest of the world believed that the days of British imperial influence were over, the defence of the Falklands proved that they were not quite. The lion could still summon up a convincing roar and its sonority transformed her ratings in the opinion polls. It proved, according to Enoch Powell, that the Iron Lady had 'ferrous matter of the highest quality'. Powell became one of her champions. Although he was now an Ulster Unionist, and not a member of her party, he seems to have profoundly influenced her thinking on such matters as immigration and the EEC. The National Front, which had grown in strength during the 1970s, went into a decline and many of its members joined the Conservatives.

The statistics of the war make uncomfortable reading. There were fewer than 3,000 residents of the Falklands, but 900 British lives were lost in their defence. The war cost £700 million, according to Mrs Thatcher's statement to the Commons, and more, if the costs of maintaining an army garrison at Port Stanley are taken into account. Despite this, Thatcher's poll ratings rose by 10 per cent and more. This may have been the most significant statistic of them all, for it may have encouraged other leaders, Tony Blair among them, to believe that waging far-flung wars did no harm whatsoever to their personal reputations.

Perhaps it made Britain feel great again.

(iii)

Big Bang Monday came at a key time in international relations for, in the previous year, 1985, the last of the ancient Soviet warriors finally left the service of his country. Konstantin Chernenko, died after a short time in office as the General Secretary of the Soviet Communist Party. The new Soviet leader, Mikhail Gorbachev, was a younger man, still in his forties, who immediately signalled his intention to dismantle the huge apparatus of the Soviet State.

He announced that the new objectives of his administration were *glasnost* (open government) and *perestroika* (reconstruction), and to bring to an end the long years of 'stagnation', which had prevailed since Brezhnev took over from Kruschev in 1964. These had seen a great increase in the Soviet Union's military strength, but no improvement at all in its chaotic, Kremlin-centred economic structure, with its gluts and famines, its rusty pre-war factories and its disgruntled workforce.

The Cold War was not over, for ballistic missiles still confronted each other from both sides of the Iron Curtain, but the curtain itself was becoming more porous and full of holes, as more families slipped across the borders and found homes in other lands. Reagan first met Gorbachev in November 1985 in Geneva, where they agreed to discuss the elimination of intermediate range nuclear missiles. Their talks continued in Reykjavik in October 1986 and again in December, when an agreement was reached to eliminate entirely the threat of nuclear missiles from the cockpit of the Cold War, Europe. This lifted a huge psychological burden from the East and West alike. It no longer felt that the end of the world was nigh.

For most people in Eastern Europe, Gorbachev's *perestroika* meant Westernisation and, in particular, the transition of their so-called 'command' economies to the equally so-called 'free market system'. After the fall of the Berlin Wall in 1989, the economic textbooks in East German universities were changed within weeks. Out went the horror stories of how hardened capitalists exploited the poor. In came Milton Friedman and the three primary rules on how to create a successful business model, as taught by Harvard Business School: market research, maximising assets and marketing.

From 1985 to 1992, I was a regular visitor to the Soviet Union, until it finally evolved – or collapsed, what you will – into a commonwealth of independent states, with Russia as the mother country. I made programmes for the BBC. I wrote articles from Eastern Europe for an American magazine, *The World and I*, and for British magazines as well. In 1985 in Rome, I was elected President of the International Association of Theatre Critics (IATC), a non-governmental agency, affiliated to UNESCO. Even my election was a sign of the times: an Englishman, not a Socialist, to lead a multinational cultural agency, with its head office in Paris, a journalist, a Liberal and, politically speaking, a loose cannon. My opponent was the eminent Italian critic, Renzo Tian, a friend of Dario Fo, who wrote *The Accidental Death of an Anarchist*. But to be left wing was not fashionable. The scent of freedom was in the air. I was its beneficiary. The Russians voted for me. The French did not.

I have one vivid memory of what it was like to live within the Soviet Union's transition from a command to a free-market economy. The image stays nightmare fresh in my mind. It was of a respectably dressed, middle-aged woman – a college professor, perhaps – screaming at a corner shop baker, 'You're a robber! A bandit! You should go to prison!' while the baker was trying to explain why a loaf of bread now cost 30 roubles, or half her weekly pension. For decades, the value of the rouble had been artificially tied to that of the US dollar, one to one, for reasons of political prestige. But the official exchange rate bore no relation to the old rouble's purchasing power even within the Soviet Union. A tourist had to buy a certain number of roubles at the official exchange rate to cover the supposed costs of his or her visit, although, once inside the country, he or she could easily find currency touts, who would be prepared to offer ten roubles or more for a Western dollar.

The introduction of the new rouble was another sign of *glasnost* and *perestroika*, but it had a disastrous impact upon those who were on fixed incomes. For a period of time, which may not even now be over, it left many people in the Soviet Union feeling much poorer. They blamed the West. The visitor could wander around the street markets and find relics of the Soviet Empire, such as medals, passports and official-looking military costumes, to be bought for a few dollars. You did not have to hunt for bargains. They were thrust into your hands.

For the Western entrepreneur, everything seemed absurdly cheap, from canteens of cutlery to tins of caviar and oil wells; and foreign money flooded into the country, making instant millionaires of those who had something valuable to sell and creating the oligarchs that came to symbolise the new Russia. Luxury goods came back to the shops but, in the suburbs of Moscow and out in the countryside, there were growing colonies of beggars, who, or so I was informed, would never have been seen in the old days.

My memory of the last years of the Soviet Union was that nothing worked. There was a repair shop in every street. The shops were either empty or suddenly filled with goods that people queued for hours to buy, whether they wanted them or not. Unwanted goods could be exchanged. Restaurants had enormous menus but few available dishes. The Communist Party machinery was everywhere, and the streets were still cleared for the deputies' official cars. The real work was done by officials in government offices, who were trying to keep the spirit of the Revolution alive, despite the shortage of money. They were the ones who kept the schools open, pensions paid, hospitals equipped and the streets swept.

They reminded me of the hard-working colonial officers during the last days of the British Empire, who wanted to maintain its ideals, while packing their bags for a return home. The Soviet officials were the ones who suffered most as the process of transition began and many state-owned assets were sold, often illegally, to visiting entrepreneurs with large wallets. But their images of Western freedom were misleading as well, a violent, unmonitored individualism, like Chicago in the 1920s, or further back, like the Wild West before Washington DC took over.

When I first visited Leningrad in 1985, it was a grey and sober city, still mourning for its sacrifices in World War II; but it had a renowned opera, the Mariinsky Theatre, and a very fine acting company, the Mali (Little) Theatre. They survived, but after five years, the social atmosphere had changed, together with the name of the city itself, which reverted to its former name, St Petersburg. The youth educational centre was now a dance hall. There were nightclubs and Runyonesque speakeasies in side alleys, while on the main streets there were shops selling goods with Western labels, which were probably pirated, but nobody cared.

There were gang fights in the streets but the authorities in St Petersburg were struggling to regain control and, at the same time, to bring the services to the levels of those expected in Western Europe, at the airport, in the hotels and tourist centres. The agents of the press, subdued or suppressed by censorship for so long, were starting to find their *glasnost* voices with alarmist leaders and scurrilous news. For many who had grumbled under Soviet Communism, it came as a surprise to find how un-free a free person might be under Western laws, democratic politics, its cultures and constitutions. Those who believed that liberalism meant doing what you liked found that the reverse was often the case. In some European countries, smoking was even banned in restaurants! Whatever next?

Mrs Thatcher was not physically present at the nuclear disarmament talks between Reagan and Gorbachev; but the two leaders of the English-speaking peoples presented a united front on most matters. The Special Relationship at last seemed to contain some substance. The future lay in global trade, less government and the freedom of the individual to choose without the meddling of the bureaucrats. At the heart of these dramatic changes lay the City of London's Big Bang, which made it the transactional hub of the Free World. Hard-line socialism was dead, victory for the West was assured, and, according to the US economist and political scientist, Francis Fukuyama, the 'end of history' had come.

Neo-liberal democracy was triumphant. In Britain, Labour suffered a heavy defeat at the 1983 General Election, which revealed the split between the Marxist and Keynesian wings of the party. Its manifesto advocated more nationalisation, an increase in taxation and unilateral nuclear disarmament. It was described by a Labour supporter, Gerald Kaufman MP, as the 'longest suicide note in history'. Labour's new leader, Michael Foot, was thought to be a hard-liner, a forerunner, even in his dress sense, to Jeremy Corbyn.

In 1981 some senior centre-left Labour politicians split from the party and formed the Social Democratic Party, which polled well in the 1983 Election but not well enough to win many seats, due to the uneven nature of the electoral system. The Conservatives were also split, if less demonstrably so. The sceptics included three former Prime Ministers, Macmillan, Douglas-Home and Heath, and those on the One Nation wing of the party, the Keynesians. Macmillan likened privatisation to 'selling off the family silver'. Monetarism was like playing golf with only one club, a driver. The ball went long distances, but missed the hole. The sale of council houses was all very well but would they be replaced by new social housing? Who was building it? How would local councils raise the money to do so? Thatcher had rate-capped them.

Under any kind of proportional representation, these shades of opinion would have been reflected in parliament, but 'first-past-the-post' two-party system favoured the leadership of the winning party. Under PR, could 'Thatcherism' have happened? Probably not but, for someone like Heath, having lost the leadership, this single-minded devotion to a suspect philosophy was almost as bad as pre-war appeasement. What was the role of a government other than to solve the world's problems? Without a social vision, a politician would be using his or her privileged position merely to play games around a swimming pool.

Heath cut a lonely figure on the Conservative benches. He became a figure of fun to the right-wing media, a sulky loser, who never gave his leader the support that, in their opinion, she deserved. The press attacks on him became increasingly sleazy. He was a life-long bachelor, whose private life was a matter of speculation. Were young boys involved?

Heath may not have worn his heart on his sleeve but he was in some ways the least secretive leader of modern times. His romantic passions could be felt through his music and his love of adventure as an open-sea yachtsman. He captained the six-man crew of his own boat, *Morning Cloud*, one of several that he had built with that name, which in 1971 won the international open-sea race, the Admiral's Cup. In 1974, however, his yacht, *Morning Cloud 3*, was struck by heavy seas off the Sussex coast and sank, killing two members of his crew, Nigel Cumming and Christopher Chadd, Heath's godson. Their deaths affected him deeply. He never owned or built another yacht – and never went to sea again.

His political vision was equally passionate. It could be felt in his contribution to the Brandt Commission report, *North-South: A Programme for Survival* (1980), edited by the then German Prime Minister, Willi Brandt, a Social Democrat. It set out to describe the challenges to human survival in a Cold War world, including the vast gap in wealth between the rich North and the poor sub-Saharan South. Capitalism was part of the solution, but only a part. Neither Brandt nor Heath was a monetarist. Heath used his memory of the 1930s to warn against the rise of nationalism and the risks of destroying the pride and well-being of the defeated countries. The report outlined the problems of climate change, nuclear disarmament, Civil Rights and problems that required the concerted action of like-minded countries. It provided a road map for the new Europe and assumed that there were leaders in the West, who might be prepared to read it.

Where were they?

***

Chapter Eight
Perspectives

(i)

Six months after winning her first General Election as the leader of the Conservative party, Margaret Thatcher attended a meeting of Heads of State at a European Summit in Dublin in 1979. It was at the end of November, when the grey and listless days of late autumn were cheered up by the first signs of Christmas. Little else augured well. France was in recession. The EEC's prosperous years were coming to an end and negotiations were under way for more countries to join as full members, Greece among them.

Applications had been received from Spain and Portugal, whose wartime fascist leaders, Franco and Salazar, died during the 1970s. They were seeking to become members, which meant that their credentials as democracies had to be examined. With the admission of the UK, Denmark and the Republic of Ireland in 1973, the EEC was already greatly enlarged and, with each new member, the balance of political and economic interests shifted, becoming more unstable, until the reform of its structure seemed inevitable.

Thatcher came to the Summit with a specific request. Britain was paying too much annually into the EEC's budget and receiving too little in return. She insisted on being repaid and received an offer of £350 million, which she rejected. It was far too small. She demanded a return of one billion pounds. 'Let me be very clear,' she insisted, 'I am not asking the Community for money. I am asking for my money back.'

Britain was the third poorest member, the 'sick man of Europe', but it was paying almost as much into the Community's budget as its two richest members, West Germany and France. West Germany, unlike Britain, did not have to carry such a large burden of NATO's defence costs; and France, unlike Britain, received large sums to support its farmers through the Common Agricultural Policy. Britain would soon become the EEC's largest net contributor. This was, according to Thatcher, obviously unfair.

The battle for the rebate lasted for five years. It was settled at the Fontainebleau Summit of 1984, which arrived at a complicated formula, whereby Britain received back two thirds of its net contribution from the previous year – the difference between what it paid into the Community and what it received back in the form of subsidies and regeneration grants. It was a unique formula. Other countries received temporary rebates but not Britain, which would be repaid annually. The significance of the rebate was not merely financial. It demonstrated to the British public that Mrs Thatcher was a doughty leader, who would fight for their national interests in defiance of the somewhat patriarchal comments from two French presidents, Valéry Giscard d'Estaing and François Mitterrand.

To the right wing of her party, it was an illustration of how a tough and independent Britain should stand up to its continental neighbours, whose lust for expansion overcame what should have been their painful lessons from history. It also revealed Mrs Thatcher's vision for Europe as a club of sovereign states, which should pursue their national interests, while joining together on matters of common concern, such as reducing barriers to trade. She did not engage with the idea that, through the EEC, politicians in Europe might be seeking to construct a new civilisation. On the BBC Radio 2's *Jimmy Young Show,*[i] she condemned those people 'who spent far too much time talking about these airy-fairy ideas'.

But President Mitterrand was among those who believed that she could have achieved more for Britain, both financially and in terms of influence, if she had taken a different approach. The Community was already engaged in a wide-ranging review of its affairs, led by the energetic chair of its economic and monetary committee in the European Parliament, the Christian Socialist, Jacques Delors. Without the mood of confrontation that Mrs Thatcher relished, Britain could have become, in Mitterrand's view, a more effective contributor and, as a result, more of a beneficiary.

As a former French Minister for Finance, Delors pursued moderately monetarist policies. He did not try to overturn the market economy but sought to work within it. He did not want to destroy the French government's social policies, but to curb them with measures that were almost austere. He was considered to be 'a safe pair of hands'. He was already trying to transform the CAP. The aim had been to redress the balance in wealth between the industrialised and the agricultural regions of Europe. But to subsidise farmers for growing more without taking into account the extent of public demand was wasteful. It destroyed other countries' agricultural economies by dumping unwanted goods on the world markets.

He sought to change CAP into a policy for regional regeneration with a wider remit. It included the development of tourism, transport, ecology and information technology (IT), which was starting to absorb swathes of academia throughout Europe. It could include the participation in joint medical research programmes, in space projects, and financial services, for which the City of London was already world-renowned. It meant carrying out Monnet's original aims by developing a single market, which combined economic with social reform. But this also required a more united Europe, creeping towards federalism.

Delors' canvas was broad. It embraced the nations who had joined the Community, the ones who were about to join and those from the other side of the Iron Curtain, which might in time be persuaded to join, for the signs from the east were of stagnant economies, low standards of living and discontent. Could the EEC offer them a better way? His aim was to build a Social Democratic Europe, which offered the economic growth of the West with the social services (much reformed) of the East.

In contrast, Mrs Thatcher's drawing pad was crammed with punctilious detail – who owed what to whom – and with red lines, as she sought to isolate the examples of injustice, as she saw them, committed by the EEC in its attempt to protect itself from the rest of the world. She pursued her aims with a tenacity that brooked no opposition.

The difference between these two perspectives coloured the negotiations that led to the Single European Act, which she signed on Britain's behalf in February 1986. Its purpose was to amend the Treaty of Rome and smooth the way towards a unified Common Market, with most of its barriers removed, by a newly targeted deadline, 1992. It had also to take into account the arrival of its new members, which was making the old EEC constitution cumbersome, if not unworkable. The old Treaty was slowing down the process of integration.

Under the original Treaty of Rome, the Council of Ministers, the highest authority, consisted of representatives from the elected governments of the original six members, each of which had the right of veto over its decisions, thus guaranteeing equality between the sovereign states, despite their different sizes and wealth. But as the Community expanded to nine countries, and then to twelve, with the prospect of more, it was felt that, with safeguards, 'majority' voting within the Council should be allowed. Otherwise, the progress towards a unified market might grind to a halt.

But this change was not merely technical. It altered the nature of the club. Instead of being a voluntary club with relaxed membership rules, it became one where the collective view might override the interests of a particular member. It was a step towards federalism, which Mrs Thatcher wanted to resist. A system of concessions was devised in the form of 'opt-outs', whereby some countries could refuse to take part in particular EEC projects, such as a common currency, while still remaining members of the Community. But this might lead to a two-speed Europe, with the inner six racing ahead towards integration, while the outer six, seven or eight dawdled behind, with Britain often leading the laggards.

The Single European Act had many dimensions. It took several years to negotiate. The reforms started in 1983 with the Stuttgart Declaration, proposed by the German Foreign Minister, Hans-Dietrich Genscher, and supported by his Italian counterpart, Emilio Colombo. The EEC faced a problem with its new admissions. It was agreed that the Community should consist only of genuine democracies, unlike those countries that claimed to be democracies, such as East Germany, but were in reality totalitarian states in disguise. A democracy should have a transparent voting system, a free press and laws that prevented bribery and coercion. But none of these were 'absolutes'. There might be many ways in which a national government could be elected, but the principle of majority rule should always be observed; and the Community had to decide whether, in an applicant country, it was honestly being so.

The arrival of Britain in 1973 as a member was welcomed. It was a well-established democracy, a large-scale trading partner, and provided a model for other applicants, against which their standards of democratic government could be measured. Greece had been a military dictatorship between 1967 and 1974: Spain and Portugal had struggled under fascist rule, until the restoration of democracy in 1978 and 1976, respectively. When Gorbachev became the General Secretary of the Soviet Union, and talked of *glasnost* and *perestroika*, the prospect arose that countries from the Eastern bloc, freed from the grip of the Kremlin, might wish to apply. The time had come to decide what was meant by 'democracy' and to transform last year's good resolutions into formal codes of behaviour. Did every member country share a common understanding of what was meant by 'Human Rights'?

In January 1985, Delors was appointed as the new President of the EEC Commission. His responsibilities were immense. He was in a position to decide what was meant by democracy for the purpose of admitting new member states or, at least, to establish the negotiating machinery whereby such decisions could be taken by majority opinion. This was merely the beginning. The EEC had to agree on what was meant by 'a level playing field' within the different sectors to ensure fair competition or, at least, to build up the machinery within the different layers of government that could negotiate such agreements.

But a commonly agreed principle like 'fair trading' could lead on to other matters, such as 'equality', 'workers' rights' and the wider laws of employment, which touched upon questions of identity and national cultures. Some could be bypassed, ignored or kicked into the long grass, but others could not be so easily avoided. It would be unfair if a company in one country could undercut another by being state subsidised or by employing what amounted to slave labour. These were often matters of degree. Some state aid to industry might be acceptable: too much would breach the principle of fair competition.

On 8 September 1988, Delors came to the British Trades Union Congress at its annual meeting in Bournemouth and his speech transformed the negative attitude of the Labour Party towards what many of its members still considered to be a rich man's club. He offered a vision in which the conditions of fair employment, such as collective bargaining, would be respected throughout the member states, in what became known as the Social Chapter. The workers of the world were starting to unite. The Congress ended by singing his praises as 'Frère Jacques'. Many Labour members were converted and became firm Europhiles.

The powers of the trade unions in Britain had already been curbed by Mrs Thatcher's government and the prospect that the EEC might overrule a British administration in matters of employment law was very appealing. But the Social Chapter went even further, in that Delors floated the idea that health and safety regulations should be agreed throughout the Community, as should the protection of the environment, the conservation of fish stocks, electoral law, guaranteed holidays and many other matters of Community concern.

By 1992, he predicted that 80 per cent of the legislation that governed trade, labour relations and human rights throughout the EEC would be decided by common agreement in Brussels.[ii] What did the Common Market mean other than harmonisation of its laws in the interests of the Community as a whole? This did not mean that foreigners would rule the country, but that Britain would negotiate the rules in consultation with its European Community partners. But the way in which his prophecy was worded inflamed every brand of nationalist opinion in Britain. It shocked not only the right wing, but also many of those who were, in principle, in favour of being good Europeans but did not want to sacrifice all their rights as British citizens to be so.

Within a fortnight of his speech to the TUC, on 20 September 1988, Mrs Thatcher replied to Delors, without naming him, in a speech given to the College of Europe in Bruges, which contrasted his vision for Europe with her own. During the EU Referendum in 2016, Mrs Thatcher's Bruges speech was cited as a rebuff to all things European, although she went out of her way to confirm that Britain's place was, and always had been, at the heart of Europe. But Delors and Mrs Thatcher had different kinds of Europe in mind. These were not necessarily left or right wing. They were speaking to different publics, one of which was frightened of too much state control and the other of too much individualism. Their world perspectives were at odds.

Delors was addressing a European public, which from one side of the Iron Curtain was emerging from decades of Communist rule. He offered a vision of a democratic Europe that retained state benefits for its citizens; that retained state benefits for its citizens, upon which those who were brought up within the USSR had come to rely. He dangled the prospect of a Europe with legal safeguards against the fascist tyrannies of the past and guaranteed human rights, ethnic tolerance and free speech. He proposed the idea of a new Europe rising from the ashes of its past to become the third world force. Europe should be the leader in tackling the new challenges from global warming to digital communication. It should send up a satellite of its own.

But Thatcher had no such concerns. Britain had not been occupied. It was satisfied with its junior role in the Special Relationship and had nothing to learn from the Continent, or so she believed, in such matters as democratic government and the protection of human rights. It had its submarines and nuclear missiles; and a civilisation that stretched back (almost) unbroken for a thousand years. What more did a federal Europe have to offer?

(ii)

In 1983, two Home Office researchers, C.G. Veljanovski and W.D. Bishop, published a short book, *Cable by Choice*. It described the recent advances in telecommunications, the new satellites, the receiving stations and, in particular, optical fibre cable. Under the old methods that my father knew, cables consisted of strands of wires, coaxial cable, usually of copper alloy, twisted together so that they could conduct electrical impulses that could be converted into heat, light or, as with telephones, human voices. But metal wire was wasteful and expensive, and limited in its capacity. Optical fibre was different: almost infinite in its capacity, cheap and, in transmission, lightning swift.

Optical fibre cables consisted of thin strands of glass, lying side by side, not twisted, through which signals could be passed with very little resistance. Together with satellites, they transformed the prospects of all communication systems. The old broadcasting system was terrestrial. It had to contend with such matters as the curvature of the earth, the limited capacity of coaxial cable and the need for relay stations. By the 1970s, as the researchers pointed out, few of these restrictions still applied. There could be as many channels as there were names in a telephone directory. The way was open to install an optical-fibre cable network for what was called the 'information highway' – or broadband.

Its potential usefulness was almost too great to be predicted. It was compared to the invention of the printing press. Large quantities of news and scientific data could be transferred across the globe, eliminating at a stroke one of the main disadvantages between the affluent North and the poverty-stricken South, the knowledge deficit. It transformed the prospects of Harold Wilson's project, the Open University. Its students, whose studies might be hampered by the lack of local libraries, would be able to open up an online encyclopaedia of factual information and research. It democratised knowledge.

Previously, commercial and industrial activity had developed around urban 'clusters', where factories, research centres and shops provided pockets of wealth around the country, which attracted the ambitious and the upwardly mobile away from rural areas where the business opportunities were less apparent. With broadband, it was possible to set up factories in remote parts of the country and still be in touch with retailers and distributors elsewhere, and communicate directly with the companies' investors and bankers in London. It might even reverse the centuries-old drift towards the prosperous South East of England.

But the cables still had to be installed, with other parts of the technical jigsaw that would link cables with satellites, receivers with transmitters, scramblers with de-scramblers, and computers that understood each other. It would require a great deal of investment and where would the money come from? In the 1930s, the rapid development of the BBC's broadcasting services was helped by its Royal Charter, a *de facto* state monopoly. Britain was then an imperial nation, whose military and commercial interests demanded the best possible system for staying in touch. Could a poorer, post-Suez Britain face up to a similar challenge?

There was another problem. British Telecom was a nationalised company, formed in 1980 as a separate offshoot of the Post Office. It was in an ideal situation to install the cables and develop the technical infrastructure that the country's future needed. It should have been one of the nation's assets, the prize plate in the family's silver, but it was also towards the top of Mrs Thatcher's list of companies to be privatised. She did not want to complicate the sale of British Telecom, launched in 1984, with an expensive commitment to install broadband.

In 1988, the government published a White Paper, *Broadcasting in the Nineties*, which proposed that broadband should be installed at 'a rate determined by the market'. It envisaged a future in which a number of companies, small and large, operating a variety of new channels, would be regulated along the lines of the existing private companies. But it failed, however, to take into account what was happening elsewhere, in places such as Singapore, which was seeking to become the information hub of the South, or around San José in California, which became known as Silicon Valley. In San José, a cluster of smaller towns was attracting firms to explore the potential of the silicon chip, the main source of its manufacture.

It may seem unfair to blame the government for failing to forecast the explosion of hi-tech companies that burst upon the scene in the 1990s, the decade that it was claiming to predict. Could it have anticipated the astonishing rise of NASDAQ, the world's first electronic stock market, founded in 1971, which linked with the London Stock Exchange in 1992, to finance companies such as Apple, Microsoft and Google? Their worldwide assets rapidly exceeded the GDP of several sovereign states within the Common Market. Nor could it have predicted the success of the World Wide Web, founded in 1989 by the British inventor, Tim Berners-Lee, which rapidly turned the planet into a global village.

Yet the tunnel vision of this Home Office document was still depressing. It seemed to think that it could impose the same 'Consumer Protection Requirements' upon the brave new world of satellite and cable that it could in the old days of terrestrial broadcasting. It still expected that those who wanted to apply for a broadcasting licence to run a new channel could be forced to meet the Home Office's standards in decency, fairness and impartiality. It ignored the advice of its researchers, as well as books about the subject, such as *The Gutenberg Galaxy* (1962) by the Canadian media analyst, Marshall McLuhan.

McLuhan forecast the arrival of international media companies, whose power to spread political and commercial misinformation vastly exceeded that of a national newspaper. Vance Packard's *The Hidden Persuaders* (1957) had described the ways in which skilful advertising could trick the consumer into buying things that he or she did not really want; but McLuhan raised the stakes to include geopolitical propaganda as well, prevalent throughout the Cold War. The new NASDAQ companies extended this power as a world community service, social media writ large, for the World Wide Web, Facebook, Wikipedia and others were all formed with the highest hopes for mankind in mind.

In short, there was little excuse for the government to produce so myopic a document as *Broadcasting in the Nineties* at a time when the broad- and narrowcasting industries were going through such fundamental changes.

Monetarism, Friedman's free-market philosophy, had so colonised the British government's thinking that it could contemplate few exceptions to the rule. The privatisation of British Telecom took place at the time when the government was preoccupied with reversing the trend towards state ownership and could conceive of no other circumstances where this might not be to the benefit of the country.

The commitment to install broadband 'at a rate to be determined by the market' contained other risks, for private companies would seek franchises in cities and large towns, where there were the opportunities for quick returns. They could not be blamed for doing so; it was an expensive business to dig up roads and pavements. But the result was that smaller towns and rural districts would slip further behind urban clusters. The inequalities in wealth and opportunity that existed between different regions in Britain could only become more extreme. Information was, is, and always has been, power.

The way in which broadband was installed operated against a long-standing British tradition that such communication services should be evenly spread around the country. In 1840, the national postal services offered a flat-rate delivery service to every part of the United Kingdom. They were officially required to do so. The telephone system was developed as an offshoot of the Post Office as a national service. In the 1920s, the BBC received its Royal Charter by promising to provide its services throughout the kingdom. To install broadband only where it was profitable to do so imitated the US business model. It was almost against the Britishness of being British.

The BBC was not one of Mrs Thatcher's favourite organisations, as her memoirs reveal.[iii] One incident in particular infuriated her. It concerned a BBC interview, conducted by Robin Day, with her Minister for Defence, John Nott MP, in the aftermath of the Falklands War. Nott was seeking to cut the costs of maintaining the navy, against the advice of his senior military advisers; and Day asked, 'Why should the public believe on this issue you, a transient, here-today-and-gone-tomorrow politician rather than a senior officer of many years' experience.' Nott unclipped his microphone and walked out of the studio.[iv]

Thatcher interpreted this incident as defiance of her government, one of many from the BBC, and, as her status grew, she sought to curb its influence. Robin Day, who had done so much to transform the incisiveness of political interviews in the 1950s, added fuel to the fire. In March 1985, Mrs Thatcher's government initiated the Peacock inquiry into the corporation's funding arrangements and the future of the licence fee. It took more than 25 years for broadband services to be provided for most (but not all) of the country. In this case, privately-owned companies did not beat the public ones for efficiency. One BBC executive insisted that there was no demand for broadband. It was often claimed that Britain had the best television in the world. Why was there any need for change?

But it did not require a prophet or techno-wizard to guess that a cultural revolution was at hand. I was neither, but in 1978 I was asked to write a Green Paper[v] for the Liberals that might form the basis for a new arts policy. There was already a Liberal commitment to protect and promote 'free speech' but what, in practical terms, did this mean? Was there a free press, despite private ownership of newspapers? No censorship? None whatsoever? If we were serious about free speech, the first step was that we should install broadband as a public service. Then, if necessary, we should think about the ways in which its power to change our lives could be in some measure democratically controlled.

In the late 1970s, there was no ministry of culture, or anything like it. Broadcasting was the responsibility of the Postmaster General, while the Arts Council (ACGB) was supported through the Office of Arts and Libraries, a small department in the Department of Education and Science. The prospect of broadband required a government department of sufficient stature to ensure that its services would be widely spread. The history of the twentieth century gave ministries of culture a dismal reputation. They were vehicles for state propaganda. Throughout the Soviet bloc, *samizdat* (self-published) books and newspapers were valued above the impressive tomes from the state publishing houses. Subsidies to the arts, as to broadcasters, potentially threatened their independence. Governments cannot hand out money for nothing. It would be illegal.

In my Green Paper for the Liberal Party, I wanted to find the middle way between supporting the arts and interfering with them. All the political parties paid tribute to the 'arm's length principle', whereby those who provided public support for the arts were not in the position to decide upon the artistic policies. We all distinguished between the provision of services for the arts, which was acceptable, and financing particular productions, which was not. We were in favour of free speech, for the weight of political correctness had not yet descended upon our backs. But how could we square the circle? How could we provide the circumstances in which the arts and, broadly, our culture, could thrive, without deciding what artists should do, for 'freedom', as we all agreed, was essential to their inspiration?

Then, like a *deus ex machina*, the technical solution came down from the skies, via satellite dishes, broadband. Anybody could become a broadcaster. There was no need for licensed TV channels. Anybody could make a film or a soundtrack, and distribute it online, without having to build cinemas. Anybody could publish a book. Anyone who could speak, act, sing or play the penny whistle could find an audience somewhere in the world.

Our document, *The Arts, Artists and the Community*, to be presented to the Liberals' annual conference in September 1982, was hailed in the Guardian as 'a cultural revolution'.[vi] There was a headline to this effect. It offered a 'blueprint for the arts' in the twenty-first century. These were the heady days when the Liberals with the SDP as the Alliance were running neck-and-neck in the polls with the other main parties. All seemed possible. But I was warned that British revolutions happen more discreetly: not with headlines but by making the right appointments to the civil service; not by confronting the media companies but by secretly pointing out how they could outmanoeuvre their rivals.

The best revolutions happen when no one is looking. From the British government's point of view, the most important aspect of broadband was that it threatened the BBC and could force Auntie back into line. Since the days of Carleton Greene, the Moral Majority, in the disguise of the National Viewers and Listeners Association, had concluded that the BBC was too broadminded and independent for its own good. Nobody could object to more 'free speech' but, in practice, broadband lessened the power of the broadcasting *élite* who had seized the microphone and did not want to let go. According to the Liberals' parliamentary spokesman for the arts, Clement Freud MP, Mrs Thatcher wanted as many broadcasting channels as possible, provided that they all spoke with one voice, her own.

'And so', he mournfully added, 'does everyone else.'

(iii)

Mrs Thatcher's speech to the College of Europe in Bruges in 1988 had been arranged by the Foreign and Commonwealth Office (FCO) several months in advance. It was intended to be a positive, pro-Community speech. But as the day approached, the circumstances so altered what she was expected to say that the FCO had to mount what its Assistant Under Secretary, John Kerr, described as a 'damage limitation exercise', which was about '90 per cent successful'. This was a somewhat optimistic assessment. Her words irritated her partners in Europe, divided the Conservative party, led to the resignation of her Foreign Secretary, Geoffrey Howe, and contributed to her downfall. But it entered into the annals of those who had never wanted to be part of the Community as the definitive statement of what was wrong with the EEC.

For a long time in the British press, the EEC had received unfavourable and sometimes xenophobic coverage. It was linked with the CAP's butter mountains and battles over the rebate, which left the impression that the Community was full of extravagant foreigners, who wanted to squeeze Britain dry. The Foreign Office hoped to redress the balance. It wanted Mrs Thatcher to congratulate the Community on its successes and to remind its partners in a quiet and not too censorious a way how the British economy had been transformed through the application of monetarist principles. The FCO wanted to extend the UK's influence in Europe, not diminish it.

But Delors' speech to the Trades Union Congress on 8 September brought out Mrs Thatcher's combative streak, which was never far below the surface. On 20 September, at the the Belfry of Bruges, the historic centre of the medieval city, she roared back. 'Let me say bluntly on behalf of Britain. We have not embarked on the business of throwing back the frontiers of the state at home, only to see a European superstate getting ready to exercise a new dominance from Brussels.' This was a highly provocative remark, as it was meant to be.

Geoffrey Howe saw a draft of her speech in advance and commented that there were some 'plain and fundamental errors'. His comments were circulated around a discreet circle within the Foreign Office.[vii] 'A stronger Europe does not mean the creation of a European superstate but it does, has and will require the sacrifice of political independence and the rights of national parliaments. That is inherent in the treaties.' Mrs Thatcher's speech gave the impression that Britain would not adhere to the treaties that it had signed, but regarded them as unnecessary rules and regulations, imposed by a foreign government in Brussels. It sent out the wrong signals to our partners in Europe, those of 'perfidious Albion'.

If Mrs Thatcher saw his comments, she ignored them. This was not a casual occasion. The College of Europe was established in 1946 as a higher academy for European civil servants at a community level. Churchill and the Belgian Prime Minister, Paul-Henri Spaak, were among its founding fathers; Nick Clegg, the future Liberal Deputy Prime Minister in David Cameron's coalition government, was among its alumni. The guest lecture by a distinguished visiting politician was the inaugural event of each academic year. President Mitterrand delivered it in 1987 and the Foreign Office had sought a similar invitation for Mrs Thatcher, while appreciating that this opportunity carried risks. She was her own woman. Nobody could be quite sure of what she was going to say.

She began, as was the custom, with a historical survey. She reminded her audience that Britain was an integral part of Europe, 'as much heirs to the legacy of European culture as any other nation'. She had no intention of allowing Britain to be upstaged in its claims by the French or the Germans. Within this heritage, Britain had made a unique contribution:

> We are rightly proud of the way in which, since Magna Carta in 1215, we have pioneered and developed representative institutions to stand as bastions of freedom. And proud of the way in which for centuries Britain was a home for people from the rest of Europe who sought sanctuary from tyranny.

This was another way of pointing out that Britain won the war. 'Over the centuries, we have fought to prevent Europe from falling under the dominance of a single great power. . . . And it was from our island fortress that the liberation of Europe itself was mounted.' She placed her own political battle with Delors within the British national narrative that stretched back over centuries, before World War II to the Napoleonic Wars, the Spanish Armada, the Reformation and even Agincourt. 'All these things alone,' she continued, 'are proof of our commitment to Europe's future,' which was presumably to save Europe from itself.

'Nor should we forget,' she added, 'that our European values have helped to make the United States of America into the valiant defender of freedom which she has become.' Wherever there were painful toes upon which she could tread, she went out of her way to tread on them. She was, by implication, likening the European superstate to the Third Reich, the US, which had just disentangled itself from its futile war in Vietnam, to the Champion of Freedom, and placing Britain with its monarchy and imperial history firmly as the pioneer of democracy.

National narratives can be persuasive to those who believe in them, destructive to those who do not. There would be many in Middle England who would accept her version of events as self-evidently true. Of course, this was what happened! We were taught it at school. Decades of World War II films and docudramas told the same story. But for those on the Continent who had suffered under oppression, who knew the jungle of mixed motives that even resistance fighters had to endure and who were now embarked upon an ambitious project of reconstruction, her language must have seemed insufferably complacent, mocking at scars from one who never felt a wound.

There were also those within her own party, even within her own cabinet, who were squirming with embarrassment. They included Heath on the Conservative backbench who was watching the mauling of his life's work, Howe and those on the centre-left, such as Michael Heseltine, a previous defence secretary, Leon Brittan and Douglas Hurd, who succeeded Brittan as Home Secretary. But after winning the 1987 General Election, Mrs Thatcher was riding high in the polls, boosted by her reputation as the 'Iron Lady', who had defeated the trade unions, the Argentine colonels, the Labour Party and the SDP-Liberal Alliance, and helped to secure a points win in the Cold War with her staunch companion, US President Reagan.

Domestically, her battles with Delors and the European Commission were seen within a similar context; and, when she laid down her five guiding principles, few on the right wing thought it necessary to inquire whether they had been tried before, or were in the process of being tried, or had been tried before and found wanting. She began with the Gaullist principle of maintaining the independent sovereignty of the member states. 'Europe will be stronger precisely because it has France as France, Spain as Spain, Britain as Britain, each with its own customs, traditions and identity. It would be folly to try to fit them into some sort of identikit European personality.'

This was not Delors' aim, nor that of any other member of the Commission, the Council of Ministers or the European Parliament. His intention was to secure an agreement on the principle of democracy, not on the details of any electoral system, in which Britain with its unelected upper chamber might have been seen in an unfavourable light. Should any country with a one-party system or ruled by an army dictatorship be admitted to the club? That was the top-down principle that Delors sought to be accepted. If he did have a specific target in mind, it might have been de Gaulle's proposed amendments to the constitution of the Fifth Republic in 1968 that Mitterrand had denounced as the voice of dictatorship.

Mrs Thatcher's second and third principles similarly gave the impression of pushing at a half-open door with an unnecessary degree of force. She urged the Commission to reform itself with slow, practical steps – which is what it thought it was doing – taking the reform of the CAP, which had already begun, as her prime example. The Community should encourage enterprise, which meant the removal of its rules and restrictions, although the liberalisation of capital controls, one of her key demands, was already secured under the Single European Act. She went out of her way to specify the 'free movement of capital', 'the abolition of exchange controls', a 'free market in financial services' and, curiously in light of her opposition to the Euro, 'a greater use of the ecu', the European currency that came before the Euro.

None of these would have caused dismay to Delors, except through the vehemence with which she demanded them, as if she and she alone, on behalf of Britain, had thought of them first. Her fourth principle was that

'Europe should not be protectionist', which implied that it was in danger of being so. But this was not the Commission's intention. Its aim was to negotiate favourable agreements with other trading blocs, believing that the strength of the Community, its size, would produce better results than each nation negotiating on its own. There were some countries, who wanted limited protection for sections of their economy, but the official aim of the Community was to liberalise world trade, not to set up more barriers.

But it did have ambitions to set higher standards in world trade, in such matters as environmental protection, labour relations, health and safety and arms control. The different measures, each designed with the best motives in mind, could quickly accumulate into a mountainous pile of legislation. The intention might not be protectionist, but the results might be so, and they required a larger-than-average bureaucracy to monitor all the required legislation. Mrs Thatcher insisted on tighter accountancy to keep the institutions of the Community in check, a principle with which nobody was likely to disagree, although it required tighter control from Brussels than she would have been willing to allow.

Her fifth principle concerned 'the most fundamental issue', defence through NATO, which meant being grateful to the United States for carrying the burden of Western defence, modernising its arsenal of nuclear weapons and contributing a fair share of the defence costs. 'There can be no question of relaxing our efforts, even though it means taking difficult decisions.' At the same time, Europe should secure 'better value for money', a tricky demand. It was taken to mean that it should not waste money in developing its own weapons, but buy from the US, if their companies could supply what NATO needed at a lower price.

This issue had already split the British cabinet. In 1985, a British company, Westland Helicopters, was facing bankruptcy. The Defence Secretary, Michael Heseltine, was seeking to bring together a European consortium to rescue it, which consisted of French, German and Italian companies, and build the combat helicopter that NATO needed. But a US consortium, United Technologies Corporation, intervened and, with Mrs Thatcher's approval, offered a similar but cheaper product. It was a geopolitical decision, rather than an economic one, and when her cabinet chose the US over Europe, Heseltine resigned.

Similar decisions, taken over time, would reduce the Community's capacity to defend itself while increasing the costs of its defence. But Mrs Thatcher saw no problems. 'The fact is things *are* going our way: the democratic model of a free enterprise society *has* proved itself superior; freedom is on the offensive, a peaceful offensive the world over, for the first time in my lifetime.' But talking about freedom as if the English-speaking peoples owned the copyright did not endear her to those who wanted to pursue the social democratic alternative to neo-liberalism. It did not impress those who feared the freedom of US gun laws, which reduced the costs of weaponry to the point where the EEC did not need to manufacture its own.

Parts of her speech were expressed in a more friendly way. 'Britain does not dream of some cosy, isolated existence on the fringes of the European Community. Our destiny is in Europe, as part of the Community.' Even when she was at her most positive, she seemed reluctant to acknowledge the advances that had been made and the nature of the struggles ahead. 'Certainly we want to see Europe more united and with a greater sense of common purpose. But it must be in a way which preserves the different traditions, parliamentary powers and sense of national pride.'

Perhaps that was another example of what Monnet might have meant when, or if, he admitted that he should have started with culture. There may be a trait in the Anglo-American cast of mind which believes that, once a war has been won, the institutions of peace and freedom will develop of their own accord. 'We Europeans,' said Mrs Thatcher, 'cannot afford to waste our energies on internal disputes or arcane institutional debates.' Why not, if it meant the reduction in the risks of fascism, phony politics, the oppression of minorities, trafficking and massive tax fraud? The fact that Britain has no written constitution seemed to lead Mrs Thatcher to believe that no other country needed one either. Roger Scruton argued in *The Salisbury Review* that a national constitution was something that grew up over time, which in Britain began even before the Magna Carta, and then became accepted as a way of life. It would have been more accurate to say that Britain's constitution was written over time through its legal and parliamentary decisions, its precedents, its religion and its language, within libraries of written documents. Other societies could not wait so long. Mrs Thatcher had evidently decided that, if she spoke in a loud enough voice, foreigners would understand her and recognise what was good for them.

***

Chapter Nine
Maastricht and the Bastards

(i)

'Some of the founding fathers of the Community,' said Mrs Thatcher in her Bruges speech, 'thought that the United States of America might be its model. But the whole history of America is quite different from Europe. People went there to escape from the intolerance and constraints of life in Europe.'

She was offering a historical narrative in which the United States and Britain stood firm as the bastions of freedom against the dictatorships of Europe, which might seem to be a fair description of the twentieth century. But the longer picture told a different story. The Declaration of Independence in 1776 severed the United States' imperial ties with Britain, not the Continent, and the first large-scale wave of immigrants came from Ireland in the 1840s, fleeing from famine and injustice in the United Kingdom.

Half-truths can be as misleading as fake facts, because they can sound more convincing. Despite breaking these ties, the US Constitution of 1788 retained many laws and customs that it had inherited from Britain, including *habeas corpus* and the right to bear arms, a law promulgated in 1689 to protect English Protestants from Continental Catholics. The refugees from Europe, according to Mrs Thatcher, 'sought liberty and opportunity; and their strong sense of purpose has, over two centuries, helped to create a new unity and pride in being American'. But this 'strong sense of purpose' applied less to the slaves brought over from Africa, who also built America, and the two centuries over which modern America developed its sense of identity included a civil war and the suppression of the Native Americans.

Perhaps the most misleading aspect of Mrs Thatcher's version of history was the way in which she failed to acknowledge the interdependence of Europe and the United States, how they have influenced each other over time, so that what we have come to mean by such ideas as 'liberty' and 'democracy' are an amalgam of the wisdom and experience of many countries. No one country, not even the Special Relationship, can claim authorship. 'Liberty, Equality, Fraternity' can claim its rightful place as well.

As the President of the Commission, Delors was instructed by the Council to bring together a new treaty of European Union, which would streamline the many amendments and additions to the Treaty of Rome that had been accepted over the previous 45 years. After years of negotiation, it was signed by twelve heads of state, which included six monarchs and six presidents, or their representatives, in the Dutch town of Maastricht in February 1992. The Maastricht Treaty, as it became known, was intended to provide the next stage in European integration but it carefully left the door open for new member states from the former Soviet Union to join, if they wanted to do so.

This was one of the many ways in which the Maastricht Treaty resembled the US Constitution, which was signed by thirteen member states but designed in such a way that it could admit other states, as they came into existence. But the applicants had to accept the same aims and principles as the original members and, to that extent, the US Constitution was not just constructing a new economic zone but laying the foundations for a new civilisation. The Maastricht Treaty had a similar purpose.

The US Constitution envisaged two forms of democratic control over the executive, the role fulfilled by the US President. These were the House of Representatives, directly elected through its member states, and the Senate, whose senators were appointed through the elected state governments. This system of checks and balances was reflected in the Treaties of Rome and Maastricht. There was a directly elected European Parliament, and a Council of Ministers, appointed through the elected national governments.

There was no European equivalent to match the powers of the US President. Some presidential powers lay in the hands of the rotating chairs of the Council, the President of the European Parliament and the heads of its Commission, but the title and role of a president was a more contentious issue, which Delors' Commission decided to postpone.

The US Constitution proposed a common citizenship, although the legal systems might vary from state to state. So did the Maastricht Treaty. The US Constitution sought a common defence policy and so (after time) did Maastricht. It demanded a common currency, the US dollar, whose value should be defended against foreign currencies, even though this might be to the economic disadvantage of some member states; Maastricht sought something similar and offered the ecu, which became the euro, seeking a transition period for those countries that could not meet the criteria that the Eurozone required.

But the similarities between these two constitutional treaties, separated by more than two centuries, are most evident in their wider aims. The Preamble to the US Constitution states that: 'We, the People of the United States, in order to form a more perfect Union, establish Justice, insure domestic tranquillity, provide for the common defence, promote the general welfare and secure the Blessings of Liberty to ourselves and our posterity, do ordain and establish this Constitution.' The similar foreword to the Maastricht Treaty announced its intention to reach the next stage in European integration, and to seek an 'ever-closer union', bearing in mind 'the historic importance of the ending of the divisions in Europe'.

The Maastricht Treaty 'confirmed its attachment to the principles of democracy, liberty, the respect for human rights and the fundamental freedoms and the rule of law'. It intended to 'deepen the solidarity between their peoples, while respecting their history, their cultures and their traditions'. It sought to achieve 'the strengthening and convergence of their economies' and 'to promote social progress for their peoples'. It reaffirmed the 'free movement of people' within the Community, while securing common borders. The two treaties might be expressed differently, they might have had different areas of concern, but unmistakeably they shared a common DNA. One evolved from the other.

Taken together, the US Constitution and the Maastricht Treaty, with their previous treaties, amendments and cautiously phrased *caveats*, provided the fullest expression of what was legally meant by 'freedom' in the 'free' West. Through the words that were chosen, the strands and sinews of their thought can be detected, together with the range of their authorities, from Adam Smith to Milton Friedman, St Augustine to Martin Luther King, Hegel to John Stuart Mill, each contributing a phantom presence within the Grand Hall of Signatories. Neither document is inward-looking or self-protective. Both looked outwards to recruit new members, but on terms that retained the vision in which they were conceived.

Nor were these ideals overprescriptive. Some were principles, like 'democracy', which were obligatory, but others were civic aims, like 'domestic tranquillity', which were not, and several were moral aspirations, like 'Justice', of which only God could be the judge. Where the Maastricht Treaty most differs from the spirit of the US Constitution was where it sought to accommodate the wishes of its member states. Where the American Founding Fathers were able to draw straight lines on the constitutional map, like the roads in yet-to-be-built cities, Delors' Commission had to make allowance for the quirks of national systems, monarchies and republics together, in a confused Continent of once-great powers.

These explain the stress in the Maastricht Treaty on respecting the cultures and traditions of their member states, which was indispensable to secure agreement. No country, and certainly not Britain, was prepared to throw away its entire heritage to become a member. At the same time, no national narrative was free from deeds and blemishes that the country would rather forget. Should these be respected as well? Anti-Semitism, the Reign of Terror, the Spanish Inquisition? Or should the EU, in the spirit of common politeness, ignore the darker side of its national cultures and concentrate on the bright spots instead?

Throughout the Maastricht Treaty, Delors used the word 'culture' in a positive sense to mean values that had led to a more civilised way of life: its arts, its manners, its rituals of birth, marriage and death. But some cultures were bloodthirsty, some were xenophobic and many more were hierarchical, favouring one section of humanity over another, men over women, whites over blacks. They could not all be respected. Instead they needed to be 'deconstructed', to use a favourite word of the 1990s, analysed and unpacked, so that the corruptions of history could be exposed, and the half-truths of national narratives could be seen for what they were. But this was dangerous territory.

Delors had to placate those who, like Mrs Thatcher, felt that their national identity was under threat and so he pretended that all national cultures were good and should be respected, except when they were bad, in which case they should not be called 'culture'. If Monnet was right to think that his plan for a new Europe should have begun with 'culture', Delors painted over that starting point with a thick layer of diplomatic tact.

He also tried to detach 'culture' from the efficient workings of the market place, another near-impossibility, but one which had to be attempted, if free trade within the Community were to become more than a tempting dream. What people like and dislike, and what they want to buy or not, are closely connected with their national cultures. Trademarks and regional specialities needed to be respected and thus protected. But the rules that insisted that champagne should come from the Champagne district in France and Scotch whisky from Scotland should not be allowed, or so the Commission believed, to disrupt the founding principles of the EEC: the free movement of goods, capital, services and labour.

At the heart of these riddles, as it had been for the Founding Fathers, was the proposed currency. The physical manifestation of a currency, a coin or note, has no value. It derives its value as a symbol of exchange. To adopt a common currency, whatever it was, sent out a signal to the rest of the world that the countries of Europe were working together for their common prosperity, the international exchange value of their currency being their joint concern. Within the EU, a common currency would prevent one country from gaining an unfair advantage over the others by manipulating its exchange rates.

Britain played its part in drafting the Maastricht Treaty. Delors was the longest serving President of the Commission, serving three terms, but there were representatives from the British government at each stage of the process. But their freedom to negotiate, however, was hampered by Mrs Thatcher herself, who had made up her mind that the Community was a threat to national sovereignty, and probably always would be.

In 1989, she dismissed her Foreign Secretary, Geoffrey Howe, one of her most loyal supporters, and his subsequent speech from the backbenches contributed to her downfall. From being the Iron Lady who could do no wrong, she was widely seen in her own party as being rigid, authoritarian and out of touch. Howe criticised Mrs Thatcher for undermining all the efforts to achieve economic and monetary union in Europe:

> We commit a serious error if we always think in terms of surrendering sovereignty and seek always to stand pat upon a given deal by proclaiming, as the Prime Minister did two weeks ago, that we have surrendered enough! . . . The European enterprise is not and should not be seen like that, as some kind of zero-sum game.

He deplored 'foghorn' diplomacy, shouting across at the other heads of state, and likened his task as her Foreign Secretary to being 'sent out to the crease as an opening batsman, only to find from the moment that the first balls are bowled that the bats have been broken by the team captain'.

Other stories emerged of her stubbornness. One of her ministers, Douglas Hurd, confided that only three topics were discussed in the Cabinet: parliamentary affairs, home affairs and xenophobia. Sir Patrick Wright, formerly the Head of the Diplomatic Service, spoke of her hatred of Germany. While other European leaders welcomed the fall of the Berlin Wall, Mrs Thatcher was hostile to the prospect of a reunited Germany; and wanted Gorbachev to keep Soviet troops in the former East Germany.

While she claimed credit, with Reagan, for rolling back the spread of socialism from Eastern Europe, she was less interested in offering an alternative system of government. This was another example of where a bottom-up philosophy differs from a top-down one. After World War II and after the Second Iraq War, the pragmatic British were content with a poll of the people to mean democracy and a free-market economy to solve other ills. Many other issues had to be settled as well, preferably through a reasoned debate.

The Maastricht Treaty was finally signed in February 1992 by Douglas Hurd on behalf of Britain and the new Prime Minister, John Major, who succeeded Mrs Thatcher. She left behind a divided and hostile Party, one side of which shared her version of history, distrusted all things European and assumed that compromise was a sign of betrayal. The struggle to maintain a balance between the pro- and anti-Europe wings of the party dominated Major's time in office, led to thirteen years when the Conservative Party was out of office and returned to haunt another Conservative Prime Minister, David Cameron, some eighteen years later.

During the EU Referendum in 2016, her voice spoke from beyond the grave. She died in 2013. But for those in Britain who hoped that Maastricht would become, like the US Constitution, a testament to the moral strength of the Free World, the damage had already been done. To placate both wings of the Tory Party, Major's government had already adopted a half-in, half-out stance towards the European Union, within the Europe exchange rate mechanism but outside the Eurozone, not quite borderless, not quite integrated and not quite European.

'No, no, no!' insisted Mrs Thatcher in the Commons in 1990, dismissing the common European currency as another step towards federalism. 'Up yours, Delors!' echoed the headline in *The Sun*, lending its support.

(ii)

Behind Mrs Thatcher's and Jacques Delors' two perspectives lay the foggy question of 'culture', and what was meant by 'culture'. She was an energetic Minister for Education in Edward Heath's administration, determined to raise standards in all state schools and to ensure that all students were well equipped to earn their livings in the market-places ahead. Delors was an educationalist as well as an economist, and chaired UNESCO's Commission on Education for the Twenty-first Century, which stressed the values of lifelong learning. His report, *Learning: The Treasure Within* (1996), provided the conceptual basis for Canada's *Composite Learning Index* and the *European Lifelong Learning Indicators*.

During the 1979 election campaign, Mrs Thatcher was asked whether 'monetarism' meant cutting back on the grants to the Arts Council. She dismissed the question as trivial. Her government was not interested in 'candle-end' economies, the tiny amounts given to support the arts through the Office of Arts and Libraries within the Department of Education and Science. She had something more fundamental in mind, the transformation of the British economy.

But arts lobbyists complained that she was underrating the financial contribution of the 'arts-based' industries, in which the provision of grants through the Arts Council and the local authorities played a small but significant part. The British music industry was booming, fashion was swinging, publishing was thriving and, as a result, tourism and the advertising industries were doing very well. British theatre was an international attraction and West End restaurants were full to capacity for seven days a week.

In 1978, as the newly appointed arts and broadcasting spokesman for the Liberals, I expressed my surprise in a cross-party debate, that subsidies given to the car industry were considered to be investments, although usually they lost money, whereas grants given to the arts were treated as charity, although often they made money. What was the difference?

I had shocked phone calls from party headquarters. Of course, the car industry was more important to the economy than the arts. Had I forgotten the small suppliers? But some economists came to my rescue, including Professor John Pick, who conducted case studies on the annual impact of the Edinburgh International Festival upon the city's economy. These demonstrated that the arts could be a more profitable investment than the automobile industry, although not inevitably so. Certain socio-scientific distinctions needed to be made. Economists proposed two categories in the arts industries, 'cultural' and 'creative', of which one was profitable, but the other speculative. They were often confused, since they both employed artists, and even the British Council could not tell the difference between them. In the terrain of the arts, however, they were separated by a large spiritual and intellectual gulf.

In an age of monetarism, when every last penny of public money had to be justified in terms of its economic return, the idea that the arts too were an industry, and part of a wider field of commercial activity, was very appealing. It changed the way in which financial support was given to the arts. Commercial sponsorship was encouraged, so that the swinging heart of London could be supported by the firms who most benefited. When local authorities were rate-capped and not allowed to spend more than their authorised limits, sponsorship took their place. Under John Major, lottery funding was introduced and Britain's first 'ministry of culture' was established in 1994, the Department of National Heritage.

It was often asserted that Mrs Thatcher cut the state subsidies to the arts but she actually increased them. The money given through the Arts Council rose during her time in office but *how* this money was spent was transformed. The spending was justified by indicators other than the merely artistic. At Stratford-upon-Avon, there was a thriving tourist industry, based upon Shakespeare. The Shakespearian heritage spread prosperity throughout the region. Stratford had its research centre, which attracted international scholars, its sites of special interest, such as Anne Hathaway's cottage, and its shops of Shakespeare memorabilia.

Against that background, the public funding of the Royal Shakespeare Company, one of the finest in the world, made commercial common sense. It was a showplace for Britain, a prime example of a cultural industry. As modern Europe was under construction, there were many such places. The 'Cities of Culture' celebrated them all, with a European Committee to decide whose turn was next. In Paris 'les grands projets' of François Mitterrand were intended to build centres for the arts to celebrate French culture. It included the transformation of the Louvre and the modern music centre, IRCAM, at the Pompidou Centre, which was in itself a triumph of modernist architecture.

It was challenged in London by the development of the South Bank, with the presence of the new National Theatre, Tate Modern, a National Film Centre and the transformed Festival Hall with its three concert platforms. These large-scale and expensive schemes were not intended merely to attract tourists, but also to demonstrate the scale and provenance of a national culture, even its identity, and to provide what the advertising industry called a brand image. The economic benefits were sometimes more hard to measure. The 'cultural industries' could not be allowed to fail or to seem less than they were expected to be. National prestige was at stake. Critics had to be kept in line. Journalists were warned by their editors not to make facetious remarks about them.

In contrast, the 'creative' industries were by nature speculative. They were supposed to be breaking new ground. They might either strike gold or alluvial swamp. They could not guarantee success. 'Creativity' itself was a problem word. To what extent could human beings ever be considered 'creative', as a god might be creative or a technological wizard? What did 'creativity' mean? Was it more than inventiveness, so that one who discovered new sounds from synthesisers in a radiophonic workshop might be called 'creative'? Or did it have a socio-psychological import, so that novels by minorities were being creative, because they opposed the typical WASP's version of 'reality'?

Or was it a matter of training our senses, so that we looked at the world around us with a heightened appreciation? When I first saw a Ben Nicholson painting, a brown square upon a purple ground, I left the gallery to find a brick wall beautiful and intriguing, rich with colours that I had never noticed before. Or was 'creativity' a matter of philosophy? In our daily lives, we notice what we are trained to see, through our education, childhood and social narratives. We are conditioned by our myths, but with the help of the arts, we can alter our assumptions, and transform the way in which we interpret the world. For literary critics, influenced by Structuralism, that was what creativity really meant.

There was an even broader definition, supported by centuries of religious thought, to the effect that we are surrounded by 'the Cloud of Unknowing'. The mystery of creation was and always would be beyond the reach of understanding. But through our senses, our imaginations and our capacity to reason, which were all gifts from God, we could appreciate aspects of the divine universe of which we were part. The creativity of the arts came from exploring that border country, where the known met the unknown, and we could sense the glory of God intuitively through what lay beyond our factual knowledge.

From that point of view, the 'creative' arts were more of a process of understanding than a collection of skills that produced marketable products. This was recognised by Delors, who, in his work for UNESCO, distinguished between four goals of education: learning to know, which included research and the discovery of facts; learning to do, how this knowledge could be applied; learning to be, how our minds and spiritual lives were transformed by what we were discovering; and learning to be with, the social implications of lifelong learning.

These were identical to the aims of the adult education institutes during the 1960s, where I taught, to those of the Open University and to those of the development of the regional repertory theatres, where 'Theatre in Education' was considered to be a necessary part of the activities. The rise of the reps was supported by the belief that there were many different local cultures in Britain, each of which should be given their chance to flourish. Reps were supposed to have their own small companies, drawn from local talents, with the means to encourage local playwrights and composers, and to offer fringe facilities for experiments in studio theatres.

During the 1960s, the arts were considered to be not so much of a product but a process. It was how we learnt to adjust our minds to the changing world around us – the threats and promises of its new technologies, its environmentalism and its classlessness. Some companies preferred to call themselves workshops or research centres rather than theatres, such as Joan Littlewood's Theatre Workshop in Stratford East or Peter Brook's International Centre for Theatre Research in Paris, his new home in the early 1970s.

But the 'creative' industries were much harder to finance than the 'cultural'. It was difficult to know in advance what the returns will be. No politician, no commercial sponsor, wants to be associated with a venture that may flop. Like any other research department, some efforts might be wasted, although others might be triumphantly successful. The value of the activity did not lie in ticket sales, which might be small, but in how it influenced the minds of those who took part, both as artists and as audiences.

This might not be measurable. The creative industries did not fit in easily with a monetarist philosophy. During the financial crises of the 1970s, the motives for funding the arts started to change at a political level. Sponsors wanted to know precisely what they were receiving for their money. This was partly due to the arrival in the mid-1970s of the new National Theatre building. The NT had cost the taxpayer a great deal of money, far more than the original estimates. It was delayed in its completion and its Brutalist exterior, all concrete and wood patterned slabs, was likened in the press to a nuclear bunker. It had to be seen to be successful. Otherwise heads would roll.

The National Theatre Company had been housed in the nineteenth-century Old Vic theatre;, but it now occupied a much larger space with two main auditoria and a small adaptable stage, together with extensive foyer spaces for exhibitions and platform performances. The management had changed, Laurence Olivier giving way to Peter Hall, who was expected to turn the place into an instant success. To achieve this result, its funding was greatly increased, until it took about a third of the public spending devoted to the theatres throughout Britain.

The regional reps suffered in two ways. In some cases, their Arts Council support was frozen, or fell, while their best actors, directors and designers were lured to London with the promise of higher wages and international publicity. At the Old Vic, the NT Company had been a closely knit group, inspired by social-democratic ideals. This approach did not fit easily with the new management philosophy, which took Broadway and the West End as its model. Box office success was its main criterion. Hall described his NT as an 'industrial-commercial complex', which required top talents to be hired at competitive rates with the international stars of the transatlantic entertainment and media companies.

Hall himself, unlike Olivier, was not employed directly by the NT, but hired through an independent company, according to commercial practice. This enabled him to spread the tax burden, to accept other commissions and to gain the financial advantage of any transfers to Broadway, which included Peter Shaffer's *Amadeus*. His exact salary was not published. At that time, I had been commissioned to write a history of the National Theatre,[i] taking over from the journalist and writer, Nicholas Tomalin, who had been killed on the Golan Heights on the frontier between Israel and Syria. Like him, I wanted to march to the sound of gunfire.

In common with other journalists, I wanted to know more about Hall's salary and the nature of his contract with the NT. I asked the chair of the NT's Board, Lord Rayne, and was told that this was highly confidential. I asked a former chairman of the Arts Council, Lord Goodman, the same question, making it clear that I was not concerned with the exact figure but whether the director of the NT was allowed to receive income from the commercial transfers of NT productions, as well as his salary as its artistic director.

Goodman took time to reply. 'I do hope that you will be a responsible journalist,' he said, 'because I should warn you that irresponsible journalists get a very bad reputation. I should know, because I am the Chairman of the Newspaper Proprietors' Association.'

With those words, a wider chill descended. In the interests of national prestige, the cultural industries would soon overwhelm and swamp the creative ones. The time might come when the process meant nothing at all, but only the profitability of the product.

(iii)

In September 1990, Mrs Thatcher resigned, having faced a challenge from the pro-Europe candidate, Michael Heseltine, which she won, but not by a sufficient margin to guarantee her survival. The split within the Conservative Party over Europe was an open chasm and would remain so for almost three decades. Each of its subsequent leaders – Major, Haig, Duncan Smith, Howard, Cameron and May – tried to stay in control of the party, whose members were at odds over this fundamental issue. A leader famously opposed to compromise left her party so divided that its future leaders were forced to compromise. They had no alternative.

When Heseltine's bid for leadership failed, John Major was chosen as the new leader of the Conservative Party and the *de facto* Prime Minister, who had the support of Mrs Thatcher but was not considered to be an anti-European. Labour had a substantial lead in the opinion polls but, when the next general election was called in 1992, Major won an unexpected victory. He had only a narrow majority in the Commons and throughout his period in office, he knew that the anti-Europe rebels within his own party could overthrow his government. His own cabinet represented a delicate balance between the pro-Europeans, led by Heseltine, Kenneth Clarke and Douglas Hurd, and the Eurosceptics, Peter Lilley, Michael Howard, John Redwood and Michael Portillo, whom he called (but not by name) in one unguarded television interview, 'the bastards'.

The Maastricht Treaty was signed in February 1992. Major called an election in April and in May the House of Commons had the opportunity to debate what had been agreed. The general election straddled the months during which, according to Major, 'the biggest transition to democracy in our Continent in its entire history'[ii] was taking place. The Conservative manifesto was bullish, fighting back at a resurgent Labour. It summarised the achievements of the Thatcher-led Tory governments since 1979 and announced several new proposals, among them a Citizens' Charter and Britain's first Ministry of Culture.

The Conservatives, according to its manifesto, had inherited a 'depressed and divided country', which it had transformed, and was now the centre for a thriving business culture. The City of London contributed more than £11 billion to the economy. It was at the heart of Europe and soon it would be Britain's turn to preside over the Council of Ministers. To appease the Eurosceptics, it listed the ways in which the government opted out of the Social Chapter and refused to commit itself to a single currency; and it steered a careful path between praising and criticising the Maastricht Treaty. The key principle, which Major claimed to have introduced, was that of 'subsidiarity', whereby no issue should be decided at a Community level that could be settled by the nation state.

But this did not go far enough for many Eurosceptics because, although the actual word 'federal' had been omitted from the document, it implied that there would be a level of government above that of the nation-state, and therefore federal by nature, if not by name. The significance was often revealed in the small print. The government would ensure 'that the renegotiation of the Common Fisheries Policy protects the interests of UK fishermen and retains their share of the Community's fishing opportunities'. For those who believed that the coastal waters were British anyway, this sounded like surrender to a superstate.

To appease the Eurosceptics, the manifesto presented the European Union always in a less than positive light. It failed to acknowledge that our membership was based upon treaties which our governments helped to frame and had signed on behalf of the United Kingdom. It seemed as if the Maastricht Treaty was a hostile plot against Britishness. To that extent, it was Thatcherite in tone, if not in content.

It was, as all the commentators agreed, a pivotal moment. The Cold War was over. The whole Continent was engaged in building a model for its future, which would take into account the global challenges of a nuclear age. Space travel was now feasible. Communication satellites had shrunk the physical divisions between nations across the world to the click of a button. Nevertheless, the political debate remained focussed upon domestic issues. Either the politicians did not trust the public to speculate about world events or they were so divided that they could not venture an opinion without starting another quarrel.

Already the two world powers, armed with their weapons of mass destruction, were starting to look old-fashioned, as if from another generation. The Soviet Union had collapsed, while one of the two halves in the Special Relationship seemed uncertain of the way ahead, sentimental about its past, fretfully aggressive to those who disagreed with it and distrustful of foreigners who wanted to share in its prosperity. 1992 should have been the time to debate the future of the free world. Instead, the government's election campaign began with a death-defying compromise and ended with a squeak of self-satisfaction. We were still a sovereign nation but had opted out of a full commitment to the EU.

The smaller parties – the Liberal Democrats, Greens and National Front – complained about the political system. Under any form of proportional representation, it should have been possible to distinguish between those party candidates who were Eurosceptic and those who were not. Under the British 'first-past-the-post' system, this was difficult. The main political parties, Conservative and Labour were both divided, officially in favour of the Community but with strong dissenting minorities. To win, they had to pretend to be more united than they were.

There were alternatives. It was possible to argue that the trading agreements that held the Community together and put forward as the chief justification for our membership could have been reached by other means. Instead of trying to pile everything together into one Treaty, the social with the economic, the environment with industry, there could have been many separate treaties between independent countries. A proposal along these lines was put forward by a lecturer at the London School of Economics, Dr Alan Sked, who founded the Anti-Federalist League in 1991 and fought two elections under this banner.

He was a former Liberal, converted by Mrs Thatcher's speech in Bruges. He had studied the details of the Maastricht Treaty and decided that they were incompatible with national sovereignty. His new party was unsuccessful at the ballot box and part of the trouble, he concluded, lay in its name. 'Anti-Federalist' was too clumsy. 'Independence' was better, but a name like the 'British Independence Party' ran the risk of confusion with the British National Party (BNP), whose racism Sked abhorred. He and his supporters settled on a new name, the United Kingdom Independence Party – or UKIP.

Sked was its founding member and first chair. Under his leadership, UKIP joined the cluster of small parties at the bottom of the political pile, a respectable single-purpose pressure group with little chance of power. He was joined by a former Conservative candidate, Nigel Farage, who wanted to broaden its appeal. As a supporter of Enoch Powell, Farage linked the party's anti-federalism with anti-immigration. Whereas Powell had immigration from the Caribbean and East Africa in mind, Farage expanded these warnings to include immigration from the continent of Europe as well and the 'free movement of labour'. In his view, sovereignty was not the only issue at stake but national identity as well.

In the 1994 European Parliament Election and the 1997 British General Election, UKIP did badly. It was outpolled by the Referendum Party, funded by the multimillionaire Sir James Goldsmith, and Sked himself was thought to be a poor campaigner, too cerebral, lacking in popular appeal. He was replaced by Michael Holmes, a dedicated anti-Europe campaigner. With the death of Goldsmith in 1997, the Referendum Party collapsed and many of its members joined UKIP. But UKIP was still a small party. In 1997, it fielded 197 candidates but received only 0.3 per cent of the national vote. In the 1999 European Parliament Election, which used proportional representation, the party did better, winning three seats. Farage gained one of them and entered the European Parliament as an MEP for South East England.

Gradually, the party's fortunes improved. In the 2001 General Election, it secured 1.5 per cent of the national vote, but no seats in parliament, and in the 2004 European Parliament Election, it did even better, gaining twelve seats and 16.1 per cent of the national vote in a low and apathetic poll. Holmes was a moderate leader. Although he wanted Britain to leave the Community, he was prepared to settle for reform, in which the European Parliament would be given greater powers over the Commission and the Council of Ministers. He wanted to extend democratic control over the Executive, which he considered to be largely self-appointed.

UKIP was never a party of reform, only of trenchant opposition. Election analysts studied its gradual rise in the polls and discovered that it appealed to blue-collar, middle-aged workers, white, nearing on the brink of retirement, a section of the population that was similarly attracted to the British National Party (BNP). Farage, who took over from Holmes as UKIP's national president in 2006, ruled out the prospect of a merger with the BNP. Like Sked, he feared that the outright racism of the BNP, and its reputation for violence, would deter those respectable Conservative and Labour supporters whom he hoped to attract. However, he held firm to the simple UKIP message. Foreign workers took British jobs, exploited the welfare system and depressed wages. They brought in foreign diseases, smuggled in drugs and terrorism, and despised British values. They did not play cricket, either physically or spiritually, and the prime source for this foreign meddling in our affairs was Brussels, the organ of the EU.

'The instinctive prejudices and wisdom of street politicians,' prophesied John Biffen, MP, in 1992, 'hold the key to Europe's future, not the great and the good.'[iii] Ten years later, he was starting to be proved right. UKIP outpolled the BNP in local and national elections, and attracted their old members, as well as many traditional Conservatives, who were alarmed by Major's apparent equivocation over Europe. When Major's government was defeated in 1997 by Tony Blair's New Labour, UKIP's support continued to rise, outperforming the BNP, which dwindled accordingly, and it became Britain's third largest party in the 2014 European Parliament Election, ahead of the Liberal Democrats, polling 27.5 per cent and sending 24 MEPs to the European Parliament.

Was this street wisdom 'instinctive' or 'acquired'? Was it the result of a natural human instinct to protect the family, the community or the race, from outside interference? Or were these prejudices derived from our British culture, the stories that we told each other, incidents that we remembered or wanted to forget? The rise of UKIP illustrated how a single issue of lesser importance could pick up other grievances, as it rolled like a stone downhill, until it became a mountain-slide of everything else that was wrong with our society.

UKIP was not just a political party. It was more of a mid-life crisis. Its manifestos could appear contradictory in that they offered ideas that were economically neo-liberal, in that UKIP favoured the free market and less interference from government, but socially conservative, in that the party knew what Britishness was really like and would summon up the full authority of the state to impose it. These, as Mrs Thatcher discovered, were incompatible aims and in both cases, when Margaret Thatcher and Nigel Farage left the political stage, their houses of cards collapsed . . .

. . . Or nearly collapsed, for even when their causes had been won or lost, and there no longer seemed to be a reason to prolong their campaigns, a residue of the struggle lingered on and polluted or, some might think, enriched the ground upon which it was fought. In UKIP's case, what started as a battle for national sovereignty became the war against immigration, and then an assertion of national identity, bringing the 'greatness' back to Great Britain. Any problem which could not be tackled at a national level and required cooperation with others, such as global warming, was ignored or disparaged. Nigel Lawson and others who campaigned for Brexit denied climate change as well. To be consistent, they had to do so.

If there was a weight of academic opinion against them, this had to be disparaged as elitism or 'airy-fairy' nonsense. Class entered the equation. Those who had not earned their livings in business or by the sweat of their brows were out of touch with real life. They came from the privileged few who had been to university and so, naturally, their findings were biased toward the fortunate section of society from which they came. Any grievances, any feeling of failure, could be laid at the door of the Establishment, preferably in Brussels. So ingrained was the longing that dated back to Suez and the loss of the Empire that no honest supporter of UKIP could doubt that somewhere along the road we had been betrayed.

'You are a useless lot,' cried out Nigel Farage to the European Parliament. 'None of you has done an honest day's work in your life!' The man who sat beside him in the debating chamber scribbled a notice for the TV cameras. 'He is lying!'

***

Chapter Ten
Breaking the Mould

(i)

In *The Search for the Perfect Language* (1997), the Italian novelist and semiotician, Umberto Eco, described how the seventeenth century mathematician and philosopher, Gottfried Wilhelm von Leibnitz, pioneered the binary language that we now use in our computers and thus left an indelible mark upon our cultures and the ways in which we think.

Leibnitz was a pioneer of the Enlightenment, the great rationalist movement that swept across Europe during the eighteenth century. A key feature of the Enlightenment was the separation of publicly verifiable 'facts', or 'objectivity', from private dreams or intuitions, 'subjectivity'. Scientific knowledge was supposedly based upon facts, not guesswork or emotions, and the common acceptance of these facts led to the Industrial Revolution, modern medicine and everything that we now assume to be an objective response to the real world.

To share this knowledge required a language that was equally 'objective', whose signs could not be misunderstood or lead to false conclusions. Medieval philosophers had used Latin as a common language, and scientists had followed their example, because words in the vernacular might not be understood by anyone that lived outside their districts. But Latin had become corrupted and fell short of the all-embracing language that the Enlightenment required, one that could accurately convey every detail of human experience, every observation of nature, every unexpected discovery. And so the search went on.

There were several attempts to develop a new international language, like Esperanto, which could be quickly learnt and used by travellers around Europe. There were sections of the colonial worlds where French was the common language, or Spanish, German or Dutch, although the native tongues might be richer in detail and more expressive. In the twentieth century, English became the dominant world language, written and spoken by more people even than Chinese. A common language suggested a common culture, replacing the slang and quirks of a local vocabulary with something more easily understood by a foreign traveller.

None of these matched the aspirations of Leibnitz, who in 1703 published his *Explication de l'Arithmétique Binaire*, in which he explained how a system of binary numbers, 0 and 1, could be infinitely extended to provide a symbolic language in which all known things, 'facts', could be listed and categorised. Unfortunately, as Eco pointed out, it was socially unusable. It could not be spoken or easily written. But it came into its own in the twentieth century when, in conjunction with computers, optical fibre and satellites, it became the operating language for a worldwide communications system.

It was very precise. Instead of mimicking a sound or an image, as with 'analogue' technology, it converted it into its binary equivalent, a process known as digitalisation, which greatly improved the accuracy and quality of its reception. It was infinitely versatile. It did not confine itself to verbal languages, but could encompass music, film and the visual arts, and prepared the way for the all-round headsets for virtual reality machines. It was no longer socially unusable, for its use was everywhere, but it was socially limited, in that it lacked many elements that normal speech inherently contains.

This is why 'emojis' were invented. In ordinary conversation, you can usually tell if a word is used ironically, very sincerely or as a joke. In a screen chat, this is more difficult, and so emojis were created to convey the intentions behind the word. Yet these little images such as 'rolling around with laughter' or 'heartbroken' are crude and simple. They have to be interpreted. Does he or she really mean it? No emojis can replace the variety of signals that we receive during the course of an ordinary conversation and incline us to like or dislike, trust or doubt, the words of the person who is speaking to us.

There is another problem. A digital language can exactly label a fact or a thing, which is one important function, but many words, when we use them in conversation, bring with them a context, which might be a motive, a history or a narrative. We can often guess at the word, such as 'Hello', by recognising its context – and how, why and where it is being used. The context can be more complicated. It may contain memories of previous meetings. There are some 'Hellos' that we may want to avoid, others that we might welcome, and, if we substitute the greeting for something more substantial, such as 'May we have a little chat?' a whole orchestra of alarm bells might jangle. This depends on how the words are spoken, where they are said and the history behind them.

In real life, words cannot be divorced from the relationships of which they are part and which a digital language can never match. But for many purposes, the digital language was found to be efficient and useful. It could list those who were unemployed, suffered from cancer, missed school for more than four days in a term or were disabled. In the 1930s, in the days before computers and digitalisation, this information usually had to be gathered by meeting people, recorded in a notebook, filed and placed in filing cabinets; but by the 1990s, it could be digitalised and placed on databases, which could be linked with other databases and exchanged. Whole populations could be thus categorised.

This was very useful. It meant that a government, a local authority or an advertising agency could compile a statistical profile of a neighbourhood, or a whole country, which would greatly improve the efficiency of its services. By the end of the twentieth century, any modern government had at its fingertips information about its population that would have previously required a large bureaucracy to compile. Most people could be persuaded to fill in their own forms themselves, and provide details of their lives, such as their religions, marital statuses and ethnic identities, which might have seemed intrusive if a public official had asked them point-blank. In the old days, we needed a dictator to compile the structure of a police state. By the turn of the twenty-first century, we could have the benefits of such a structure without the dictator. This may or may not be a comforting thought.

This flow of information enabled governments and anyone else who had access to it to attempt bold and ambitious tasks of social engineering that would have defeated previous administrations. Like the Big Bang, which opened out the City of London's banking services to instant trading from across the world, so those who wanted to trace their ancestries, or to compare salary levels between men and women, could trawl the Internet for useful 'facts'. But the mountainous piles of collectible details, which could be sifted through and selected in 0.03 seconds, could not compensate for the fatal flaw of all digital language. It could list the word but not its context, the fact but not the motive, the event but not why it happened. It could catalogue the entire library of human behaviour but, if you lifted a book from one of its shelves, its pages were almost bare. This had consequences.

The financial crisis of 2008 became the cautionary tale that revealed how much the Internet and digitalisation had changed the way in which we organised our affairs, not wisely but too well. We could learn from its lesson and eventually profit from it. In the years that led to the turn of the century and a new millennium, we could all bask in the glow of the Internet, the vast expansion of our sources of knowledge and the websites that had suddenly appeared on our desktop computers. The negative side-effects, even the near-collapse of the banking system, could not suppress the optimism with which the digital age was greeted.

It was like the first walk on the moon. For the first time in history, it was possible for one person with a computer to have access to worldwide databases, surpassing the resources of even the most comprehensive library – another giant step for mankind! Or theoretically possible, for the databases still had to be built, the connecting links had to be constructed and, as its pioneers soon realised, the Internet had to be kept free from censorship and the intrigues of politicians.

At the European Organisation for Nuclear Research (CERN) in Zurich, an English scientist, Tim Berners-Lee, developed an information management system, based upon links embedded in a readable text, which referred the researcher to other websites, globally. 'Imagine,' he told his colleagues, 'the references in this document all being associated with the network address of the thing to which they referred, so that, while reading this document, you could skip to them with the click of a mouse!' He refined his idea and with his colleague, the Belgian scientist, Robert Cailliau, he presented a proposal to CERN in 1990, which he called the World Wide Web.

The usefulness of the web soon became apparent. Although it was no more than a large-scale management tool to assist global browsing, it opened up other possibilities that we are still exploring. It enabled Internet trading and threatened the high-street shops. Berners-Lee and his colleagues were determined that so powerful a tool should not fall into the hands of politicians. It should provide a service to everyone, regardless of nationality, religious belief or wealth. It should become the servant of the common man. Accordingly, they formed an international consortium, W3C, to develop the web for its 'social value . . . in that it enables human communication, commerce and the opportunity to share knowledge'.

Unlike the Microsoft Corporation and similar companies, W3C was a 'not-for-profit' organisation and became the model for other consortia, such as Wikipedia, which raised the money to keep them afloat through charitable donations and the support of the universities. The Internet was never entirely free from the ideological dividing lines of the twentieth century, between socialism and capitalism, and those who believed that its services should be free for all and those who saw it as an opportunity to make money. But this was not an Iron Curtain. Both were partners and neither occupied the moral high ground unchallenged.

This was the time for visionaries, as the new century approached and, gradually, like a blood-red sun, the twentieth century sank into history. Every department in government, every company large and small, every independent entrepreneur with the chance to build a website, was planning how best to digitalise its affairs and take advantage of globalisation. There were multiple glitches on the way. Hackers and fraudsters were learning their trades as well; and even those with honourable motives could make mistakes that imperilled the medical records of an entire hospital or lose the entrance visas of the Windrush generation.

That was one of the problems. When digitalisation went wrong, it often went wrong in a big way. When governments started to rely on their computers and statistical analyses were built into their systems, a small error could have devastating consequences. But managements that did not take advantage of the digital age also made mistakes, and were less efficient as well, and so the wise director employed the best available IT experts and crossed his fingers. When mistakes were made, he or she would hire the best PR consultancy to cover up the damage.

This was not to suggest that the benefits of digitalisation did not outweigh the risks, for gradually, as in all forms of progress, lessons were slowly learnt and the dangers avoided. But while this was happening, there could be a rash of unintended consequences. One was that political leaders got delusions of grandeur. They forgot the lesson of King Canute. They started to think that immigration could be cut by half or social benefits could be stream-lined by bringing them all into one package. Governments promised as much. They taught us to tick boxes and brought in various systems to grade schools, to admit refugees and migrants and to license medicines. They were relentlessly topical.

Governments also forgot how each of these 'reforms', if they were seen as such, could cause chaos within the lives of those that suffered from them, the families and individuals who may have slipped between the boxes or otherwise failed to fit. The troubles of the digital age were caused by the limitations of the digital language itself. We should start by blaming Leibnitz and the Enlightenment.

There were also those who might be described as suffering from a sense of worthlessness, a nationwide inferiority complex. Few people wanted to be catalogued against their will and put into a section of the human race that felt like a colonial outpost. Some women want to be listed on their National Insurance forms as housewives. Others do not. Some do not want to be labelled for benefit purposes as 'unemployed', when they are really self-employed and waiting for their next big break. My passport tells me that I was born in Leigh-on-Sea, Essex, which I remember as a place where Cockneys go to die. In my mind, I am a child of the Cotswolds, which was where I grew up. Why should my official description differ so much from my image of myself? Whose life is it anyway?

The result of the 2016 Brexit Referendum has been blamed by commentators on class alienation. It was a rebellion against the Westminster *élite*, but, if you have been told that your family is number 83 on the council's waiting list but that you have not ticked enough boxes to qualify, you can feel that the whole system is humiliating. You do not have to blame the upper classes. Anyone in authority is rotten. Modern cities are paved by the unwilling victims of bureaucracy, who have not necessarily been badly treated. They may not have suffered from cutbacks or excess charges. But they have been digitalised to the core.

(ii)

Both main political parties in Britain were split and had to contend with large breakaway fragments that threatened to destroy them or, at best, to ruin their electoral chances.

In 1983, at a time when the monetarist policies of Mrs Thatcher's government had caused a large increase in unemployment, Labour went into the general election with what one member described as 'the longest suicide note in history'.[i] It advocated unilateral nuclear disarmament, leaving the European Economic Community, getting rid of the House of Lords and nationalising large sections of industry. The manifesto itself, which was enormously wordy, was an exercise in grassroots democracy. It contained a long wishlist of things to be remembered from previous party conferences.

Its leader, Michael Foot MP, was a member of a well-known Liberal political family, who had converted to socialism in the 1930s; he was elected leader of the Labour Party as a left-winger, someone whom the trade unions respected and had the support of the radicals, led by Tony Benn MP. The challenge to his brand of politics came from the right, the neo-Keynesians, the pro-Europe MPs and the social democrats, some of whom broke away from Labour to form a new political party, the SDP.

Following the victory in the Falklands War, the Conservatives won by a landslide, Labour lost three million votes and was reduced to its smallest number in the House of Commons since the 1930s, 209 MPs. But the party with the largest grievance was the SDP, which had formed an alliance with the Liberals to fight the election. The Alliance parties won 25 per cent of the vote and came within 700,000 votes of Labour, but gained only 23 parliamentary seats. This led to renewed calls to change the political system towards some form of proportional representation. Only the Conservatives were still happy with 'first past the post'.

Ten years later, the situation changed. After Maastricht, the rise of UKIP started to threaten the Conservatives in a similar way; but Europe was not the only issue that divided the party. Immigration, law and order and a resurgent nationalism were other factors. Major's government was seen as a weak administration, which was trying to bridge the gap between two incompatible groups – those who wanted to work within the European Union and those who hankered after a stronger Commonwealth and the closer harmony of the English-speaking races. The divisions within the party were at least as great as those within Labour and sometimes, as in a large family, more bitterly fought.

Without proportional representation, which would have allowed the electors to decide which faction they wanted to support, the main political parties had to change. They had to develop a very broad consensus to hold their parties together. In this evolutionary process, Labour had the head-start. The debacle of the 1983 election concentrated the minds of those who followed Foot as the Labour leaders, Neil Kinnock, John Smith and two young MPs, Tony Blair and Gordon Brown, who (with Jeremy Corbyn) were elected in that same year. Kinnock led the battle against the far left, the Militant Tendency, in an effort to win back the supporters of the SDP; and, when Kinnock failed against Major, and Smith unexpectedly died, the young Turks took over – Peter Mandelson, who had been Neil Kinnock's assistant, Tony Blair and Gordon Brown. In 1994, it was announced that Labour had changed its name. It would now be known as New Labour.

Just as some army generals are accused of fighting yesterday's battles, so the leaders of New Labour were determined not to repeat the mistakes of the early 1980s. In 1995, Clause 4 was dropped from the Labour Party constitution. It had been written in 1917 to call for the 'common ownership of the means of production, distribution and exchange of goods'. Whereas Old Labour had called for more nationalisation, New Labour respected the market economy, and ostentatiously said so, and looked for public-private partnerships. Whereas Michael Foot was a pacifist, Blair wanted to prove that he was someone like Thatcher who stood up for Britain, and did so in small wars, before joining US President George W. Bush in a major one against Saddam Hussein's Iraq. Foot was against the EEC; Blair was a wholehearted supporter of the EU.

In the effort to win back those Labour voters who had defected to the SDP, the entire political programme on which the party had fought the 1983 election was turned inside out. New Labour was now a comfortable ally of big business and self-described as the party of modernisation. It was highly successful. It won the 1997 General Election, after which John Major resigned, and went on to become the party of government for thirteen years.

The Conservatives went through a similar transformation during their years out of office, but in an opposite direction, becoming increasingly hostile to the EU. This was partly to meet the rise of UKIP, but also to reflect the growing nationalism, which took Mrs Thatcher's Bruges speech as its unofficial manifesto. But it was still divided. When three Eurosceptic leaders, William Hague, Iain Duncan Smith and Michael Howard, all failed to muster the support to defeat New Labour, the Conservatives turned to one of their own young Turks, who, like Tony Blair, might lead them out of the wilderness, David Cameron, pro-EU but a reformer. He promised to cut immigration and to reform the EU by using Britain's privileged status as a world power to change some of its rules, including mobility of labour. This proved to be easier said than done.

Although these metamorphoses were in opposite directions, they had something in common. Both Labour and the Conservatives were responding to the arrival of new parties, the SDP and UKIP, which funnelled away their traditional support. The older parties were struggling to rebrand themselves. But it was still extraordinary to watch how they could change their minds about the future of Britain within the space of ten years, and persuade so many of their followers to do the same. It was like a mass conversion. The anti-EEC party, Labour, became the pro-EU party, New Labour. The Conservatives, who, from Macmillan to Major, had built their economic strategy around membership of the European project, were slowly starting to edge their way out of the Community's back door.

Some voters were very perplexed. Why should they continue to support a party that had promised one thing at a general election – and its exact opposite at the next? Where were its principles, its philosophy? Perhaps the answer was that, in the modern age, ideologies were starting to count for very little. The nature of politics was changing. It was becoming more managerial, less (for want of a better word) 'theoretical'? Why talk about Utopia when what the public really wanted were better bus services? Seminars were held on this question.

The trend started when, in 1979, the Conservatives turned to Saatchi and Saatchi, the 'global communications and advertising agency', founded in 1970, for their professional assistance. It delivered a poster of long dole queues with the slogan, 'Labour Isn't Working'; no philosophy, a gut image of hopelessness, job done. It was criticised for being misleading and untruthful but, as the Conservative campaign message, it worked very well. Saatchi's managing director, Tim Bell, advised Thatcher on her three election campaigns, as well as her vocal delivery and dress sense, and she nominated him for a knighthood. Tony Blair acknowledged his value.

He supported his elevation to the Lords as Baron Bell of Belgravia. PR consultants, once the party's window dressers, now occupied a place at the top table.

Blair had similar advisers, Philip Gould, an expert in market research, and Alastair Campbell, a former journalist, who was his election strategist and became his Director of Communications. Gould pioneered the use of focus groups in politics to trace how opinions were changing and how certain words or slogans had a more powerful effect than others. He became Lord Gould of Brookwood but died at an early age. Both had been nominated by Neil Kinnock's Director of Communications, Peter Mandelson, the mastermind behind the branding of New Labour, the future Lord Mandelson. He came from a political family. He was the grandson of Herbert Morrison, the Deputy Prime Minister in Attlee's post-war government. He could present himself as an authentic Morrisonite, a centrist, not a Bevanite, after Bevan, Morrison's rival, the orator of the radical left.

Mandelson and Gould studied the election strategy that had brought Bill Clinton to the White House, and borrowed his election software, Excalibur, to analyse public opinion. It helped them to compile a statistical profile of key constituencies, so that their campaign leaflets could be targeted to meet the known likes and dislikes of the voters. This was presented as a giant step forward in democratic politics. Through market research, a party could find out what the public really wanted, instead of just thinking up policies that it hoped the electorate would like. Politics was changing. It was becoming digitalised.

All political parties have differences of opinion, inevitably so. All change direction under the pressure of events, and would be foolish not to do so. But the Conservative and the Labour parties were bitterly divided within themselves, particularly over Europe. Market research came to their aid without ruffling any more feathers. Statistics told them what to do. Opinion polls and focus groups provided an objective snapshot of popular opinion but, at the turn of the twenty-first century, it was often hard to decide what either party stood for and what were the reasons for its existence. 'New Labour, New Danger' was the Conservative poster for the 1997 General Election, with a picture of Blair wearing a highwayman's mask. What did it mean?

In *The Blair Revolution* (1997), Peter Mandelson and Roger Liddle tried to explain. The British felt 'increasingly insecure' at a time of 'rapid economic and technological change'. The country was in decline and 'badly equipped to meet the challenge of change'. The answer was to tackle the 'vested interests and class barriers' that held Britain back and release 'the dynamism and entrepreneurial energy of its people'. 'The fundamental question is whether we can compete successfully in the global marketplace and still live in a decent society.' New Labour's answer was 'modernisation'. What did that mean?

The threads and links of the political debate were sacrificed to the topic of the day, pragmatism run wild; but the true strength of a democracy lies in the culture that surrounds it. Before the NHS was launched in 1946, there had been some 30 years of discussion about the prospect of state-run social services that could replace the previous mixture of private philanthropy and the charity of the churches. It may be said to have begun in 1906 when the Liberals introduced their plans for an old-age state pension. It continued in the interwar years with proposals for unemployment benefits, paid sick leave and similar matters, which led to the Beveridge Report in 1942. This was given a full lecture slot on the BBC. Among the issues concerned was the massive extension of the powers of the state.

The New Left Book Club, the manifestos, articles in the press, sermons in pulpits, speeches in the Commons and the Lords, all made their contributions to a national debate. Although the NHS was brought into being against much opposition at the end of World War II, it had its roots in the conscience-driven exchange of ideas about the sort of Britain that our great-grandparents wanted to build, a 'land fit for heroes'.

There was no such debate about Europe. This was not a British project. Although the political exchanges went on for even longer, it was presented to the British people in less than idealistic terms. It was a way of strengthening our economy, a trading area, nothing more, a rich man's club. The six countries that first signed the Treaty of Rome had peace on their minds, Britain its balance of payments. As the Cold War came to an end, this justification for membership was taken away and, led by Mrs Thatcher, the anti-Europe bickering began and spread throughout the Conservatives, UKIP and the country. It mangled history, turned a blind eye to the EU's achievements and promoted the white Commonwealth, the Anglosphere, as if it were an alternative.

In 2012, the European Union received a Nobel Peace Prize for 'advancing the causes of peace, reconciliation, democracy and human rights over six decades in Europe'. The citation praised the founders of the European Union for demonstrating that 'historic enemies can become close partners'. The prize was worth £1 million, to which the EU added another £1 million, to fund four emergency education projects in Syria, Colombia, Pakistan and the Congo, so that 'the children of war should become the children of peace'.

In Britain, the EU's Nobel Prize was greeted in the right-wing press with derision. According to Iain Martin in *The Daily Telegraph*, it was 'at best premature. . . . We have no idea how the experiment to create an anti-democratic federation will end'. He pointed out that 'Greek protesters are wearing Nazi uniforms and Spanish youth unemployment is running at 50 per cent'. From a Continental perspective, such a response was merely ill-willed and grudging. Was the EU responsible for these social disorders? It was self-evident that Europe in the second half of the twentieth century was a more peaceful place than it had been during the first half. Why should the British deny the obvious?

The British Prime Minister, David Cameron, a Conservative, chose not to join the other EU leaders at the award ceremony. He sent along his LibDem deputy in the coalition, Nick Clegg, to go in his place, because otherwise he might have annoyed the anti-Europeans. By now, the battle lines were drawn up. Further discussion was useless: any idealism would be airy-fairy. But the real victim of entrenchment was not the EU but the political culture in Britain. It was becoming very difficult to talk about Europe at all without abusing the other side. The standards of debate seemed to be declining. What was the cause? Market research revealed a divided country. What was the answer?

Surely not a referendum?

(iii)

I work at my computer all the time. I write on it, research on it, send messages and play games on it. If I am temporarily separated from my desktop computer, there is no reason to despair, because I can take away my laptop, which is connected to my desktop through something which is called the Cloud. If I do not want to carry a briefcase with my laptop, I do not have to tear my hair out with frustration, because I have my mobile phone, which picks up my messages and has a thousand apps, which I rarely use. The ad for my phone said that I need never be away from my office. What a relief!

My phone is connected to the Internet of Things. I can measure my heartrate, my speed of travel and my body mass index. I can switch on the lights in my room, lower the temperature and see who is coming to the front door. I am never lost. I have a satnav to tell me where I am and how to get to Central London or anywhere else from my house in Kingston. I can pay bills from it. I can transfer money from one account to another and I really do not need cash at all. I have got rid of my cheque book. I am completely in control – unless, of course, I leave my mobile at the check-out!

But I am not wholly out of control even then, because my laptop can trace my mobile, unless, of course, I have forgotten to bring my laptop, in which case I have to go back home to my desktop and hope that it has not been hacked.

In which case, I would be totally and completely lost. What could I do?

Fortunately, in my case, the worst has never happened. There have been minor glitches and my heart still sinks when a software programme upon which I depend tells me to update. I often have to reset my passwords. But none of that really matters. I rely on my computers and the systems behind them; and I can sit on a train, close my eyes and feel in control, thanks to Leibnitz, of 'the best of all possible worlds'.

But I can remember the time when all this technical support was not part of my life. I wrote on a non-electronic typewriter, used Tippex to correct errors and went to libraries to research. I would browse the bookshelves, instead of websites, and would pick out books to read on the advice of my teachers, employers or columns in the press. I would submit an article to an editor, instead of putting it online, and hope that it would not be rejected, and waited to see what mistakes the Neanderthal sub-editors might make on publication.

I received information in a different way. Its provenance mattered. Did it come from a reliable source? There were several kinds of sources. Some came from my education. I chose a particular subject to study at university, because a teacher at school fired my enthusiasm, but then changed my course, because I was influenced by somebody else. Some came from my family life. As an Anglican Christian, I was wary of anything too High Church. It might lean towards Catholicism. Some came from my social life or my hobbies but, at every stage, there was a filtering process, whereby the information I received came through other people's hands and minds before it reached me. It came down to me, vertically.

Of course, this meant censorship. It always did. It might not have been the 'burning-of-books' type of censorship but, in the early 1960s, there were laws against blasphemy, pornography and sedition. By the end of the decade, many of these had been relaxed or annulled, but some had been replaced by new laws against racial or ethnic discrimination, incitement to violence and criminal libel. But formal censorship was less prevalent than the informal. Cover-up censorship was one brand. Almost everyone practised it. Companies protected their reputations, local authorities the abuse in their care homes, churches their paedophile priests and the NHS its death rates. It was sometimes called discretion.

There were other forms of censorship. 'Protecting the young' covered a large area and men's magazines were placed on the top shelf at the newsagent's, out of reach of the twelve year-olds, unless they had older brothers – or inquisitive sisters. One difference between British newsagents and those in the United States was the absence of magazines about guns. You could not pick up information about assault rifles from your local supermarket shelves, as you could in New York. Was this censorship, a lack of public demand – or both? There was no rifle lobby in the UK. The law restricted the ownership of guns and so there may have been little demand for magazines on the subject but which came first, the ban on guns or the lack of newsprint about guns?

There is no country in the world without censorship. There may be degrees of press freedom, different levels of tolerance and of good will towards strangers; but no society is without a kind of filtering process, whereby some values are encouraged and others are not. To that extent, talk of Free Speech is mainly propaganda. Language itself is a filter. Some words are insulting and rarely used, whereas others are polite or politically correct.

These values are always changing from generation to generation and even within the mini-sub-divisions inside a generation. Some words may be sexist and others are merely flirtatious, although they may be the same words. Sometimes a society may want to uphold a strict domestic code, with parents, children and lifelong mortgages, and, at other times, it matters less who sleeps with whom, provided that they are all happy.

Censorship is part of a wide spectrum of active choices, in which we develop the kind of life that we want to live, the society that we want to build and our culture. Most of these rules have been handed down to us from parents to children, teachers to students, priests to worshippers. We can rebel. We can do exactly what the powers-that-be do not want us to do. But if we try to get rid of their influence altogether, and all the authorities from the past who influenced them, we would be defeated. The wholesale clearance of our mental lofts would be an impossible task. It would be easier to build a new house.

But the Internet cuts across our vertical information systems, horizontally. We can hear about a disaster in Borneo as soon as it happens. We can be Skyped by a total stranger. The news that we receive is not filtered through layers of authority, such as the BBC, but fixed by time and news deadlines. In Britain, we could find out about the therapeutic qualities of cannabis oil, while it was still on the police list as a banned substance. The World Wide Web was meant to be a service to mankind, free from political or commercial meddling. Nothing would be censored. It was intended to be an online temple to Free Speech.

'I'm trying to make the world a more open place,' said Mark Zuckerberg, the founder and chief executive of Facebook, described on its website as an 'online social media and social marketing service company'. Facebook was meant to be an open platform for opinion, a site on the Internet where people could exchange experiences, rant if they liked, but freely promote their own ideas and companies. Zuckerberg was shocked to discover that it could be used for nefarious purposes as well and admitted as much before a US Congressional Committee.

To protect its reputation, Facebook introduced monitoring and vetting procedures, which might not have been quite the same as vertical filtering through top-down authorities, but often sounded very similar. Other platforms were not so scrupulous but, under pressure, brought in improved security and age identification regulations. It was still possible to access the dark web, the unregulated areas of the Internet which could be reached without platforms or websites, but this required greater technical knowledge than most users possessed. In any case such sophistication was rarely necessary. There were enough ways to manipulate the Internet without resorting to cyber infiltration.

At the turn of the twenty-first century, while New Labour was modernising an 'increasingly insecure' Britain, many were just browsing the websites and fascinated by what they found. Small items of information came in from all over the world: a beached whale in Northumberland, a forest fire, a strange murder. No other generation in history had access to so much news, to so many campaigns and lobbies, with prizes, threats and the full gamut of other inducements. The web was full of factual sites, semi-factual sites and fake-factual sites, and sites that came without any provenance at all but expected you to believe in them. A teenager could learn with experts how to send rockets to Mars – or how to manufacture the bomb to carry on a bus. Fortunately, the social media sites were usually more fun.

Horizontal information very often crossed swords with the vertical variety. A priest at Sunday school might discover that a ten year-old knew more about sexual behaviour than he did. A sixth form student might pick up the tests from a research paper on the web before his or her teacher, who relied on university textbooks, had even heard of it. Time and distance were not the barriers that once they were. An elderly gentleman in Australia could form a profound online relationship with a boy from Thailand, who was pretending to be a girl. Their feelings might be genuine and mutual, although the situation was a complete fantasy.

This kind of conflict had political consequences as well. An old-fashioned politician, a Churchill, a Macmillan or a Foot, would approach a modern crisis from a background of past experience, which was both personal and collective. A history had been handed down vertically through which the present was interpreted. This had its strengths and weaknesses. Fighting last year's battles might be the recipe for defeat, but to have little experience at all was even more likely to lead to disaster. But to learn from playing war games on the Internet could be an even worse education, vast dreams of power, undiluted by the pain.

We are, of course, not dealing with absolutes. Everybody learns through both vertical and horizontal systems, facts and ideas that are inherited from parents and teachers, and those that come from today's experiences or by browsing the web. Culture is a blend of both. But the Internet tilted the balance away from the vertical towards the horizontal, so that in the debate about Brexit, the narrative that connected the formation of the European Union to the turmoil of the 1930s was sacrificed to a host of other issues, such as fish dumping or migrant workers in trouble with the police, because they had cropped up in that day's tweets.

Horizontal information frequently undermines the vertical narrative and, where it does not destroy, simplifies it. The flood of daily news half-drowns the echoes of the past, which linger on as ghostly alarm bells. 'We fought against Germany fifty, sixty, seventy years ago and, although they are now supposed to be our allies, we should be wary of them. They pinch deckchairs on the beach. It is a sign of their national character.' Similar arguments can be found in almost any British newspaper, broadsheet and redtop alike – and in French and German papers about the English.

Societies are normally held together more by their vertical narrative rather than the horizontal. When this is called into question, it becomes more difficult to hold on to an identity and to guess where you came from, as well as where you are going. Public opinion becomes more volatile, which may not be due to unemployment or another economic factor, but because there is an unease that what was once assumed to be reliable and truthful no longer seems so. One of the side-effects of the World Wide Web was to spread the idea that the information picked up on the Internet was more reliable than that from official sources, which would be filtered and censored through layers of authority.

This led to the demand that all the authorities should be held to account; and, in 1997, New Labour went into the election with a proposal for a new Freedom of Information Bill, its version of Gorbachev's *glasnost*, which was passed as an act of parliament in 2000. It was like a public declaration that, in future, the People would be in Control. In practice, it was less revolutionary, with many exemptions from disclosure, but top salaries in the public sector were revealed – which would have helped with my history of the National Theatre. In 2008, using the Act, *The Daily Telegraph* published the expenses of MPs, which stirred up a major political scandal resulting in the resignation of some MPs and the deselection of others.

This was a little local difficulty compared to the upheavals elsewhere. In 2006, an Australian computer programmer, Julian Assange, formed a new company, WikiLeaks, with its website located in Iceland. Its aim was to publish confidential documents, leaked from government and big business sources, and to distribute them widely through the Internet. He was accused by the US government of being a spy and a traitor. An international arrest warrant was issued against him by Sweden, following accusations of sexual assault and rape, he handed himself in to the British police but jumped bail and found sanctuary in the Embassy of Ecuador in London.

But this did not stop his activities or those of his company. In 2010, he published a large number of US Army files, which he had obtained through a US soldier, Bradley (later Chelsea) Manning, who had access to a secret US military archive. These included logs of the wars in Afghanistan and Iraq, as well as the files from the detention centre in Guantanamo Bay. Three years later, WikiLeaks published a similarly huge tranche of documents, leaked from the US National Security Agency by a former operating officer, Edward Snowden, who escaped from an international arrest warrant by refusing to leave Moscow's Sheremetyevo airport. He was granted asylum by the Russian authorities.

Taken together, the information provided by Manning and Snowden through WikiLeaks did more than just disclose how the US and British armies, and their security services, had violated the codes of war. It revealed the hollowness of the claims that the West was standing up for freedom. The moral authority that the West had claimed during the years of the Cold War was severely damaged. The United States, the principal defender of freedom, was revealed to be a serious offender, with the United Kingdom as its principal ally.

It was a bad time to run for office if you were a liberal member of an orthodox party. Politicians were tarred with the same brush. It was the dawn of the age of the right-wing outsiders: Farage with his pint of beer; Trump, the golden-haired TV celebrity; Steve Bannon, a plain-speaking media executive from Breitbart News; Arron Banks, the rich philanthropist; and Robert Mercer, who kept himself away from the spotlight. Whether they all knew Assange is a moot point. Whether Farage was the only man to visit him at the Embassy of Ecuador or whether others knew him through their Russian contacts are disputed questions. This was a time when rumours could be as useful as leaks, if they were backed up by digital marketing.

'Things fall apart,' wrote W.B. Yeats in 1920 in *The Second Coming*, when the European governments had no answer to the distress left by World War I, 'the centre cannot hold. . . . And what rough beast, its hour come round at last, Slouches towards Bethlehem to be born?'

***

Chapter Eleven
The Third Way

(i)

Many British politicians, trapped by the confrontational, first-past-the-post system for running the country, looked for the middle way. It was like trying to find the northwest passage across the top of Canada to nineteenth-century explorers. Most felt sure that it was there. It just had to be found. Some claimed to have got through, but had difficulties in getting back. Several got stuck in the ice and they all had trouble staying in touch with their home bases. The Norwegian explorer, Roald Amundsen, led the first fully documented expedition to reach this goal, but it took three years. Since his aim was to find the quickest trading route between West and East, even his success was not encouraging.

So it was with the political thinkers in their search for the middle way. In 1938, when Harold Macmillan as a young Conservative MP published *The Middle Way*, he sought a route between 'the unfettered abuse' of the free market and 'the intolerable restrictions' of the state – or between capitalism, as he saw it, and communism. Like Keynes and Beveridge, two Liberals, he advocated a 'conscious' role for government, which stopped short of interfering with the rights of the individual citizen. He wanted to devise a system that would 'retain our heritage of political, intellectual and cultural freedom, while . . . opening the way to higher standards of social welfare and economic security'. But there was a grey area where to protect 'welfare', it might be necessary to restrict 'freedom', and vice versa, which was the duty of the 'conscious' government to balance and decide.

In 1956, the Labour MP, Anthony Crosland, published *The Future of Socialism*, in which he tried to bridge the gap between those party members, who called for full nationalisation along the lines of Clause 4 on their membership cards, and those who feared that the country would become another proletarian dictatorship, like Stalinist Russia. Crosland distinguished between the 'ends' and 'means' of socialism. The 'ends' were to improve welfare, to seek equality and to distribute the rewards and privileges of society more fairly; but was it necessary to seize all the 'means of production' to do so? He thought not.

In 1998, the Director of the London School of Economics, Dr Anthony Giddens, published *The Third Way: The Renewal of Social Democracy*, which became the textbook for New Labour. He reacted against the way in which Thatcherism had seized the imagination of the Free World. Her 'neo-liberalism' was anti-state, pro-market and defended the rights of the family against those of society at large, which, in her opinion, 'did not exist'. Mrs Thatcher held most forms of social equality, the Welfare State and Social Chapter, in deep suspicion; but her key point was that governments could never succeed, where the markets had failed. Hard-working individuals created wealth. Governments were at best a service industry.

Giddens took her political achievements into account, but went on to describe how our lives were changing – with globalisation, post-industrialisation, the digital society and the green revolution. The individual or even a medium-sized nation could only achieve a certain amount by itself. The Free World had to develop a new socially-democratic 'Third Way'. New Labour should link arms with the progressive forces in other countries, the new Democrats in the US under Bill Clinton, the Scandinavians and the EU to build a modernised Britain that could take on the challenge of the brave and technologically mind-blowing New World.

In addition to these well-known and influential works, there were thousands of other similar tracts, promoting liberalism, social democracy and variants. There were also attempts to form new centrist parties, such as the SDP in the 1980s, the LibDems and New Labour at the turn of the century. They did not exactly fail. Centrism, in government or out, prevailed in the 50 years that separated the end of World War II from the turn of the century; and led to many reforms. Most centrist politicians favoured closer ties with Europe.

But the centrists left the impression that they were compromise parties, well-intentioned but lacking the courage of their convictions. In times of crisis, they gave way, either by calling for a general election, as was the case with Heath's government in its battle with the miners, or by holding a referendum, as with Wilson's, when his cabinet was split over Europe. They turned to public opinion as their ally in the belief that the wisdom of the British would make up their minds for them. This was an escape clause that they could use once too often.

Thatcher called their bluff. 'What great cause,' she asked, 'would have been fought and won under a banner "I Believe in Consensus"?' She accused the centrist parties, including her own under Heath, of 'abandoning all beliefs, principles, values and policies in search of something in which no one believes, but to which no one objects'. Compromise in her mind was an ugly word. It suggested weakness, endless concessions and giving way before evil. She herself was a conviction politician. On the basis of her Christian beliefs, she formed her vision as to what was right for the country. There was no alternative.

That was the challenge that faced all centrist parties. They were defining themselves against the extremes without having a philosophy of their own. They had to borrow from one side to pay the other. New Labour was in favour of the free market, because it produced the wealth that paid for the social services, but there were always conflicts of interests. To what extent should New Labour curb big business to protect the nation's health? Tobacco was an example. Should cigarettes be banned? There were pragmatic solutions, such as raising taxes and all the carrots and sticks of the nanny state, but what was the philosophy behind them? Did any philosophy matter to a public opinion that always thought 'bottom-up'?

The word, philosophy, was losing its meaning. It was too abstract. Most political commentators preferred to use 'ideology' to describe a system of ideas and opinions that a political party might share. Was nationalisation a better solution to the problems of transport than competition between private companies? That was an ideological question. It could be answered by statistics and a plausible theory. But a political philosophy started out by trying to understand what was meant by Reality and the riddles of human existence. To what extent, as the environmentalist James Lovelock asked, did 'egalitarianism' interfere with evolution and the survival of the fittest? Should we even try to protect the weak? Did we have any responsibility for the immigrants from war-torn countries, pounding at our borders?

That sort of question could only be answered through a faith or a system of beliefs, although *how* it was answered might influence almost every other area of public life. How much of our national income should we spend on looking after the vulnerable, as opposed to strengthening our defence system and building more houses? How much should be spent on improving our own standards of living, as opposed to responding to famines elsewhere? In Europe, how much sovereignty should be sacrificed to a federal structure? The world was full of middle ways but they all needed to be charted.

The missing factor, as with the Arctic explorers, was a reliable compass. We could not pinpoint exactly what we were or what we should be doing. This was a philosophical, not an ideological, problem. Ideologically, we were very good at measuring our rate of progress but very bad at deciding in which direction we should be going. This was why our political parties were split and why, in conversation, there were sudden and irreconcilable polarities of opinion. There was no common structure of belief, to which each side might refer. In an earlier age, this could have been Christianity, at another time science, but, at the dawn of a new millennium, the lack of a philosophy for the Middle Way hampered the search for one. We all knew that space and time were relative but where were we in the flow of variables?

'Back to basics,' said John Major in his search for something completely different. He may have meant a return to cricket, church bells, family life and care in the community. 'Community participation,' said Giddens, as if he had just discovered it. 'You can call it liberalism,' said David Cameron in 2010, the Prime Minister of a new coalition government, 'You can call it empowerment. You can call it responsibility. I call it The Big Society.'

The 'Big Society' represented:

> a huge culture change, where people in their everyday lives, in their homes, in their neighbourhood and in their workplace don't always turn to officials, local authorities or central government for the answers to the problems they face, but instead feel free enough and powerful enough to help themselves and their own communities.

This represented 'the most dramatic redistribution of power from the *élites* in Whitehall to the man and woman in the street'. Freedom at last! But there was another interpretation. The country had run out of money and his government needed to offload its responsibilities before embarking upon the new age of austerity. Cameron, like everyone else, was looking for the middle way.

This sounded like classical liberalism – less government intervention, more freedom – but it was far from being so. Liberalism was born at the end of the seventeenth century, when the aim was to protect the individual from oppression either by the Church or the monarchy. It was the political expression of Protestantism, whose first principle was to affirm the right of Christian believers to pray directly to God without the intervention of a priest to tell them how to do so. It was the affirmation of the private conscience, whose moral authority outranked that of the King, the Church, the government or the Pope.

From that wellspring of faith flowed all the other streams and tributaries of liberal democracy, influencing the Social Contract and both sides of what the political writer, Yuval Levin called the 'Great Debate'[i] between two eighteenth-century philosophers, Edmund Burke and Thomas Paine 'that still defines our politics'. Burke, the conservative, believed that the individual could only improve his or her calling in life, and thus society at large, by working within those institutions that he or she had inherited and seeking to improve them. The established church should not be seen as an oppressor but rather the institution within which collectively we were still learning to pray. Paine was the radical, who believed that government was at best 'a necessary evil, at worst an intolerable one'. 'My mind,' he boldly asserted, 'is my own church.'

It was the dispute, as Levin pointed out, between 'universal principles and historical precedents' – and similar to the arguments between the political left and the right. But it was not quite the same, because the original religious beliefs were missing, even among those who were dedicated Christians. The British did not automatically go to church before the polling booth, as they do in many Islamic countries. This removed an important element from the debate. 'We don't do God,' advised Alastair Campbell, Tony Blair's Director of Communications, fearful that Blair, a Christian, might blurt out some incriminating evidence in an unguarded moment. Most centrist politicians agreed with him.

Since Darwin, the drift had been in another direction. We were encouraged to think about ourselves as a species in the process of evolution which could be examined 'objectively', as we might study any other animal behaviour. Extraordinary scientific advances were made in the way in which we decoded our DNA and traced it to more primitive versions of ourselves. We analysed the electrical activity in the brain that told us what emotions were being stirred, what memories stored, and whether we could be kept alive with someone else's heart. If 'God was dead', as Nietzsche asserted, what was the point of praying to him?

Through market research, we could discover what words and images stimulated a positive or negative response within the public, and among what age and income groups, and then break down these broader findings into smaller units, through the use of focus groups, and analyse the websites that our subjects visit, and draw our conclusions from this data, adding a little guesswork of our own. But could we detect a place in the brain for the 'private conscience'? That remained an enigma of its own – if, of course, it existed.

This should have made the debate as to whether Britain should or should not be a member of the European Union much easier to resolve. It should have been an ideological rather than a philosophical question. It should have been a matter of general prosperity, the size of the markets, who was in control of the borders and other factual issues. Generally, that was how it was perceived on the English side of the Channel.

But for those countries on the other side which had suffered under fascism or whose families had been sliced apart by the Iron Curtain, it was more philosophical than ideological. The conscience was not just a function of the brain. It meant taking someone else's place in the cattle wagons. It meant hiding a Jew or selling a coat to buy food for the family. It was the force that stood out against military dictatorships of the left or the right. Under these circumstances, Liberalism, the philosophy that drew its strength from Protestant Christianity, was not, and never could be, just a middle way. It was the very core of humanity.

Whereas Anglo-American films, books and video games were flooded with stories of how we won the war and stood firm against world communism, those of middle Europe were awash with tales of secret resistance against the odds, to which families could add their own examples. However they might place themselves within the political spectrum of the left and the right, the great names of European literature during the second half of the twentieth century – Bernhardt, Grass, Dürrenmatt, Frisch, Konwicki, Kundera and Levy – were all concerned with how to protect the private conscience against the intolerable pressures from the state.

Similarly, the founding fathers of the European Union – Schuman, Keynes, Monnet and Churchill – were preoccupied with the problem of how to devise a political system that safeguarded human rights, including freedom of conscience, while maintaining the security and guiding rules of an economic zone. The four principles of the Treaty of Rome – the free movement of goods, services, labour and capital – supported a wider philosophical vision. Like the US Declaration of Independence, the Treaty was meant to safeguard the citizen against abuse from any particular faction within the club of sovereign nations, including a populist uprising. To that extent, liberalism was at the heart of the Common Market.

But freedom was perceived differently by those who took it for granted and those who had suffered under oppression. Hollywood heroes fought fistfights in bars, carried rifles, outwitted (like Bond) a global conspiracy and saved the People from the malign forces that operated within the government. The heroes from central Europe sat in coffee shops, exchanged glances, trod the underground sewers and engaged in arguments with scientists, who did not know right from wrong.

They both wanted freedom. They were both prepared to fight for what they believed, but one took more belligerent risks than the other. Was there a northwest passage between the brash Americans and the cautious Europeans? British governments believed so. They lived under the cover of NATO, the Special Relationship and the EU, the geopolitical Middle Way – but they too could get stuck in the ice.

(ii)

The neo-liberals placed such trust in the free market to regulate itself without interference from the state that the economic crisis of 2008 came as a serious shock. It threatened the globalised banking system and the optimism that came with the ending of the Cold War. It fulfilled the prediction that capitalism would collapse from its internal contradictions, but since Marxism-Leninism had already collapsed in Eastern Europe, the command economies of the Eastern bloc offered little hope of a solution. The times demanded a Third Way.

The days were over when an old-fashioned bank manager sat behind a desk and examined the client's assets before sternly granting a small overdraft. He had been replaced by holes-in-the-wall or ATMs, standard borrowing limits, credit and debit cards, online banking and all the advantages of a digitalised age. Since the City's Big Bang, investment banking had gone global. Vast sums of money criss-crossed the planet without one trader leaving his or her desk.

The benefits were immediate and, in some cases, spectacular. According to the World Hunger and Poverty Statistics published in 2016, the number of those living under famine conditions or in absolute poverty declined by nearly 50 per cent in the years between 1992 and 2012. The countries that benefitted most were those of South East Asia and China, where Western entrepreneurs outsourced manufacturing processes to places where labour costs were cheaper. The opportunities for increased investment also helped countries with untapped mineral and oil reserves, such as Kazakhstan. Where there were unstable governments, as in sub-Saharan Africa, the investors fought shy, demonstrating the virtuous circle of neo-liberalism. Peaceful trade produced stable governments, and vice versa, to the end of history.

The UK under New Labour did well. According to the Office of National Statistics, 2004 was a boom year for inward and outward investment. Foreign companies invested £30.7 billion in Britain, an increase of two thirds over the previous year, of which £20.4 billion came from Europe. British companies invested £51.8 billion abroad, mainly to the US and Canada, but the investment towards the EU decreased somewhat to £10.4 billion. In total, including the accumulated foreign investment from previous years, British investment abroad amounted to £656.8 billion, from which it received £63.8 billion in annual income. Foreign investment in the UK amounted to £336.5 billion, from which it received £26.1 billion. Japanese companies built or acquired car plants in the UK, French firms invested in the energy sector, Indian in steel.

These figures indicate the extent to which the British economy was enmeshed not only within the EU's trading area, but also within a global system where few nations lived from their own resources but trusted in the strength and competitive forces of world trade to keep the wolf from the door.

New Labour's mission was to modernise Britain, which meant building new hospitals and schools, investing in green energy and transforming all public services to take advantage of the digital age. Unlike the Keynesians, who borrowed nationally to pay for infrastructure, New Labour sought a third way, public-private partnerships, to raise the investment required. These were similar to very large-scale hire purchase agreements. The government, national or local, would commission with a downpayment a new project, which would be completed by a private company, using its own resources. The private investment would then be paid back over a period of years, with interest, until the project could be described as publicly owned.

Such agreements required a certain degree of financial stability. New Labour prepared the way by giving independence to the Bank of England, so governments were no longer in a position to raise or lower interest rates to suit the needs of the moment. No party would be able to fiddle the exchange rates to produce a pre-election boom. The free market was acknowledged to be a more accurate guide to the state of the economy than the partisan guesswork of a Treasury minister. With this single gesture, New Labour cut free from its economic theories of the past – and, for the time being, from its socialist roots.

For a few brief years around the millennium, the world glittered with investment opportunities. The traders in the City had never had it so good. They were the new Masters of the Universe. The banks were remaking the world in their own image and, by investing where there seemed to be the best chance of profit, they were harnessing the evolutionary impulses of mankind into schemes, whose aspirations glittered the skyline with tall glass buildings. But soon the cracks in this smooth-as-a-button ideological framework began to appear.

The real problem, although it seems pious and anti-monetarist to call it so, was greed. In order to finance the shining possibilities, traders borrowed money at easy rates of interest in order to invest, but they became less fussy about the assets that acted as security for the loans. In most cases, they were borrowing on other people's behalf and receiving commissions on the deals, and, so, if one of their clients defaulted and the deal fell through, the brokers themselves did not suffer. Large bonuses were paid to successful dealers, but they did not have to stick around to find out whether what they invested on other people's behalf had delivered according to its prospectus. In the world of global trading, it was sometimes quite difficult to do so.

Property, like gold, was thought to be a safe asset which rarely declined in value. In Thatcher's Britain and George W. Bush's America, property ownership was encouraged, because it was assumed that, if you owned a house, you were a respectable citizen and held a stake in society. While the property market stayed firm, traders could borrow against its assumed value; but, as borrowing rose and the property market failed to keep pace, or declined, the boom in investment bubbled and eventually burst.

The trouble first became apparent in what was known as the US 'sub-prime' mortgage market. After years of growth, the property market stalled and those with high mortgages sometimes found that the value of their houses did not match the sums that they had borrowed. A 'sub-prime' mortgage was given to those who might have some difficulty in honouring its repayments; and so the interest rates on a sub-prime mortgage were higher than those on prime mortgages. If it was honoured, it would be more profitable to the lender. When sub-prime mortgages were used as collateral for other loans, there was a serious risk that the accumulation of debts could lead to the collapse of the mortgage companies or of the banks themselves. But few economists forecast that this might happen or heard the rumble of the descending avalanche.

Systematic deregulation added to the problems. In 1999, the US Glass-Steagall Act was repealed. This had separated investment and commercial banking activities and was enacted in 1933 in the wake of the 1929 stock market crash. The repeal of the Glass-Steagall Act was intended to free up resources of capital that lay within personal bank accounts. This meant that the investment portfolios of insurance companies were no longer kept apart from the day-to-day transactions of small businessmen in market towns. The collapse of the big schemes led to the failure of much smaller ones, so that the effect of the financial crisis in 2008 was felt at every level of Western society. It led to mass unemployment in Europe, austerity in Britain and the failure to modernise US manufacturing industries and so to the dystopian rust cities of the Midwest that in 2016 voted heavily for Donald Trump.

In September 2007, an independent bank in Britain, Northern Rock, sought help from the Labour government. It was thought to be an isolated case, a building society that had turned itself into a bank and required an injection of new funds to meet the demands from its customers. It was temporarily nationalised in 2008 and, in 2010, it was divided into two companies, for assets and daily banking, with a view to selling its banking side to another company, Virgin Money. Its assets, including mortgages, were kept within public ownership.

But the collapse of Northern Rock was primarily caused by the fact that it had been borrowing money on the international market, where the boom years were coming to an end. It was the symptom of a wider malaise. A more dramatic collapse came with the bankruptcy of the US investment bankers, Lehman Brothers, in September 2008, after experiencing losses of $3.9 billion from their investments in the mortgage market. It was the largest bankruptcy filing in US history. Attempts were made to save Lehman Brothers, but to no effect. A bid to buy the company by the British bank, Barclays, was blocked by the Bank of England, on the grounds that Britain itself could not afford to take the risk.

Two US mortgage companies, 'Fannie Mae' and 'Freddie Mac', which had offered cheap mortgages to encourage home ownership, fell into difficulties and had to be bailed out by the US Federal Government. The failures were cumulative, as one company after another defaulted on debts which were supported by assets whose value was rapidly declining. In 2009 the International Monetary Fund estimated that worldwide losses from the crisis were as high as $4.1 trillion, with gross domestic product (GDP) contracting across the world for the first time since World War II.

The European Central Bank estimated that its losses on loans and securities amounted to about $650 billion in the years between 2007 and 2010. The GDP of the European Union fell by 4 per cent, in which the poorer countries were worst hit by rising unemployment and declining income. For the first time in its history, the predictions of Jean Monnet that free trade within the community would lead to greater prosperity for all of its members were shown to be far too optimistic. Some countries fared better than others. In 2007, the German government was forced to bail out the IKB Deutsche Industriebank, but it could afford to do so. In France, BNP Paribas suspended three of its investment funds, citing a 'complete evaporation of liquidity in certain market segments of the US securitisation market'. In Spain, Greece and the newly arrived countries from the Eastern bloc, the financial crisis hit even harder, leading to widespread unemployment and economic stagnation. The boom ended with a severe jolt.

The British government responded quickly, as the scale of the problems became apparent. In October 2008, the new Prime Minister, Gordon Brown, and his Chancellor, Alastair Darling, announced plans for immediate equity injections into British banks. The prime example was the Royal Bank of Scotland (RBS), the second largest bank in Europe. It had acquired the Citizens Financial Group in the United States and was the second largest shareholder in the Bank of China. In the millennium years, it had been on a spending spree and was suffering the consequences. It had assets of £1.9 trillion and liabilities of £1.8 trillion, which made it briefly the largest bank in the world. But the margins for error were slight and the chance that RBS, with all its subsidiaries and partners, might collapse threatened a worldwide financial catastrophe.

The British government stepped in and bought 58 per cent of its shares, effectively placing the company into public ownership. It amounted to a grand act of nationalisation, which cost every British citizen about £650, although the government announced its intention to sell the shares on the open market, when the time was right. It prevented any further run on the banks and temporarily stabilised what had become a very precarious and volatile situation.

If Britain had acted on its own, it would have delayed, but not prevented, the dangers to come. Instead, Gordon Brown called for an emergency summit of EU heads of state, at which a European rescue plan was agreed, which proposed an injection of €2 trillion to recapitalise and, if necessary, take shares in other European banks. This was rapidly endorsed by the European Council, the European Central Bank and individually by member states. It was an example of how the European Union, acting together, could achieve a result that no nation, acting its own, could deliver.

The European example was followed by Bush's government, when the US Treasury Secretary, Henry Paulson, announced that it would buy equity stakes in its banking sector. The risk of a collapse of the world's financial system, which might have led to a depression exceeding that of the 1930s, was narrowly avoided; the slow recovery began, which lasted for more than ten years. In 2018, 10 per cent of the British stake in RBS was offered to the market, but the government retained 48 per cent to be sold at a later date.

Although the final crash was averted and the democratic West heaved a sigh of relief, the 2008 crisis still left its mark upon the world's geopolitics. The large trading areas in the Far East suffered far less from the uncertainties of the times and seized chances that Western entrepreneurs were forced to neglect. The balance of financial power started to shift from Europe and the US towards China, India and South East Asia.

In Britain, the government had to borrow so much money to cover its commitments that the national debt increased to a level which was widely considered to be unsustainable. In 2010, a general election year, it amounted to £960 billion or 62 per cent of GDP, at a similar level to the debts that the country owed after World War II. Most individual families felt poorer and holidays had to be cancelled. Houses lost value and there was a growing sense of personal grievance. The new poverty was not caused by those who were suffering most from its effects. In every newspaper, there were stories of traders and bankers, who had escaped with their bonuses and pensions intact and were living in luxury somewhere else. Politicians, perceived as living on inflated salaries and expense accounts, were blamed as well.

The entire political system was coming under suspicion. The 2010 General Election reflected the changing mood in the country. No single political party won an overall majority but the Conservatives won the most seats (306). There was a 5 per cent swing from Labour to the Conservatives. The third party, which won 23 per cent of the vote, was the LibDems with 57 seats. It was possible for them to form a coalition with the Conservatives that could command a majority in the House of Commons. In exchange for their committed support, the LibDems demanded a referendum on proportional representation.

The big losers of the 2010 Election were not the far left, but the far right, particularly UKIP, which fielded 560 candidates, won no parliamentary seat and received only 3 per cent of the national vote. They had a different narrative to tell. UKIP spoke of the need to control our borders and restrict immigration from the EU that threatened the sovereignty of the country. Too much multiculturalism had destroyed the sense of national identity. UKIP had its Hall of Fame (Churchill, Powell and Thatcher) and its Rogues Gallery (Macmillan, Heath and Major). Who were the devils responsible for the 2008 financial crisis? The Socialist bureaucrats who ran the EU. The UK, they concluded, could do much better on its own.

(iii)

Many continental observers were puzzled by the Special Relationship. How did it work? They recognised the value of NATO, whereby an attack upon one of its member countries should be interpreted as an attack on them all. It was a necessary safeguard in the Cold War. But the Special Relationship was something different. Having taken the US dollar to build its own independent nuclear force, Britain seemed morally obliged to support the US in every other way. Why? There was no reciprocal arrangement and the relationship between the UK and its former colony seemed very one-sided. In the 1950s, Britain joined the US-led forces in Korea, but the US government had not only failed to support, but actively undermined, the Anglo-French-Israeli invasion to recapture the Suez Canal.

It was a similar story in the 1960s. Britain allowed the US to use its territory as a base for their front-line air forces, which made it the first target for a pre-emptive nuclear strike. As a friendly gesture, it had few parallels in military history. But the British government, preferring a more nuanced approach, did not subscribe to the US strategy of trying to 'contain' the spread of worldwide communism. Harold Wilson did not send British troops to support the US forces in Vietnam, pleading poverty, but convened a Commonwealth peace mission. There was very little evidence to suggest that Britain had any influence on American foreign policy at all, except on a personal level. Britain had no vote in Congress. It could not even exert any influence. Macmillan was on good terms with Kennedy, Thatcher with Reagan; but, if this chemistry was missing, there seemed little else to hold the Special Relationship together. Britain was no longer the power broker that it once assumed it was.

Even in the very Special Relationship between Thatcher and Reagan, united in their common aim to see the end of the 'Evil Empire', there were striking differences. Reagan failed to support Thatcher's task force to retake the Falkland Islands from the Argentine invasion, preferring to wait and see, but sent an army to invade Grenada, which was recently a British colony and was now a Commonwealth country. Grenada might have expected to receive British support. But Reagan did not know about its ties to Britain, did not ask Mrs Thatcher for her advice and had to phone her to apologise.

And yet, on so many other levels, there were close connections between the English-speaking races that lived on both sides of the pond, between the universities, entertainment industries, tourism and the media. They shared a history. Literally and figuratively, they spoke the same language – or very nearly the same language, for (as in other families) the differences also drove them apart. While Britain was still tidying up obligations from its imperial days, the United States was settling the mantle of *Pax Britannica* around its shoulders, the new defender of world peace.

This tangle of conflicting motives was most apparent in the Middle East. Britain and the United States shared many aims, but they approached them in different ways. Britain, like France, preferred to work indirectly by supporting the Arab ruling families, whereas the Americans preferred to keep more control, preferring to supply arms and money directly to those forces that were on their side, whichever they were.

During the Soviet-Afghan War (1979-89), the US government supplied the Mujahideen, the Afghan rebel freedom fighters, with weapons, only to discover, when the war was over, that the new Taliban government was as hostile to the West as it had been to the Russians. The arms that the Americans supplied were turned against them. When a US-led coalition invaded Afghanistan to restore a pro-West government, it resulted in the longest-running war in US history.

This was the risk of trying to understand the complicated alliances of the Middle East through a Cold War perspective. The loyalties and animosities lay much deeper. After World War I, the ancient Ottoman Empire, whose glory was still remembered by the aristocrats of the desert, was dismantled. This led to its partitioning into British and French spheres of influence. Following their imperial practice, the British government struck up alliances with patrician Arab families, allowing them to govern their countries in exchange for trading and military concessions. Some were British protectorates.

But this led to other problems. The three former Ottoman provinces of Baghdad, Basra and Mosul, were united into one nation, Iraq, which was granted independence in 1932 under the Hashemite family, who had helped the Allies against the Ottomans. T.E. Lawrence (Lawrence of Arabia) led the way. In 1958, the Hashemite dynasty in Iraq was overthrown by a popular revolution, which received military aid from Soviet Russia. Jordan, however, remained a Hashemite kingdom and aligned to the West.

Other Arabic nations around the Persian Gulf were perceived as being on the front line in the Cold War. When the Persian government nationalised the Anglo-Iranian oil company, it led to a chain of circumstances in which an Anglo-US alliance overthrew the government and installed the Shah of Iran as an absolute monarch in its place. The Shah was deposed by a religious and popular uprising in 1979, led by the Shia Muslim clerical leader, Ayatollah Khomeini; and the West's influence on Iran was ended. The United States was portrayed as the Great Satan, with Britain its Mephistopheles. The modernising influences that the Americans brought with them were treated as signs of the devil. It became a religious republic, controlled by its clerics, embracing Sharia law and non-aligned in the Cold War.

Elsewhere in the Persian Gulf, Anglo-American diplomacy was more successful. In 1981, six countries signed the treaty that established the Gulf Cooperation Council (GCC) and they were all aligned towards the West – Saudi Arabia, Kuwait, Oman, the United Arab Emirates, Qatar and Bahrain. They were predominantly Sunni Muslim countries, rather than Shia. The bitter struggles in Islam between the Sunnis and Shias, like the Catholics and Protestants in Europe, were added to the polarities of the Cold War. In Iraq, the Shias outnumbered the Sunnis by three to one, although it had a secular Ba'athist government, mainly run by Sunnis.

Shortly after Khomeini had taken control in Iran, Iraq invaded its Shia neighbour, hoping to become the dominant power in the region. Iraq was a secular Arab republic. It was opposed to clerical rule. It was the kind of state that the West understood. This led to an eight-year war, conducted along the lines of the 1914-18 war, with trenches and machine guns, during which the United States and Britain supplied the Iraqi leader, Saddam Hussein, with arms as a gesture of friendship. More than a million soldiers were killed or injured.

The war came to an end in 1988 through a peace settlement, brokered by the UN, but two years later, a new war broke out, shuffling the allies. With the support of Iran, Iraq's army, under Saddam Hussein, invaded the oil-rich Gulf state of Kuwait, which was a British protectorate until 1961. The invasion was condemned by the UN's Security Council and a coalition force from 35 countries, led by the United States, was assembled. Following several failed attempts to negotiate Iraq's withdrawal and following other UN resolutions, the coalition army, in an operation codenamed Desert Storm, drove the Iraqi forces out of Kuwait, leaving a trail of torched and burning oil wells behind them.

The first Iraq War was restricted by the terms of its UN mandate. It was not a licence to attack Iraq itself or to institute regime change in Baghdad, Iraq's capital city, but merely to drive Saddam's forces from Kuwait. The international coalition had been carefully brought together by British and American diplomats. It contained Arab countries, such as Syria, who were anti-Saddam Hussein but not pro-West, as well as Commonwealth countries and even Russia, for the Cold War was coming to an end.

During the course of these negotiations, there were regime changes in Washington and London. Reagan's term of office came to an end in 1989, to be followed by George H.W. Bush. Thatcher was forced to resign in 1990, to be succeeded by John Major. This did not change the overall policy, for they were of the same parties, Republican and Conservative, and outwardly subscribed to the same principles. But Bush and Major were less confrontational. They obeyed the UN's mandate and, mission accomplished, stopped at the borders of Iraq, having driven Saddam's army from Kuwait.

There were those, however, in the UK and the US, who wanted to get rid of Saddam altogether. They would have preferred the coalition forces to march on to Baghdad and install a new government. Saddam had committed 'crimes against humanity' by using chemical warfare against the Kurds and persecuting the Shia Marsh Arabs in the wetlands, a World Heritage site, to the south. For more than ten years, the British and Americans retained a hostile suspicion of Saddam, instituting no-fly zones to protect the Kurds and the Marsh Arabs. Some were seeking a fresh excuse to invade.

Their wariness was understandable, given Saddam's own behaviour. He was caught in a cleft stick. He had to convince Iran, his erstwhile enemy, that he had powerful forces at his disposal, including chemical and nuclear weapons, while reassuring the UN Security Council that he had none. Rumours abounded, among them that Saddam had secretly developed ballistic missiles capable of carrying nuclear and chemical warheads, classed as weapons of mass destruction (WMDs), They were hidden somewhere in the desert.

The UN Security Council imposed sanctions on Iraq, but, in the meantime, events were taking their own course. Could Saddam's missiles strike at London or Washington? Certainly not, but on 11 September 2001 (9/11, as the date became notoriously known) four American passenger jets were hijacked by eighteen Islamic terrorists, who belonged to the jihadist group, Al-Qaeda. Two of the jets were flown into the North and South towers of the World Trade Center in New York, while the third flew on towards Washington DC to crash into the side walls of the Pentagon in Arlington County, Virginia. The terrorists in the last flight were disarmed by the passengers and the plane crashed down into a field in Pennsylvania.

Nearly 3,000 people were killed in New York; and the dust and the rubble from the collapse of the twin towers smothered Manhattan. In the Middle East, this was widely celebrated as a triumphant victory against the Great Satan. Even in Amman in Jordan, friendly to the West, there was dancing in the streets. The 9/11 carnage revealed the extent of hatred towards the US felt by the jihadists. Although the Ba'athist government in Iraq was not responsible for these attacks, and were opponents of Al-Qaeda, what happened on 9/11 added credibility to the idea that there could be a more devastating onslaught from the nuclear missiles of Saddam Hussein, if they existed.

Saddam disassociated himself from the 9/11 attacks and to prove that Iraq was not the threat to international security that the American and British governments said it was, he complied with a UN proposal to receive a team of weapons inspectors, under the Swedish Foreign Minister, Hans Blix. But this team was never allowed to complete its work. The US government under its president, George W. Bush, the son of George Bush Snr, assembled a new fighting force and, in March 2003, launched a massive bombing attack, using the tactics of Shock and Awe to destroy the will-power of any opposition.

The bombing raids were followed by an invasion of Allied ground forces, including 177,194 US soldiers, 45,000 British soldiers, 2,000 Australian soldiers and 194 Polish soldiers; and the campaign lasted for twenty-three days, after which Bush announced, 'Mission accomplished'. But the wider war was far from being over. No WMDs were found in Iraq and no collusion was discovered between the Ba'athist government and Al-Qaeda. It was an unprovoked attack.

Unlike the First Iraq war, there was no UN mandate for the invasion, which was judged to be illegal by most international lawyers. Following the invasion, the Ba'athists in Iraq were destroyed as a national party and, as a result, there were renewed religious clashes between the Sunni and Shia Muslims. The country descended into administrative chaos, with pockets of sanity, alternating with pockets of insane violence, and became a warning to other countries in the Middle East, including Syria, which also had a Ba-athist government, secular and Socialist, under its ruler, President Assad.

The US and its allies tried to install a new secular government, indeed several, in Baghdad, democratically elected in name, if not in substance, but it required the presence of US-led forces to defend. Even its administrative buildings were under threat from jihadist guerrillas. Bush established a detention centre in Cuba, Guantanamo Bay, where terrorist suspects could be sent for interrogation, but there were persistent stories of torture – or, at least, of water-boarding (near-drowning), which many countries, including Britain, considered to be torture. This cast doubt upon the Americans' self-proclaimed moral leadership of the Free World.

There was worldwide condemnation of the Second Iraq War and even in the United States, where the Republican and Democrat Parties both supported the invasion, the poll ratings of George W. Bush sank to the lowest level recorded for an incumbent president. In Britain, Blair secured a parliamentary majority with the support of both of the main parties – not the LibDems – only by asserting that the evidence for WMDs was more conclusive than it really was. When this turned out to be untrue and confirmed by the Chilcot report, which took some ten years to compile, his reputation was near-fatally damaged.

Within the EU, the French and German Presidents, Jacques Chirac and Gerhardt Schröder, deplored the invasion; and their opposition drew the two countries together at the core of a Europe, which did not want to be too closely associated with their English-speaking partners. Britain's role as a link across the Atlantic was compromised. It was thought to be subservient in the Special Relationship. It was no longer the shaper of events but the victim.

With every effort to stabilise the politics in the Middle East, the allies of the Special Relationship seemed to make the situation worse. Blair took it personally. He saw himself as a peacemaker. He had achieved an unlikely peace agreement in Ireland. After he handed over his office as the British Prime Minister, he sought a new role as the Special Envoy for a quartet of powers, the US, UN, EU and Russia, to secure a similar peace between Israel and Palestine. But Blair could no longer pretend to be an honest broker. Nor was Britain a neutral bridge across the pond. It had been blown up by Shock and Awe.

Across the Arab world, alliances changed. Within a weakened Iraq, a new nation was brought into being, the Islamic State of Iraq and the Levant (ISIL), which occupied Iraq's second city, Mosul, as its capital. When US soldiers finally left Iraq in 2011, they left behind military advisers, whose role was to support the Iraqi army against its enemies. They had not expected to contend with this ruthless new state. ISIL financed its army from the proceeds of seized oil wells and became the new focus for global terrorism.

How could ISIL so suddenly and dramatically assemble a worldwide hidden army of sympathisers that they could train in the desert and send back to their home countries in France, Germany, the US and Britain to plant bombs indiscriminately and stir up trouble? The answer was simple. The ISIL leaders recruited the Internet.

***

Chapter Twelve
Trial by Coalition

(i)

According to the former Chief Strategist for US Counter Intelligence, David Kilcullen, 'there undeniably would be no ISIL, if we had not invaded Iraq'.

The Islamic State of Iraq and the Levant began as a movement in the late 1990s. It was an offshoot of Al-Qaeda but, after the second invasion of Iraq in 2003, it became the symbol of resistance against the US-led forces. The military and intelligence officers of Saddam's Ba'athist regime, who had been disbanded by the Allies and lost their jobs and pensions, were recruited by ISIL. They formed the new state's administration, which expanded its territory to include parts of Syria, to the alarm of its ruler, Bashar al-Assad.

The other territory claimed by its title, the Levant, corresponded to no modern nation. In English, it was an archaic term, which sometimes applied just to Syria, but historically to all those lands that bordered the Eastern Mediterranean, including Lebanon, Palestine, Israel and Jordan. In the West, it was known as ISIS, meaning the Islamic State of Iraq and Syria, but ISIL was the more ambitious title. By adopting it, its leaders were claiming the right to lead the Arabic world against the infidels' occupation of its territory, including Israel.

In 2004, an online document was published, *The Management of Savagery*,[i] by Abu Bakr Naji, whose real name was Mohammed Khalil al-Hakaymah of the Al Arabic Institute for Studies. It provided a blueprint for jihadist guerrillas to fight against the infidels by instituting a worldwide range of terrorist attacks on small and large scales. It was the jihadist version of Shock and Awe. No non-believer should feel safe. The aim was to discredit the democracies of the West and to induce panic; they would then turn towards the Quran as the only source of true knowledge and to Sharia law as the only legal system within a worldwide Islamic state.

These tactics were borrowed by ISIL and became the hallmark of the regime, for terror kept the local population in check, as well as sending out cruel messages to the infidels. The state executions were not conducted in private, but in city squares, videoed on mobiles and distributed across the web. Floggings were held in public. The lessons had to be taught. ISIL's religious leader, Abu Bakr al-Baghdadi, persuaded his followers to believe that they were facing the Day of Judgement. Sacrifices had to be made for the glory to come.

In *The Clash of Civilizations and the Remaking of the World Order* (1996), the US political historian, Samuel P. Huntington, predicted that something like this might happen. The Middle East was on the fault line between Christianity and Islam, where blood was most likely to be spilt. But for the orthodox imams within the Sunni communities worldwide, the threats of ISIL were based upon a heretical interpretation of the words of Mohammed. They were horrified by its consequences, for there were Muslim communities throughout the Western world, whose members might immediately come under suspicion as terrorists. They might be victimised by the state or lured into terrorism by ISIL's propaganda.

The Quran's message, as the orthodox imams pointed out, was of peace to mankind, not cruelty. Mohammed's words had come down to the modern world through centuries of serious interpretation, which filtered out corrupt meanings through prayer and experience. But the religious traditions of Islam, vertically inherited, were threatened by a much simplified version, horizontally conveyed across the Internet through the images and news flashes of ISIL. It portrayed Sharia law through its blood-thirsty executions, not the solving of disputes. As the Christian religion in the Middle Ages was torn apart by the excesses of the Spanish Inquisition, so Islam was now threatened by civil war from its fanatical converts.

The ambitions of Abu Bakr al-Baghdadi were not merely regional. In 2014, he called for his supporters to recognise him as the Caliph of a worldwide Islamic state, a Caliphate, which was destined to become even greater than the Ottoman Empire. It was his self-appointed task but its consequences for the world's Islamic communities were alarming. It encouraged ISIL to terrorise communities in the name of jihad. By 2014, ISIL devotees had dropped 'IL' from its title. They called it the Islamic State (IS), with no geographical boundaries, but to the orthodox Moslems, it was known by its derogatory acronym, Da'ish.

The IS terrorist attacks began as part of the war against the administration in Iraq, with car bombs launched against Shia pilgrims in Baghdad, and the Ba'athist regime in Syria. These tactics rapidly spread across the Western world – attacks in Belgium, in Canada, Australia, the United States and

France. In Nigeria, an IS-inspired gang, Boko Haram, kidnapped a whole school of 276 girls. In 2002, a terrorist car bomb in the name of Al-Qaeda killed more than 200 people in Bali, Indonesia, and was repeated in another attack in 2005. Trucks were driven into crowds in the name of IS in Nice, London, Istanbul and other cities. Even Al-Qaeda eventually disowned IS for 'exceeding the limits of extremism'.

The turn of the millennium also saw the arrival of a different kind of world war, not with mega-sized armies and WMDs, but with backpackers, home-made bombs and furniture lorries. The attacks could take place almost anywhere. They seemed arbitrary and followed no kind of strategy, and yet they were coordinated with considerable skill through the social media and various apps on the web. These were difficult to trace and intercept but security forces in the EU and the US made progress, and learnt how to trace the pattern of Internet activity, which stemmed from IS's headquarters in Mosul and Raqqa.

But IS was not the only source of instability in the Arab world. In 2010, a street trader in Tunis, Mohammed Bouaziz, was caught selling cucumbers and lettuces without an official licence. He was not arrested but stopped from running his street stall. He had a mother and a family of five – and no income. To demonstrate his anger and despair, he went to the steps of the city council in Tunis and set himself alight. Video clips of his self-immolation were transmitted across the whole region and triggered what became known as the Arab Spring, populist uprisings against their current rulers.

The Tunisian government was overthrown within a few months, but it became the only country where the Arab Spring resulted in the smooth restoration of peace and stability. There were similar demonstrations in Cairo, which led to the downfall of Egypt's President Mubarak. In Libya, the rebels brought down the regime of Colonel Gaddafi, who had ruled the country for 45 years. There were no political parties in Libya with national support to take its place. As in Iraq, after the 2003 invasion, there was a chaos of factions. The West was sympathetic to the insurgents and wanted to help, but they sought the middle way in doing so, trying not to offend their old allies and not to repeat the mistake of the 2003 invasion. This proved to be a very narrow path to follow.

In Syria, the rebels of the Arab Spring were met by Assad's militia, which was engaged simultaneously in the war against IS. At the first sign of a Syrian Arab Spring, Assad's police arrested twelve boys, who had been caught scribbling pro-democracy slogans on city walls, imprisoned and tortured them. This example drew together groups hostile to Assad and led to the rapid assembly of the Free Syrian Army to fight against the Assad regime.

They were supported with arms and money by the West and, by 2011, it seemed inevitable that Assad would soon join Gaddafi and Mubarak in the list of deposed Middle Eastern despots. A National Council established its headquarters in Turkey, which formed a Coordination Committee for Democratic Change in Syria.

But the formation of anything like a Western democracy was a long way ahead. One unresolved issue lay in the conflict between the Shias and Sunnis in the wider region. Assad was supported by the Shia governments in Iran and Iraq and by Hezbollah in Lebanon. But the rebels were helped by the Sunnis in Saudi Arabia, Qatar and Turkey, as well as by the US-led military advisers. Both the Western allies and Russia were enemies of IS, and supported the Assad troops in their effort to regain Raqqa in Northern Syria, an IS stronghold. But they were on opposite sides in the war against other rebel factions.

No fewer than fourteen countries became involved in what amounted to a Syrian civil war, which increased in cruelty and ferocity as the months wore on. The West, now led by President Barack Obama, a Democrat, and Cameron, the Conservative leader of the Conservative/LibDem coalition, warned Assad not to use chemical weapons against his own Syrian people. This was their red line, the point beyond which Assad should not stray without risking an Allied intervention. But Assad did employ chemical weapons, to terrible effect, and the choice was put to the British Parliament as to whether or not to invade. With memories of the false information that supported the 2003 invasion, the MPs refused to back the government. In Washington, Obama decided that this was not a course of action that the US could undertake on its own.

With no threat of an Allied invasion, the pro-Assad forces felt free to get rid of the opposing troops by any means at their disposal – cluster bombs dropped by Russian planes, rockets and heavy artillery. The UN Security Council, led by the United States, demanded a ceasefire, which was vetoed by the Russians and the Chinese. Various peace conferences were organised, resolutions were passed which were broken before the ink had dried, for there was no middle way. The West insisted on regime change, with Assad offered a peaceful retirement in the West, whereas Russia and the Shia countries backed Assad.

Gradually, the forces of Assad gained ground against rebel enclaves. The documented fate of the city of Raqqa between its seizure by ISIL in 2011 and its recapture by Assad's army in 2017 was distributed across the web by a group of journalists under the name Raqqa Is Being Slaughtered Silently (RIBSS). Its details can leave nobody in doubt about the extent of the suffering. This was not an isolated example. The ancient city of Aleppo, a stronghold of the rebel forces and defended by the Free Syrian Army, was besieged for nearly four years by Assad's forces, supported by Russia's bombers. Its 3,000 year-old monuments were destroyed, its schools and hospitals gutted, and its population, which totalled five million, were forced to eat rats or whatever they could find.

It was as if civilisation had come full-circle. The Mesopotamian birthplace of the modern world between the rivers of Tigris and Euphrates was reduced to a dystopian carnage. The rebel-held outskirts of the capital city of Damascus, its name so familiar from the Bible, were under constant fighting, then besieged and gutted, leaving a long trail of refugees to join those who had already been dispossessed. In February 2018, the United Nations' refugee agency, UNCHR, estimated that five and a half million people had fled from Syria, many into the growing refugee camps in Lebanon, Jordan and Turkey, while six and a half million more were displaced and roaming homeless in their own country. More than two million soldiers and civilians were killed in the air strikes and ground raids.

A man-made disaster on this scale bears comparison with the massacre of the kulaks in the USSR during the 'reconstruction' years of 1929 to 1932, when about five million property-owning peasants were slaughtered, and the Holocaust in Nazi Germany, which killed about six million Jews. The fact that these figures can only be approximated adds to the tragedy. The individual person and the family were lost in the cascade of carelessly recorded deaths. Any talk of a private conscience seemed like an academic luxury.

The war in Syria and the turmoil in the Middle East presented the European Union with a unique problem. Many Syrian refugees and asylum seekers sought to enter the EU through Turkey and, when the official border crossings were closed, they enlisted the help of people smugglers, who guided them through the hidden ways into Bulgaria, which eventually built a 174-kilometre fence of razor wire to keep them out. Others took the sea route to such Greek islands as Lesbos and Tilos, where refugee camps were built by the Greek authorities; and then into Italy and Spain.

As well as the Syrian refugees, there were those from Libya and North Africa, who took the risk of crossing the Mediterranean in overcrowded boats, which were often little better than rubber dinghies. The Libyan capital city of Tripoli was the unacknowledged centre for the people-smuggling trade, attracting asylum seekers from Somalia to Ghana and Nigeria. Possibly most of them survived. There are no reliable records; but in the first six months of 2017, UNCHR listed 2,030 deaths by drowning, including many babies and small children, and, as their bodies were washed up on the beaches of Italy or Greece, the clamour arose within the EU that something should be done. More patrol boats were sent out to rescue the survivors but, after they were picked up, soaked and shivering, what should be done with them? Sent back? Placed in camps? Allowed to settle? Where?

In 2015, in response to this humanitarian crisis, the German Chancellor Angela Merkel agreed to allow nearly one million Syrian refugees to stay temporarily in Germany, while pointing out that the European Union had a population of 508 million. Surely it would be possible for other EU countries to respond as well, to absorb an increase of less than 0.5 per cent of their numbers? David Cameron for the British coalition government agreed to accept 20,000 refugees, spread over five years, at the rate of 4,000 a year.

Both governments faced backlashes. In Germany, a new right-wing party was formed, Alternativ für Deutschland, which gained ground in local and national elections. In Britain, during the referendum, the unofficial Leave.EU campaign warned of unregulated immigration through Turkey, which Cameron denied. Turkey was not an EU member and the UK had a veto, which he would use. But a veto was not a solution to the 'swarms' of migrants, as Cameron called them, trying to find their way across the Mediterranean. A concerted EU rescue mission might have helped.

Throughout Europe, there was a surge in Islamophobia. In Holland, Geert Wilders led the new Party for Freedom, which called for no further immigration from Muslim countries and the banning of the Quran, which he compared to Hitler's *Mein Kampf*. Even in Sweden, one of the most liberal countries, there were attacks on mosques and the public burning of Islamic texts. In Hungary, the leader of the far-right Fidesz Party, Viktor Orbán, anti-Islamic and anti-Semitic, called for the EU to become a Christian federation, united by its faith.

Every IS-inspired terrorist attack added to the anti-Islam narrative. The liberalism that lay at the core of the European Union was tested to its limits. Was it possible to maintain a federation that respected different religions and beliefs, while guarding against the fanatics that threatened the safety of its citizens? Could it remember the lessons of the 1930s and World War II? Could the EU become the civilisation that matched the vision of its founders or would it become merely the sum of its trade deals?

(ii)

After the election in 2010, when the Conservative-led coalition took over from New Labour, the departing Chief Secretary to the Treasury, Liam Byrne, left a note for his successor: 'I am afraid there is no money. Kind regards and good luck!' It was meant to be no more than a comradely quip, similar to the remark that a former Conservative Chancellor, Reginald

Maudling, is said to have made to the incoming Labour minister, Jim Callaghan: 'Sorry to leave the place in such a mess, old cock!'

But the gesture badly went wrong. It was released to the press, which was another sign of the times. Such lapses in discretion should have stayed within the Treasury walls. After its publication, Byrne's note was flourished at Tory rallies as an admission that Labour profligacy had ruined the country. It was a political gaffe that Byrne bitterly regretted. With a modicum of spinning, Labour could have argued that the action of Gordon Brown, supported by the EU heads of state, had saved the country from a fiscal catastrophe. The blame would then have been placed upon Conservative deregulation of the City of London and the Big Bang. These few scribbled words altered the plot. They indicated, or so it was claimed, that New Labour's extravagance had ruined the country.

'The age of irresponsibility,' said Cameron after the election, 'is giving way to an age of austerity.' The word, austerity, was chosen with the PR skills of someone who was once a marketing consultant. It echoed the years after the war, when bread was rationed and the streets had to be cleared from the rubble of the Blitz. The British public took pride in the way in which it could tighten its belt in a crisis. The situation in 2010 was less dramatic but still very serious. The country, as Byrne had admitted, was broke. Cameron's Chancellor of the Exchequer, George Osborne, had two main aims – to make sure that after five years, Britain would be living within its means, and making a small profit, and that it could start to pay back the money that it had borrowed, which amounted to £860 billion or 62 per cent of its GDP.

His policy held a domestic appeal. Most families go through crises like that on a much smaller scale. But it begged the question as to whether the money borrowed had been well-invested in useful projects or simply frittered away. It favoured a monetarist, rather than a Keynesian, approach. Before the election, Cameron promised that the NHS and secondary education would be ring-fenced but these commitments meant that a disproportionate share of the cuts fell upon other areas of public spending, such as local authorities and social services. The balance of priorities was decided before the coalition came into being.

The effects of the spending cuts soon became apparent. The local authorities started to economise on such matters as libraries, refuse collection and road maintenance. The number of locally subsidised bus services was halved. Between 2010 and 2013, capital investment in affordable homes was cut by 60 per cent. The number of those sleeping rough on the streets more than doubled. A two-year pay freeze was imposed upon five million workers in the public sector. Some savings were made by better management, others by extending repayments, where possible, on public-private contracts; but there had to be sacrifices, for which the junior partner in the coalition, the LibDems, took much of the blame.

Their supporters were disappointed that they had not rebelled against the cuts, but their opponents hinted that they had caused them. That is the fate of junior partners. One LibDem election pledge was broken very publicly. Nick Clegg, the party's leader and Deputy Prime Minister, had made a promise to the National Union of Students that tuition fees at university would be reduced or abolished, but instead, under the austerity measures, they had to be increased. The system changed to one of student loans, rather than grants, which would be repaid after university. He apologised but it damaged his reputation and that of his party.

In the long list of broken election promises, Clegg's pledge ranks at a very low level, somewhere below Wilson's promise that the 'pound in your pocket' would not be devalued and Mrs Thatcher's to bring 'harmony where there had been discord'; but, for a party whose appeal was directed towards younger voters, it was a sad admission. It added credibility to the claim by UKIP's leader Nigel Farage that Britain was run by a 'career political class', which was out of touch with the lives of the ordinary people. Clegg was one of his prime targets.

Before the next European Parliament Election in 2014, Clegg as Deputy Prime Minister challenged Farage to two televised debates. The LibDems and UKIP, the pro- and anti-EU parties, wanted to debate the future of British membership at a time when the Conservatives and Labour were hoping to avoid the subject. They had dissenting, anti-EU minorities that they wanted to hide. Farage welcomed Clegg's challenge as the chance that he had been seeking for twenty years. He complained that the subject of EU membership had been deliberately suppressed by 'career politicians' with the support of multinational companies.

The first debate was held by LBC, the London-based news broadcasting station, on 26 March 2014, with formality. It went out on television and radio. This was not a round-the-table conversation. There were two podiums, a studio audience, phone-ins and a presenter with a stopwatch, Nick Ferrari. Farage and Clegg were polite to each other, eloquent in the sense that they were never lost for words and equipped with examples to prove their points of view. But it was hard to resist the conclusion that this was not a debate but a war of assertions, in which the image mattered as much as the argument. A smoothly-groomed Clegg, in the style of Blair and Cameron, was sent in to face a plain-speaking man of the people, Farage, who might not know much about economic theory but saw the world through the eyes of a pragmatic businessman.

In the debate, Farage often referred to his twenty years of business experience. He came from a family of stockbrokers and entered the City soon after the Big Bang.[ii] He set up his first company, Farage Futures, during the boom years. His company was moderately successful, but not a high-flier and not listed on his website, which stressed his career as the co-founder of UKIP. One of the companies that he had launched with his brother, Farage Ltd, was facing bankruptcy proceedings for failing to pay back taxes.

His career as someone who had earned his money by gambling on the stock exchange might not have impressed the directors of small businesses, who thought that he was speaking on their behalf. He did, however, offer an alternative explanation as to why the British were feeling so poor during the years of austerity. They were tied to a failing institution, the EU, whose rules and regulations prevented them from trading freely in the world's markets. The answer to their problems was to take charge of their destiny as a sovereign country, the United Kingdom. To be afraid of its future as an independent nation would be unpatriotic.

Clegg challenged his facts but Farage's strength lay in his narrative, rather than errors or lies. Did Britain send £55 million a day to Brussels? Possibly, but it received back a rebate, inward investment and the benefits of trade within the Union. On balance, it was a net contributor but not to the extent that Farage claimed. Were Britain's borders open to 450 million immigrants? That was very unlikely. 'Mobility of labour' worked in both directions. There were one and a quarter million Britons working on the Continent, one and a half million non-British EU citizens in Britain. Clegg quoted from a UKIP pamphlet, which claimed that more than the entire populations of Romania and Bulgaria were planning to settle in Britain. That was obvious nonsense.

During the debate, Farage's narrative took an unexpected turn. He claimed that the European Union harboured 'imperialist' ambitions towards Ukraine and had helped to unseat its 'democratically elected' president, Viktor Yanukovych, who fled to Moscow in 2013. As a result of this coup d'état, Russia feared that there was a threat to its borders and moved to protect its Russian-speaking comrades in Crimea, then part of Ukraine, and the provincial region surrounding the city of Donetsk. According to Farage's version of events, Putin, the Russian president, was acting in self-defence against the threat of European expansionism.

Few Western diplomats would accept this version of events. In February and March, Putin had sent troops into Crimea, annexing the peninsula as Russian territory. He installed a pro-Russian government in Sevastopol. This had been denounced as an armed invasion, illegal under international law. It broke the Helsinki Accord of 1975, which defined the borders of Ukraine, and was condemned by the UN's Security Council, which urged Russia to respect the 'territorial integrity' of Ukraine. Farage turned that version of events on its head.

This was the first indication that, behind Farage's attacks on the EU, there might be other forces at work. Clegg did not dwell upon the story but, during the following years, another version emerged from the shadows. It revealed that there was, or was likely to have been, a Kremlin-inspired conspiracy to destabilise the West by breaking up the EU. It suggested that Brexit was part of a longer-term Russian strategy.

Suspicion was aroused by Farage's claim that Yanukovych had been 'democratically elected'. Few commentators shared that view.[3] He was thought to be a Russian puppet. He spoke the Ukrainian language badly, preferring to speak Russian, and led the Party of the Regions, financed by a Russian oligarch. Shortly after his election, he sent his popular opponent, Yulia Tymoshenko, to prison. But he was also given what a US embassy official described in a cable as 'an extreme makeover' by the US marketing consultant, Paul Manafort, who became Donald Trump's campaign director.

Manafort and his assistant, Rick Gates, took charge of Yanukovych's publicity during the 2010 election, using social media through Austrian and Russian websites to do so. He continued as his adviser after the election. He was a personal friend of Yanukovych and helped to obtain the information that smeared Tymoshenko's and later Hillary Clinton's reputations. In 2018, Manafort was arrested in the United States on tax evasion charges, before facing the Special Counsel Robert Mueller's inquiry into Russian interference in the US presidential election campaign. Manafort was accused of receiving more than $60 million for his political consultancy work in Ukraine, which he had failed to declare.

Farage came to know Manafort through the circle of advisers that supported Trump's presidential campaign. He provided a Manafort-inspired version of the politics in Ukraine, which would have had the full approval of the Kremlin. If this background had been known, would it have made any difference to the debate? Perhaps not, for this was one of many charges that Farage was throwing at the EU. It did indicate, however, how the democratic system in the West was starting to change under the pressures of globalisation, the Internet and fake facts. The British electorate was asked to gamble its future by choosing between two opposite narratives that it had little chance to verify.

In the European Parliament Election of July 2014, UKIP became the leading British party in the European Parliament, beating Conservatives, Labour and LibDems, to receive 26 per cent of the votes in a low poll. Only 42 per cent of the electorate voted. UKIP had no Members of Parliament in the House of Commons before the election but, afterwards, two Conservative MPs defected and joined UKIP. Did the debates change the outcome? Perhaps not, but, to ward off the threat from UKIP, Cameron promised that, if his party came into power after the following general election, it would hold a referendum to decide, 'for a generation', whether Britain should stay as an EU member.

This pledge may have won him the 2015 election but it destroyed his political future.

(iii)

The coalition government had already held two referendums during its five years in office and it had become a feature of Cameron's managerial tactics. When in doubt, the government should go to the people and ask for its opinion. It was the democratic solution for any dissension in the ranks. In any referendum, the ruling party started with certain advantages. It could choose the question on the ballot paper, the timing of the polls and sometimes the context of the debate. Before the campaigns were launched, the government could prepare the ground by issuing advisory documents, which did not take any side, but indicated the issues at stake. The government did not have to worry about its election expenses. It was offering a service to the public and could point them in the right directions. It was what any government should try to do – to help the voters, not manipulate them.

In May 2011, in response to its prior agreement with its LibDem partners, it called a referendum on the voting system. The LibDems wanted 'proportional representation', full PR, which would have meant listing the political choices in order of preference. This, the Conservatives decided, was too complicated. It proposed an Alternative Vote (AV) system, whereby an elector could decide which candidate would receive his or her second choice. It was simpler and preserved the 'first-past-the-post' way of choosing a government, which was thought to be the more British – and more decisive. It would avoid all the complicated permutations that led to the coalition governments on the Continent.

Nick Clegg thought that AV was a 'miserable little compromise' but the LibDems hoped that it might be the first step towards a more comprehensive overhaul of the system. Their less-than-enthusiastic campaign failed and in a poll with a low turnout – only 42 per cent – the attempt to change the voting system was heavily defeated. Within a few years, the so-called decisiveness of a first-past-the-post government again came under scrutiny. Was it better to be ruled by a coalition of different parties – or by one party that was continually struggling with its own chaotic divisions?

Paradoxically, the coalition that ruled in Britain from 2010 to 2015 came to be seen as more stable and united than the Conservative governments that followed. This was not by accident. The coalition was brought into being at the time of a financial crisis. Cameron and Clegg both recognised that an unstable government would make matters worse and agreed upon a 'fixed-term' parliament of five years. This was to prevent one party from holding the other – and the country – to ransom by threatening to pull out. In the meantime, both parties were committed to a policy of reducing the level of national borrowing through austerity measures for which the junior partner often received a disproportionate share of the blame.

In 2014, Cameron allowed another referendum, in response to calls from the Scottish Nationalist government in the Holyrood Parliament in Edinburgh. There was a simple question on the ballot paper: 'Should Scotland be an independent country? Yes/No.' The poll was confined to voters in Scotland. But the Westminster government provided information that warned as well as enlightened. Scotland might lose its place within the EU, because as an independent country it would have to apply to join, maybe on less favourable terms. This was a telling argument north of the border. The bid for national independence was defeated by a conciliatory campaign, masterminded from Westminster. This had promised more powers to the Scottish government, while warning against the consequences of leaving the United Kingdom. These included the collapse of a new Scottish currency, economic isolation and border patrols, in short, 'Project Doom'.

Although there were major differences between the Conservatives and LibDems over EU membership, Cameron and Clegg both wanted to stay within the European Union and to reform it, where necessary, from within. But Cameron had to contend with some 60 backbench Conservative MPs, who kept 'banging on about Europe'. He also wanted to prevent further defections to UKIP. As the date of the next General Election approached, 7 May 2015, he went against the advice of his coalition partner, Clegg, and his Chancellor, George Osborne, by promising a binding referendum on Europe if his party topped the poll.

By now, Cameron's opponents were starting to realise how tactically referendums might be won. The secret lay in preparing the battleground. When the Conservatives won the 2015 election, due in part to the unexpected collapse in the vote for UKIP and the LibDems, the Brexiteers were already making their plans. They had wargamed the situation. They guessed the government's first moves. They anticipated that before the campaigns were announced, there would be government warnings about leaving the EU, Project Doom writ large.

When HM Treasury announced that the British economy would slide into recession with 500,000 people out of work, Brexiteers counter-claimed that this was 'Project Fear'. It was an attempt to terrorise the country into staying within the EU. The Treasury warned that families would be £4,300 worse off. Alternative economic models were produced, which presented a much rosier picture. As the opposing EU referendum campaigns developed, the forecasts became more wildly pessimistic or optimistic. They could not be proved to be exactly wrong, because they were prophecies, not end-of-the-year accounts, but the public were asked to gamble with two extremes. We were either risking 'the cliff edge', if we dropped out, or becoming a 'vassal state', if we stayed in.

The government published a pamphlet with the lengthy title: 'Why the Government believes that voting to remain in the European Union is the best decision for the UK.' It promised that the UK would not join the euro, that it would keep its border controls, not be part of further European political integration and would impose 'tough new restrictions on access to our welfare system for new EU migrants'. But it listed the benefits to our economy of belonging to the Common Market and the dangers to our security, if we decided to go it alone.

His cabinet itself was divided. It contained ardent Leavers, such Chris Grayling and Teresa Villiers, and passionate Remainers, such as Ken Clarke and George Osborne; but Cameron wanted his government to present a united front, which was why the pamphlet was worded very carefully. His Education Secretary, Michael Gove, was his close friend. Cameron expected Gove to support him. The red lines were a little fuzzy: retaining border controls did not exactly mean restricting the EU's mobility of labour, one of its first principles. It did not contain any commitment to the ideals of the EU nor to that global vision that had inspired Edward Heath. It was a compromise document that raised as many questions as it answered, and so was vulnerable to attacks from both sides.

Its final message – 'A vote to leave could mean a decade or more of uncertainty' – was accurate but it hardly blew many trumpets. On the other hand, those who planned to campaign against the EU were equally divided. There were two camps. In April 2016, the Electoral Commission nominated Vote Leave as the official campaign. Its Chief Executive was Michael Elliott, a former head of the Taxpayers' Alliance, who had run the campaign against proportional representation. Its rival, Leave.EU, was led by Nigel Farage, supported by UKIP and largely financed by a millionaire from South Africa, Arron Banks, who claimed to have made a fortune from his diamond mines in the African kingdom of Lesotho. They called themselves 'the Bad Boys of Brexit', who were not only against the EU, but against the 'political establishment' that had taken Britain into the EU.

Their rivalry bordered upon contempt. The Vote Leave team were the Westminster professionals, who sought to calm the fears of the middle classes and win over the undecided. Elliott was on good terms with the media and enlisted the help of those who were in the best position to contradict Project Fear – the business leaders who thought that the country might do better outside, the Eurosceptic economists and academics, the heritage worshippers. Dominic Cummings was his campaign director, a market analyst, who had worked as Gove's Chief of Staff at the Department of Education and earned a reputation for being talented, stubborn and afraid of no one, particularly those nobodies in authority.

Their tactics, plotted before the dates of the referendum were known, were to support Cameron in his efforts to seek better terms within the EU, so that they could pounce upon him when he failed. Under their guidance, Gove and the former Mayor of London, Boris Johnson, re-elected in 2015 as MP for Uxbridge and South Ruislip, delayed announcing their intentions to vote for Brexit, until the campaign to remain was under way. From Cameron's point of view, it looked like deliberate treachery.

Vote Leave's tactics aroused the suspicions of Farage and his supporters as well, who formed the opinion that their rivals were less than gung-ho for the fight. Leave.EU was much brasher in its approach, led by someone renowned for speaking his mind. It did not matter that Farage had fought six national elections as a Conservative or UKIP candidate and had lost each one. His lack of success added to his plausibility, for at a time when the establishment was discredited, an outsider was the more to be admired. He had fought on against the odds.

The battle between the two campaigns was one of 'class', but not in the old-fashioned sense of bosses versus workers, but of smooth intellectuals against the rough but streetwise, self-made businessmen. It was an essential part of Leave.EU's message that they should be seen to be in a better position to represent the people against those in the Westminster bubble. It claimed that there was a 'disconnect' between the 'career politicians' and those whom they were supposed to represent. A populist movement, expressed through referendums, was a clearer expression of the Will of the People than representative democracy; and so, in its modest way, Leave.EU was prepared to rip up the British constitution.

On their part, the leaders of Vote Leave were alarmed that Farage might say something so politically incorrect – or factually so wrong – that it might ruin their campaign. Cummings studied the polls, analysed the data from the Internet and ensured that the Vote Leave messages were carefully targeted. He knew that the future of the NHS was a major concern for most voters and so, if the EU could be seen to be as a threat to the NHS, it would be a powerful argument for leaving. He knew that certain phrases, such as 'take control', had a strong resonance. Nearly everyone was worried about the future. Nearly everyone believed that, if they were better organised, they might escape the troubles ahead. 'Take control' was a battle cry as well as a promise, like 'When the Saints Go Marching In'.

In many ways, Britain was and is still a prosperous country, the fifth largest economy in the world, the fastest growing in Europe. It was part of the second wealthiest trading zone, the EU, and claimed a Special Relationship with the first, the US. It was at the forefront of global trade but the benefits were unevenly spread. Large areas had suffered from modernisation. The mining communities were gone: the steel industries were under threat. Other cities had felt the impact of globalisation, the mill towns of the north. Others were putting up with the restrictions imposed by well-meaning causes. The fishing ports were suffering from the efforts of the EU to conserve fish stocks. It was of little comfort to those who wandered the streets in derelict urban sprawls to know that the City of London was doing rather well.

The government's austerity measures hit those who were poorest and in the minds of those who were old enough to remember, the loss of the Empire still rankled. To some, the very presence of workers from countries with which within living memory we had been at war was an affront. What were they doing on our side of the Channel? Those who wanted to stay in the EU dismissed this resentment as xenophobia. Mobility of labour benefited us all but those who lived in areas where there were few workers from the Continent, such as Canvey Island or Brecon, cited immigration as a main reason for wanting to leave the EU. Paradoxically, those who lived in metropolitan areas, such as Manchester and London, which had varied and cosmopolitan communities, saw no problem with immigration at all.

Before the election, Cameron had promised that his party, if elected, would reduce the levels of immigration from hundreds of thousands to tens of thousands. This was an easier promise to make than to keep. It caused a great deal of distress, not only to those of the Windrush generation, who found that they were suddenly living in a 'hostile environment', but also to those who during the 45 years of EU membership had settled in the UK. In the minds of many who voted to leave, the real danger did not come from those who had already made their home in the country, but from the tide of refugees who were waiting to be admitted to the EU. They came from war-torn countries such as Syria, Libya and Somalia, and, although most were desperately in need, a few might be terrorists, trained by ISIL.

Cameron was dealing with a divided party. He could not hold his supporters together, the right wing with the moderates, without promising such a poll, which he felt confident that he could win. In British law, the sovereign body was Parliament, whose decisions were subject to ratification by the Crown. The referendum was a way of advising Parliament about the feeling in the country, nothing more. The EU Referendum Act did not specify that the result would be binding. But it did amount to a promise that the Conservative government would respect the result, whatever it was. It would be legally controversial and a challenge to a mandate from the people, were it to be ignored.

Distrust of referendums was once widespread in the UK. Mrs Thatcher called them 'a device of dictators and demagogues', quoting the former Labour Prime Minister, Clement Attlee. The United Kingdom has a representative democracy, which elects its MPs, constituency by constituency, to ensure that local and regional interests are fairly observed. A nationwide referendum cuts across these concerns and assumes that there is something like the Will of the People, which overrides them all, including Parliament. There is nothing in the British unwritten constitution about the Will of the People. It has no official presence.

Particularly among those EU countries that had suffered under Hitler's Third Reich, referendums were thought to be constitutionally risky. They were subject to restrictions. There might be rules requiring a minimum turn-out and, if binding on a constitutional issue, the result was expected to be not 'marginal' but 'conclusive', endorsed by sometimes as many as two thirds of those who voted. Such rules did not apply to the EU referendum, because they were not included within the original Bill. The EU observers were horrified by the lax requirements but felt reluctant to interfere.

Attlee and Thatcher had one notorious example in mind. Similar referendums brought Hitler to power in Germany during the 1930s. It began with a referendum in 1929 to renounce the Treaty of Versailles, which squarely blamed Germany for World War I. This led to the rise of the National Socialist German Workers' (Nazi) Party, of which Hitler was its most passionate speaker. This referendum failed, because the turn-out was too low but, among those who voted, there was a unanimous call for a new law against the enslavement of the German people. In Britain, the Vote Leave slogan, 'Take Back Control', sounded very similar.

The strength of feeling aroused by the first German referendum helped to bring a nationalist, right-wing minority party into the mainstream of politics. In 1928, the Nazis had twelve seats in the Reichstag but, by 1932, it had 230 seats and was the largest party. Hitler became the Chancellor and by means of another referendum in 1933, united his position with that of head of state. Further referendums followed, which effectively removed all opposition parties, the freedom of the press, *habeas corpus* and most other civil liberties, all in the name of the Will of the People. Hitler as Führer was the personification of that Will.

Could something similar happen in Britain? It seemed most unlikely. Unlike Germany in the 1920s, the UK had suffered no humiliation. It was prosperous. There were those who mourned the loss of the empire and had difficulty in getting along with the French; but there were no grievances to match those of the old Weimar Republic. But there were disturbing similarities, not least in the rising levels of intolerance, the rewriting of history and the thinly disguised xenophobia. As in Germany during the 1930s, there was a distrust of intellectuals and the educated voices of the Establishment.

Even Michael Gove MP warned the country not to listen to experts. While this did not amount to a British *Kristallnacht*, there was an alarming increase in tension. In the annual police statistics, race-hate crimes rose by 58 per cent. On 16 June, a week before the referendum, the MP for Batley, Jo Cox, who campaigned for Britain Stronger in Europe, the remain campaign, was murdered outside the library in her constituency, where she was due to hold a surgery, by an unemployed gardener, Thomas Mair. He gave his name in court as 'death to traitors, freedom for Britain'.

Surely, there was calm about the British character, which negated the hysteria of Nazi-like rallies and found its true voice within the balanced programming of the BBC, the nation's comfort blanket? A country that so loved *The Archers*, the long-running tale of country folk, was hardly likely to be won over by a man with a loud voice and a spotlit podium. After Jo Cox's murder, the opposing parties temporarily suspended their campaigning – despite the fact, as Nigel Farage complained, that it stopped Leave.Eu's momentum. He sincerely hoped that the Remain campaign would not try to take advantage of that unfortunate incident.

***

Chapter Thirteen
Raw Brexit

(i)

The EU referendum in 2016 left British politics in such a mess that it might be more tactful to draw a veil. The result came as a considerable surprise. Previous opinion polls indicated a win for Remain and, even before the votes were fully counted, Nigel Farage was calling for another referendum. But the polls were mistaken. Leave won by a margin of 52 per cent to 48 per cent, but the turnout was high, 72 per cent, which meant that there was a majority of more than a million. The referendum was not legally binding but the Conservatives had promised to leave the EU if the People willed it so. It would 'settle the matter for a generation'. The government had not expected Leave to win. It was completely unprepared.

The process of renegotiating 45 years of trade deals would soon have to begin, as well as 45 years of agreements to protect the environment, social rights and a thousand other matters. But none of these negotiations could start until Britain formally had withdrawn as a member of the EU and become a Third Country. This was where some Leave campaigners had miscalculated. They wanted to have the certainty of trade agreements before the uncertainties of leaving. This was impossible. It was the wrong way round. The terms of the renegotiation depended upon the terms of the divorce.

There was scarcely even a government. Cameron, who campaigned for Remain, had intended to stay on until a new party leader could be chosen at the Conservative Party Conference in October but it would have led to months of instability. This was reduced to about six weeks. Five names for the leadership election were put before Conservative MPs, who were expected to draw up a shortlist of two names to be offered to the party membership for their final decision. The front runner in the popular stakes,

Boris Johnson MP, the former Mayor of London, withdrew his name at the last minute. Some political analysts thought that he had been stabbed in the back.[i] There was much shaking of heads.

In the preliminary ballot, presented to the Conservatives in Parliament, three candidates were eliminated: Michael Gove, Stephen Crabb and Liam Fox. This left two on the list: Theresa May, the Home Secretary, a Remainer, and Andrea Leadsom, the Minister for Energy and the Environment, a Leaver. Mrs Leadsom pointed out to the press that Mrs May had no children, which might disqualify her from knowing what life was truly about. This was considered to be bad sportsmanship, which disqualified her, rather than Mrs May. Mrs Leadsom withdrew her name at the last minute and the party members were spared from having to choose between two candidates, only one.

Barely a year after the General Election in 2015, the British were ruled by a new Prime Minister, selected by the MPs, endorsed (for want of a better word) by the party membership, leading her new frontbench with ministers, some Leavers, some Remainers, committed to policies that were not included in their manifesto and took them by surprise. Where was their democratic mandate? There were too few civil servants to staff the Brexit departments. Where would they be found? Who would sit on the committees to select them?

There was a Leader of the Opposition, Jeremy Corbyn MP, who was elected as the party leader in September 2015. He was a surprising choice, lucky to be chosen at all even for the ballot paper, left-wing and loving it, opposed to New Labour and all that it stood for, and so at odds with most of his MPs. After the referendum, where he failed, according to his critics, to meet the challenge of opposition, he faced a vote of no confidence from his own parliamentary colleagues, which he lost by 172 votes to 40. There were calls for his resignation but his support within the non-parliamentary Labour movement stayed firm. Indeed, it dramatically increased, for thousands of new members joined.

Were these newcomers really Labour supporters or far-left agitators, who had paid £3 to join the party? There was a new name for this radical movement, Momentum. It was compared to the Militant Tendency that caused a former Labour leader, Neil Kinnock, so much trouble in the 1990s. The deputy leader, Tom Watson, called together the heads of four trade unions, financial backers of the Labour Party, to support an appeal for Corbyn's resignation. He called it the last throw of the dice. They did not come. Instead, there was a fresh challenge to Corbyn's leadership, which went to the full membership of the party. Unexpectedly, buoyed up by Momentum, Corbyn won.

The divisiveness of the referendum campaign left Britain's reputation for political stability in tatters. The unravelling began. It started with the unity of the country. Scotland, unlike England, voted to Remain, which led to calls for another referendum on independence. Northern Ireland voted to Remain, although the Democratic Unionists, the party in power, voted to Leave. Northern Ireland has an open border with the Republic of Ireland, which would stay in the EU. Should there be customs posts within the island of Ireland itself? Or should there be, as Sinn Fein proposed, a fresh referendum on a United Ireland, which would tear up the existing Peace Process? Wales voted with North East England to Leave, but London to Remain. The ties that held the nation together were stretched almost to breaking point.

In the midst of this confusion, a young journalist, J.D. Taylor, climbed on his old Raleigh bicycle, packed a tent and some changes of clothes in his saddlebag, and began his own investigative tour around the country. He researched in an agreeable way by talking to people in cafes and bars, and published his anecdotal findings in a book, *Island Story: Journeys Through Unfamiliar Britain* (2016). It was a study of a land that time forgot – of derelict town centres, empty churches and locked up industrial premises, where 'basic poverty was the elementary concern'. While the official figures indicated that Britain was attracting record amounts of inward investment, Taylor traipsed around the youth centres, the food banks and charity shops, gathering the views of those 'who were most affected by the nowhereness of the moment'.

There were many grievances but, underlying them all was a sense of loss, as if the days of honour and independence were in the past and sliding still further away into the deep recesses of memory. Whole towns had lost their main source of livelihood, the reason for their existence, sometimes violently, as during the Miners' Strike, or sometimes by being overtaken by events. So many local companies, with their roots in family ownership, were merged into national or international chains, whose headquarters were anywhere. A town like Halifax was no longer famous for its textiles, Sheffield for its bicycles, or Wolverhampton for its furniture. Within the subsidised arts, the local reps were sacrificed to the two Centres of Excellence. Almost everywhere the profitability of large companies took over from the local pride in making beautiful things.

In some parts of the country, the slide into obscurity seemed inexorable, starting in the 1960s, with the loss of branch-line train services, as local stations were closed under Dr Beeching and railways were streamlined. The signs of post-Imperial poverty coincided with the arrival of immigrants from the Commonwealth, an indication that labour came from somewhere else.

Freedom of movement within the EU was an extension of this intrusion. In the 1990s, the poor distribution of broadband left some areas at a disadvantage and out of touch with their retailers, customers and suppliers. Modernity was somewhere else.

In Taylor's *Unfamiliar Britain*, the decision to leave the EU was greeted with delight. It was a rude gesture to foreigners and the metropolitan *élite* alike. The EU was like a very large laundry basket into which all kinds of dirty linen could be thrown. Taylor interviewed a man in Barnsley, a former mining town, where 68 per cent of the population voted to Leave. He was told bluntly, 'It's to stop Muslims coming into this country. It's as simple as that.' The EU was blamed for white slavery in Rotherham and cheap dresses from Pakistan. Did the import of Polish coal destroy the British mining industry? Not really. Was immigration a drain on the British economy? The statistics suggested otherwise but convinced very few EU sceptics. As a background to the complaints, ran the national narrative, celebrated by World War II films on television, about how we endured the Blitz, won the war and saved civilisation.

While Taylor was cycling around the country, a new socio-economic think tank, the Legatum Institute began publishing its first research papers. The Institute was launched in 2007 as a philanthropic arm of a Dubai-based investment company. In 2015, a new chief executive was appointed, Philippa Stroud, a former civil servant, who had recently been elevated to the House of Lords. She had worked with Iain Duncan Smith, the Work and Pensions Secretary in the coalition government, and together they had devised a new system for bundling together all the social benefits into one programme, Universal Credit.

The principle was that the rewards of work should always exceed those of state aid but, for those who lived in districts where work was hard to find, the implication that those who received benefits were work-shy was felt to be offensive. The intentions of Universal Credit were as much social and moral as economic. It was believed that those who earned money through work were contributing towards a better society and thus had a higher sense of self-esteem. It was part of Cameron's Big Society but, for those whose only chances of employment lay in stacking supermarket shelves, the prospects still seemed very bleak.

The researchers of the Legatum Institute sought to measure the sense of 'prosperity' and 'wellbeing'. They constructed an index, which listed the various attributes associated with wellbeing: income levels, education, social capital, the natural environment, health and 'life choices'. In its international index, the UK was rated as the world's fourteenth most prosperous country. When its local levels were measured, constituency by constituency, there were very large differences. Waverley in Surrey was the most prosperous of 389 districts, while Hull was the least. The average per capita annual earnings were highest in Kensington and Chelsea (£40,405) and were more than twice as high as those in Blackpool (£16,384). There were more prosperous districts in the South East than the North, thus clearly indicating the North-South divide.

The more prosperous and cosmopolitan districts tended to vote Remain, while the least voted Leave. Was that an indication that the difference between Leavers and Remainers was mainly economic? Paradoxically, however, the poorer parts of the country were often those which had received most inward investment from the EU, whereas the richer were net contributors to the EU's budget. This suggested that those who benefited most from EU investment were not grateful. Perhaps they resented it – or simply did not know.

Nor was the Legatum Institute wholly impartial in its methods. Before joining the Institute, Baroness Stroud founded the Centre for Social Justice with Iain Duncan Smith, which advised the Conservatives on their social policy. It was independent of government and believed in enterprise and self-help, rather than in state aid or EU intervention. The background philosophy was 'to lift all people out of poverty', globally, 'and create pathways from poverty to prosperity'. It was also right of centre in that it was not primarily concerned with the gulf in wealth between the rich and poor. It was not obsessed by the evils of capitalism. Duncan Smith was against the EU for its bureaucracy, its social policy and its Keynesian interventions in the market. The Institute appointed Matthew Elliott as its research director, after he had successfully led the Vote Leave campaign to victory.

The two anti-EU campaigns brought together the sources of discontent in Unfamiliar Britain into one nationalist campaign. They did so against the pressures of time and Project Fear. In doing so, they cut across ordinary party loyalties and managed to persuade people to vote who may never have voted before. They drew upon a deep well of dissatisfaction, which could be traced back to the days of Suez and even before.

But it ran the risk of shrouding the nation in a fog of nostalgic self-delusion, forward to the past. Facts mattered less than gut instincts. The Vote Leave campaign sent carefully targeted messages through social media, borrowing the skills of commercial marketing. The Brexiteers were conviction politicians, but their sense of purpose led many to believe that their patriotic ends justified their dishonourable means. In cricketing terms, they were proved guilty of ball-tampering on a massive scale. My father would have been ashamed of them.

(ii)

The Electoral Reform Society, an independent charity, published a critical report. It had commissioned an opinion poll from BMG Research to monitor the responses of a cross-section of 1,000 UK-based adults from the start of the referendum campaign to the end. This revealed a slow draining away of public confidence, like a car tyre with a puncture, in the 'facts' that were given to them. The economic models from the Leave and Remain campaigns were wildly at odds, as were other forecasts. Dominic Cummings, the campaign director of Vote Leave, realised that this war would not be won on the battlefield of statistics. He also understood that 'facts', if correctly handled, could provide useful hand grenades in the trench warfare of emotions. They could be tossed into the debate, explode and cause damage to the other side, before anyone could examine how 'factual' they really were.

The much criticised slogan on the side of Boris Johnson's Brexit battle bus was a case in point. Was it factually true that £350 million was sent to Brussels every week, which could be spent on the NHS instead? The rough answer was 'Yes', because this was the amount allocated to the EU within the terms of British membership. In the eyes of those who lived in Unfamiliar Britain, this was an enormous sum. It was also misleading, because about one third was returned in the form of a rebate, one third was spent on projects that benefited the UK and the remainder was spent on European projects, including its administration, to which the UK had agreed as an EU member. Could this money be re-allocated to fund the NHS? In theory, yes, but new money would have to be found to fund the UK projects currently supported by the EU. Economists in the Remain camp doubted if there would be any money left from the 'Brexit dividend', when the costs of leaving the EU were taken into account.

During the campaign, Vote Leave invoked the Brexit dividend as a way of funding other good causes. These included building 'hundreds of schools',[ii] 'new hospitals', 'new roads',[iii] 'expanding regional airports',[iv] 'improving railways', 'supporting agriculture', 'subsidising the steel industry' and 'purchasing fourteen new Astute Class submarines'.[v] A Vote Leave pamphlet stated that 'taxpayers' money should be spent on filling the potholes in Britain, rather than squandered on foreign bridges to nowhere' in such remote places as Romania, Poland and Bulgaria. Taxpayers from other EU countries might have complained about the money spent on rescuing the derelict Swan Hunter shipyard or lent by the European Investment Bank to build the Midlands Metropolitan Hospital (£108 million). Such mutual help was, or should have been, at the heart of the European Union.

'This report,' concluded Katie Ghose, former CEO of the Electoral Reform Society, 'shows . . . just how dire the EU Referendum debate really was. There were glaring democratic deficiencies . . . with the public feeling totally ill-informed. Both sides were viewed as highly negative, while the top-down, personality-based nature of the debate failed to address major policies and issues, leaving the public in the dark'. Under these circumstances, the proud tradition of British public service broadcasting (PSB) should have come into its own. The BBC certainly tried. Throughout the referendum campaign, there were public forums, panel discussions and in-depth news reporting. The coverage may have been too glued to the events but, within the terms of its PSB mandate, the BBC maintained a balanced approach, giving both sides an equal chance to express their opposite points of view.

But 'balance' was one of the problems. Should the two sides be given equal coverage? The referendum was not like a parliamentary election and no political party could be held to account. The Brexiteers could freely attack the EU's record, whereas they had no such record to defend. They had a licence to invent. 'Balance' removed one competitive advantage from the Remain campaign. Most experts believed that Brexit would damage Britain, not just as a trading partner but as a world power. The BBC gave the impression that the experts were evenly divided. Almost certainly they were not.

There was another danger looming, the spectre of Pavlov's dogs. Might institutional impartiality confuse rather than enlighten? Ivan Pavlov was a Russian behavioural scientist, who discovered that dogs could be trained to respond to stimuli that were associated with certain events. The tick of a metronome, regularly sounded before dinner, would encourage them to salivate. If a similar, but not identical, sound, such as the tick of a clock, occurred before an unpleasant electric shock, they could detect the difference and respond in distress. If the sounds were so similar that they could not tell them apart, they became confused, quarrelsome and displayed all the signs of a nervous breakdown.

Might something similar have happened within the PSB coverage of the referendum? Both sides of the argument were given equal time, supported by similar-sounding facts, which were equally distrusted and led to opposite conclusions. Everyone knew that his or her vote was important but the enormity of the choice was not helpful. It piled on the emotions. Families were divided. In the Electoral Reform Society's poll, the most confident voices were the best believed, Farage, Johnson and the game-show host in America, Donald Trump. There was a very large gap of trust between the 'Westminster bubble' and the populist tide.

Where the experts were distrusted, gossip took over, or 'precognitive persuasion' as it was known in the trade, the formula that worked so well in commercial marketing. These techniques had been greatly refined since the days of the 1960s, when Vance Packard wrote *The Hidden Persuaders*, not least because human behaviour was now digitalised and packaged into algorithms, so that those who were marketing a product could identify the likes and dislikes of its intended clients with greatly increased precision.

These targeted ads might not mention the product at all, only hint at the need for one. They might seem to advertise something different, but related, so that the customer would be tempted to click from one post to another, each leading towards the decision to Leave. They were distributed through the social media. One showed a Spanish bullfight, with a caption 'Stop Animal Abuse'. The only link with the referendum was that Spain was part of the EU. Another showed an image of a distressed bear, stating that: 'The EU blocks our ability to speak out and protect polar bears.' For the more sophisticated, there was the picture of a young woman, burying her head in her hands in despair: 'Albania, Macedonia, Montenegro, Serbia and Turkey are joining the EU. Seriously!' They were not. It was a lie. Seriously.

Dominic Cummings was proud of one post that he called a game-changer. It did not mention the sponsor, Vote Leave. It proposed a competition with an enormous prize: 'Love Football? Win £50 million. Predict the European Championship results for 2016. Click here.' The contestants were asked to leave their e-mail addresses; but the odds against anybody winning were calculated as 5,000,000,000,000,000 to 1 – or almost infinite. What was the intention? The Vote Leave team had been told that football fans were likely to vote against the EU out of patriotic pride but that they were harder to reach through the normal websites. The competition gave the Vote Leave campaign a list of supporters that could be targeted.

It was not usually necessary to go to such lengths. There were companies that sold targeting lists. Some went into great detail. The Vote Leave campaign employed the services of Cambridge Analytica (CA), a 'global election management company', whose Vice-President was Steve Bannon. It was founded in 2015 and owned by the family of Robert Mercer, a billionaire hedge-fund manager. Its methods were based on the research of Michal Kosinski, formerly Deputy Director of the Psychometrics Centre at Cambridge University. He is a psychologist and anthropologist, who compiles profiles of the general public from evidence provided by data from Internet browsing and the usage of websites, and he has made it clear that he has nothing to do with Cambridge Analytica.

The parent company of CA was the Strategic Communications Laboratory (SCL), which specialised in providing military disinformation, but CA's skills lay with political marketing. It had masterminded election campaigns in Nigeria, Kenya and elsewhere in Africa. In 2016, it claimed to have run Trump's digital campaign for the US presidency. But in 2017, a whistleblower, Chris Wylie, who had helped to create the company, revealed some secrets of its success. He explained how CA had harvested and retained illegally the online information provided unwittingly by at least 50 million Facebook users.

From this information, it had commissioned a Canadian company, Aggregate IQ, to create digital ads, targeted at selected groups of voters in the EU referendum. No fewer than 1.5 billion social media posts were sent out to seven million voters during the final days of the campaign. The cost to the Vote Leave campaign was calculated to be £3.5 million.

In 2017, CA was caught in a carefully planned press sting, in which a journalist, posing as an agent from the Sri Lankan government, sought its services. The CA's managing director, Alexander Nix, gave an unguarded interview filmed in a restaurant. Nix revealed CA's package of dirty political tricks, which included entrapment, spreading false information and bribery. He later denied that he had intended to commit these crimes but the damage had been done. The company could not recover from this blow to its reputation. It was declared bankrupt, but within a few months, a similar organisation was formed, Auspex International, which included former members of its staff. It remains to be seen whether CA's digital skills and ethics have been wholly lost. Its website proclaims its honourable intentions.

Was the EU referendum won through 'precognitive persuasion' and untruthful ads? Possibly not, but this did not mean that the Vote Leave money was wasted. It was argued that precognitive persuasion only works where there is a predisposition to believe what the ads say. Nobody who knew anything about European affairs could believe that Brussels would get in the way of helping polar bears or (as in another post) threaten the 'British cuppa'. But if somebody were already under the impression that the EU was a Continental conspiracy, he or she might be happy to add another fantasy to the list for disliking it.

Was this how future elections and referendums would be won, not by appealing to the mind, but by triggering knee-jerk reactions? Did we always respond like automata if the appropriate buttons in our psyche were pressed? There are mental illusionists in the theatre, like the British magician Derren Brown, who provide astonishing feats of auto-suggestion, in which members of the audience might be persuaded to rob a bank or commit a murder while under his spell, but Brown would be the first to disclaim any supernatural powers. If voters knew how they were being manipulated, they might be less likely to be so. But few people want to spend their lives studying the rights and wrongs of EU membership. They might have better things to do.

From the Electoral Reform Society's view, the worst feature of the referendum was that it helped to undermine faith in the democratic process itself. It undermined representative democracy and questioned the right of Members of Parliament to make decisions on the public's behalf. The use of commercial marketing tactics to promote a political campaign was dangerous, because no one could be held responsible for making irresponsible promises. It undermined the integrity of the political debate. The risks were made worse by the unscrupulous use of the Internet. 'Britain's electoral laws,' concluded Martin Moore, Director of the Centre for Media Studies at King's College, London, 'are weak and helpless in face of digital campaigning.'

Brexiteers hailed their victory as the largest democratic mandate in British history: 33,551,983 people voted, a turnout of 72.2 per cent. The scale demonstrated the extent of the country's concern and although the margin of 4 per cent between the Leavers and Remainers was less than overwhelming, the result was still conclusive. The Conservative government was committed to delivering on its promise to the people.

Anything less would be seen as a betrayal.

(iii)

Leave.EU, the rival campaign to the official Vote Leave, did not employ the services of Cambridge Analytica. They chose a New York-based political marketing company instead, Gunster Strategies Worldwide, but, in any case, as its principal benefactor, Arron Banks, told a parliamentary committee: 'Our social media campaign was more about being provocative about such topics as immigration rather than paying for adverts.'

They called themselves 'the Bad Boys of Brexit'. 'Our skill,' Banks explained, 'was in creating bushfires and then putting the fans on and letting them blow.' There was a great deal of tinder to burn. On the borders of the EU, there was the largest humanitarian crisis since World War II. Million-strong refugee camps were roughly erected in Lebanon and Jordan to shelter those who were escaping from the wars in Syria, Iraq, Afghanistan, Yemen, Libya, North Africa and elsewhere in the Middle East. Not all of the migrants wanted to travel on to Europe. Some were waiting for the fires to burn themselves out in their home countries but a sufficient number were seeking asylum, or only to escape, to arouse well justified alarm throughout Europe. Those were the flames that Leave.EU wanted to fan.

Could the EU rise to the challenge? Some believed that the EU had a moral duty to hold out the hand of friendship to those who were destitute and to find them some place within its expanding borders, where they could settle, work and raise their families without being under threat to their lives. Others, such as David Cameron, wanted to improve the circumstances in the refugee camps and search for peaceful solutions in their home countries, so that they would not attempt to travel to Europe. All the EU governments wanted to stop people-smuggling and the rackets of drugs and prostitution that flourished in the wake of despair. All agreed that the EU's borders should be strengthened and that there should be a better-managed procedure for vetting the asylum seekers. But to achieve these goals required a giant leap forward in EU cooperation.

This was not impossible, but unlikely. Angela Merkel had led the way in Germany by welcoming refugees, but other EU countries were reluctant to follow her example. And yet the terrible distress could not be ignored. It washed up on beaches, defiled the rocks and left its stench where in better times young bathers might flash their beauty. The alternative was to abandon all pretence at fellow feeling, and to take the view that these were not really human beings at all, but lesser creatures to be swept up and dumped out of sight.

The Leave.EU poster, 'Breaking Point', touched a raw nerve. There was a long queue of penniless foreigners, all but one coloured, waiting to take advantage of our social services. It was modelled on a well-known political poster, 'Labour isn't Working', or for those with longer memories, a Nazi poster from the 1930s.[vi] It was widely deplored, even by those of the Vote Leave campaign, but, among those who joined UKIP from the National Front, it was common sense to keep these migrants out. But if mobility of labour was a fundamental principle within the EU, what could the UK do to prevent them from coming? The only answer was to leave the EU.

Leave.EU did not need to buy the services of Cambridge Analytica. It relied upon the daily press to advertise its campaign. It spun the news sideways, so that the EU was not seen as an ally in the crisis, but as the weak link, the open back door through which refugees could sneak into the country. This was the tactic that Vote Leave wanted to avoid and which kept the two campaigns apart. Elliott and Cummings did not want to seem xenophobic, but ultra-discriminating, whereas Banks and Farage seized the opportunity to be ultra-patriotic. While the British are a compassionate race, according to Leave.EU, these foreign migrants should still be kept out; they brought with them AIDS, white slavery and terrorism. Each ISIL atrocity added one more banner to its campaign. British identity, no less, was at stake.

Leave.EU was the ultra-nationalistic wing to the Brexit campaign, blatantly so. The rise of UKIP scooped up the former supporters of the National Front. The Will of the People was no longer an abstract idea. It marched in the streets. There were other parties in the EU, which were patriotic in a similar way, sharing their Euroscepticism and organising national rallies: Le Pen's Front National in France, the Freedom Party of Austria, Geert Wilders' Party for Freedom in the Netherlands, Alternativ für Deutschland in Germany, the coalition United Patriots in Bulgaria, the Movement for a Better Hungary, the Swedish Democrats, the Northern League in Italy, Golden Dawn in Greece and the National Movement of Poland.

There is no country so small that it does not contain enough space for a warehouse, stacked to the rafters with patriotic yarns. These political movements were not equally strong. Some were on the verge of entering government; others were still on the fringe. Not all wanted to leave the EU, not all were anti-Islamic but, at the time of the EU Referendum in 2016, a critical observer of the EU, John R. Gillingham, surveyed all the nationalistic parties on the continent, marching as if in unison, and concluded that the days of the EU were over. He published its obituary,[vii] prematurely.

Was there collusion between them? Was there any kind of master plan? There were conspiracy theories on all sides. In the Kremlin under Putin, there was the prevailing opinion that NATO and the EU were conducting a hostile campaign to annex former Soviet territory, such as in Ukraine, which entitled the Russian government to send in forces to protect their own people. Paul Manafort, the US lobbyist and Donald Trump's Director of Operations, was paid $60 million to spread such rumours within the Western press and social media. This led to the counter-claim that Putin was spreading disinformation to break up the European Union and recapture those lands that were once part of the Soviet Union. Was this the beginning of Cold War Mark 2?

'I like to think,' said Banks in his jocular manner to the parliamentary committee, 'I'm an evil genius with a white cap that controls the whole of Western democracy, but clearly that's nonsense.' But there were connecting links between the Russian government, Trump's presidential campaign, the rise of nationalism in Europe, Cambridge Analytica and Leave.EU, which the committee was trying to investigate. Banks had lunched with the Russian ambassador, Alexander Yakovenko, just before the referendum, had visited Moscow and been put in contact with those who offered him a stake in Siberian gold mines. According to documents obtained by *The Observer*,[viii] there were eleven meetings between the Leave.EU team and senior Russian officials between November 2015 and 2017. Were these meetings coincidental or was there a deliberate attempt by the Kremlin to influence the outcome of the EU referendum?

While it might be accurate to insist that Leave.EU did not commission CA to post ads on its behalf, it would not be true to say that there had been no contact between them. There was a contract between CA and UKIP for £41,500 that, according to Andy Wigmore, an associate of Banks and Farage, was never signed, paid or acknowledged within UKIP's election expenses. Farage was a personal friend of Robert Mercer and Steve Bannon, who owned CA and the Breitbart News Network, and it was alleged that information, pirated from Facebook, was passed between CA and UKIP freely and without appearing on Leave.EU's accounts. 'Undisclosed support in kind,' concluded Dr Martin Moore of King's College, 'is extremely troubling. It undermines the whole basis of an electoral system.'

In the United States, very similar accusations were made against Trump's campaign team for presidency. These asserted that they had met Russian officials, used the help of Russian-funded websites to spread disinformation about Trump's opponents, the former US President Barack Obama and his Democratic rival, Hillary Clinton, and obtained e-mails that were supposed to be private through sources that were powerful enough to intercept the criss-crossing of cyber-chatter across the known universe. Whether there was direct collusion between Trump himself and his Russian friends remains an open question. If so, there would be grounds for impeachment. In May 2017, an investigating team from the Department of Justice, headed by a former FBI Director, Robert Mueller, as its Special Counsel, began a long investigation. Paul Manafort, already convicted on tax evasion and money-laundering charges from his activities in Ukraine, and Trump's former Security director, Michael Flynn, were subpoenaed to testify. Trump himself was granted permission not to appear before Mueller's Committee, but to submit written evidence instead.

In Britain, Banks' sources of funding have come under investigation. He claimed to have given £8.4 million pounds in donations and loans to the cause, either through funding UKIP or Leave.EU. He controlled an insurance company, Eldon Insurance, whose Bristol offices were used as headquarters by the Leave.EU campaign. It had profitable subsidiary companies – GoSkippy, Footprint and Business Choice Direct – and offices in Newcastle and South Africa, but his investment in a political cause that should bring him no material benefits was still impressive. He teased the parliamentary committee by telling them that he paid more tax than 'the lot of them put together' and walked out of the meeting because he had a prior engagement for lunch. This was part of his 'Bad Boy' image but, when some of his claims were investigated, they proved to be less than convincing. His diamond mines in Lesotho did not produce top-quality stones. They were boarded up and waiting to be sold.

'We were running a campaign,' he told MPs, 'deliberately to make fun of people,' particularly the liberal *élite*. He was within his legal rights to do so and, at the time of writing, there is no hard evidence to prove that he has committed any crime. His jokes at the expense of the political establishment were much appreciated by those who wanted to get rid of it anyway. He may not have believed that he would be so successful. There were cheerful pictures of the Bad Boys in the United States, rubbing shoulders with the mighty – Farage, Banks, Manafort, Bannon, Flynn and Trump – as the presidential candidate's bandwagon rolled on to the White House, through rally after rally. They defied politically correct opinion and none of the mud thrown at them seemed to stick.

Was there collusion between Kremlin officials and the Trump campaign? Was there definite proof of official Russian interference with the EU referendum? Was there a wider conspiracy to destabilise the West by spreading fake facts and hiding behind dummy web sites? Or were these just practical jokes from playboy anarchists? One chilling conclusion is hard to avoid. It was expressed by Alex Younger, the Head of M16, in December 2016: 'The connectivity that is the heart of globalisation can be exploited by states with hostile intent to further their aims – the risks at stake are profound and represent a fundamental threat to our sovereignty.'

***

Chapter Fourteen
A Bloody Difficult Woman

(i)

On 29 March 2017, nine months after the referendum, the British representative to the EU, Sir Tim Barrow, handed the letter to Donald Tusk, the President of the European Council, which triggered Article 50 of the Treaty of the European Union, the Lisbon Treaty. This declared the United Kingdom's formal intention to leave the EU after a period of two years, during which time the terms of the divorce settlement needed to be negotiated. 'There is no reason to pretend,' said Tusk, 'that this is a happy day.'

The letter came from the British Prime Minister, Theresa May. The decision to leave, she insisted:

> was no rejection of the values we share as fellow Europeans. Nor was it an attempt to do harm to the European Union or any of the remaining member states. On the contrary, the United Kingdom wants the European Union to succeed and prosper. Instead the Referendum was a vote to restore, as we see it, our national self-determination. We are leaving the European Union, but we are not leaving Europe.

In London, there was doubt as to whether this was the right time to trigger the Article. Jeremy Corbyn, Leader of the Opposition, believed that the letter should have been sent immediately after Parliament had endorsed the referendum's result. Others felt that it was too soon. The consequences should have been planned carefully in advance. Brexit should have been wargamed. But Mrs May was under pressure to demonstrate to the hardliners that she was determined to leave. Although the details might be vague, the intention was not. 'Brexit means Brexit,' she insisted, and went on saying so.

Theresa May (née Brasier) was born in 1956, the only daughter of an Anglican vicar and a mother who was a staunch Conservative supporter. She read geography at St Hugh's College, Oxford and became a financial consultant. She had worked at the Bank of England. She was elected as the MP for Maidenhead in 1997 and was appointed Home Secretary in Cameron's coalition government. She was a diabetic, who needed an insulin injection five times a day, but her determination to fight on was evident in all that she did, whether to control immigration or strike a good deal with the EU. Once she had made up her mind, she was deaf to other persuasions. She compared herself to Geoffrey Boycott, the obdurate Yorkshire and England opening batsman, who was notorious for running out his partners. She was, by her own admission, 'a bloody difficult woman'.

Shortly after the result of the referendum had been announced, another difficult woman, Gina Miller, a British-Guyanese business executive, challenged the government's authority. It had no right to implement the Will of the People without seeking the approval of Parliament first. The referendum was advisory. It was not and could not be a legislative act. Nor could MPs be expected to rubber-stamp whatever deal the government might propose. The vote had to be 'meaningful'. If May or her Minister for Leaving the EU, David Davis, brought back a deal that the Commons did not like, they should have the power to reject it.

Miller took the case to the High Court, where it was upheld. This was not what the government wanted. It limited the power of its hand both with the EU and Parliament. The *Daily Mail* took up the government's cause and denounced the four law lords, who made the decision, as 'enemies of the people', an attack upon the independence of the judiciary. In the Commons, most MPs were thought to have voted to Remain. It gave them a natural majority. They had voted to respect the referendum but, if they disliked the deal, who could guess how they might react? The Conservatives had a Commons majority of seventeen, but it was not so substantial that it could survive many deaths or defections.

May's first task was to reconcile the warring factions in her own party and to steer the ship of state calmly towards the outcome, as determined by the Will of the People. But this was easier said than done. During the campaigns, Vote Leave, and the MPs who spoke on its behalf, insisted that a free trade agreement with the EU would be easy to arrange. After all, EU countries sold more goods to the UK, than the UK did to them. The balance of trade was in their favour. The Brexiteers miscalculated. They had underrated the complexity of trade relations. It was no longer possible to assess who did better than whom. Brexiteers were scornful of EU rules and regulations. They dismissed those ideals which inspired many on the Continent, the vision of a new European civilisation. They did not believe that those airy-fairy ideas might get in the way of hard-nosed trade. The EU Commission thought otherwise.

It soon became apparent that within the House of Commons and in the country there were many versions of Brexit. Some MPs wanted to stay in the Customs Union but outside the Common Market, others vice versa. Some wanted to cut ties with the EU altogether. Some hoped to remove the authority of the European Court of Justice without realising what this might mean for the Withdrawal Agreement. The grand simplicities of Leaving grew more complicated day by day.

In January 2017, Mrs May expressed her priorities, her red lines, in a speech given at Lancaster House, a historic property managed by the Foreign Office. 'June the twenty-third [the date of the Referendum] was not the moment when Britain chose to step back from the world,' she said, 'It was the moment we chose to build a truly global Britain.' She did not hark back, as Mrs Thatcher might have done to the saving of civilisation in 1939, but to the Commonwealth and the Imperial links:

> Many in Britain have always felt that the UK's place in Europe came at the expense of our global ties. . . . Our political traditions are different. . . . We have no written constitution. . . . The public expects to be able to hold their governments to account very directly and as a result supranational institutions as strong as those created by the EU sit very uneasily in relation to our political history and way of life. That is why we seek a new and equal partnership between an independent, self-governing, global Britain, and our friends and allies in the EU, not a partial membership; or anything that leaves us half-in, half-out.

The first stage was to incorporate the body of existing EU law into British law, so that it could be changed or modified unilaterally by the British parliament. This was to allow continuity of trade: 'We will take back control of our laws and bring to an end the jurisdiction of the European Court of Justice (ECJ). Our laws will be made in Westminster, Edinburgh, Cardiff and Belfast.'

This was the bold declaration that the Brexiteers welcomed but, practically speaking, did this mean that the British government would not acknowledge the ECJ in those matters where both parties were concerned? Would British courts always claim supremacy over the ECJ in such matters as environmental protection, conservation, security, nuclear safeguards, the Internet, the rights of British citizens in the EU and EU citizens in the UK? 'Under my leadership,' Mrs May continued, 'not only will the government protect the rights of workers, set out in European legislation, we will build on them . . . [to make sure] that the voices of workers are heard in the boards of publicly listed companies for the first time.'

Opponents of Mrs May seized upon her Lancaster House speech as proof of her failure to understand the philosophy of the EU, nothing less than the safeguarding of democratic rights in an age of globalisation and technological change. No one nation, not even Britain, would be strong enough to resist all the pressures. It could never guarantee to protect the values that Mrs May insisted that Britain shared with her Continental neighbours.

'As a priority,' she continued, 'we will pursue a bold and ambitious free trade agreement with the EU,' which should allow for 'the freest possible trade with and operate within the European markets and let European businesses do the same in Britain.' This agreement should not be allowed to interfere with the UK's freedom to negotiate with non-European countries around the world. Nor did it imply that Britain would accept the four freedoms of 'goods, capital, services and people'. Nor did it indicate that Britain would comply with the 'EU's rules and regulations that implement those freedoms', because this would 'to all intents and purposes mean not leaving the EU at all'.

'After all the division and discord,' she concluded, 'the country is coming together. The overwhelming majority of people, however they voted, want us to get on with it, not merely forming a new partnership with Europe, but building a stronger, fairer, more global Britain too. And let that be the lesson of our times.'

This was starting to sound more like campaign rhetoric than a negotiating position. How did Mrs May know what the 'overwhelming majority' wanted? For which Brexit? How could Britain negotiate a frictionless trade agreement with the EU and pursue a policy of global Britain at the same time? Cynics noted that one of her first visits to promote global Britain was to Saudi Arabia, which had more money than European values. Another was to pay a courtesy call on President Trump, who had just pulled his country out of the Paris Agreement on climate change.

Members of her cabinet were getting restless. Mrs May had no mandate of her own. She had been appointed to her position as Prime Minister, when others backed away. Although she had frequently denied that she would seek a general election, and the fixed-term Parliament still had two years to run, the Conservatives were twenty percentage points ahead of Labour in the opinion polls. Corbyn was widely considered to be unelectable. His kind of socialism died with Leonid Brezhnev.

After a walking holiday in the Alps with her husband, Mrs May decided that now was the time to win a stronger mandate. She needed more Members of Parliament, a united party and the approval of the country. She called a general election.

'Now more than ever,' ran the Conservative manifesto, 'Britain needs a strong and stable government to get the best Brexit deal for our country and our people. Now more than ever Britain needs strong and stable leadership. Now more than ever Britain needs a clear plan.' Many Conservatives were convinced that they would be in power for at least a generation, perhaps longer. They talked about 'crushing socialism for ever'.

This boisterous confidence was starting to sound familiar. It had the ring of party triumphalism. May's rallies were like mini-coronations. Her rhetoric grew in scale and ambition. Once the UK had gained control of its borders, its laws and its sovereignty, it would negotiate a new partnership with its Continental neighbours, based upon independence and mutual respect. If other countries behaved in an unfriendly way, that was their problem. Their task (although the Conservatives did not precisely say so) was to make Britain Great again.

'We are already,' ran the Conservative manifesto, 'the fifth largest economy in the world, the biggest recipient of foreign investment in Europe and the fastest growing economy in the G7.' Britain was 'the world's greatest meritocracy' and holds 'global leadership in [world] development'. It contained 'the world's most dynamic digital economy', three of the world's ten leading universities and more Nobel Prize Winners than any country other than the United States'. It did particularly well in London's 2012 Summer Olympics. 'Leaving the EU would mean that for the first time in decades, we will be able to control immigration.'

'In this period of profound national change,' the manifesto concluded, 'we will only achieve our ambitions, if we have the strong and stable leadership our national interest demands.' Mrs May's campaign was presidential. She did not want to take part in the TV debates with other party leaders. She did not wish to give them any sign of parity. She was careful not to get trapped in long interviews, but kept repeating her slogans, 'Brexit means Brexit' and 'strong and stable', as recommended by her advisers.

Gradually the country stopped listening. She began to be ridiculed as 'Maybot', a wind-up robot toy. Perhaps the British do not like the sound of dictatorial pretensions. During the election campaign, the Conservatives' lead in the opinion polls started to slide. When the booths opened, the two main parties were nearly level. When they closed, the result was not what anyone had expected. Labour gained thirty seats, the Conservatives lost thirteen and the government lost its majority in parliament. Mrs May contemplated resigning but negotiated a 'Confidence and Supply' agreement with the ten Democratic Unionist MPs from Northern Ireland, which kept her in power. She sweetened their deal with a handshake of £1 billion to pay for vital local services.

Parliament was comprehensively hung.

(ii)

Northern Ireland featured very little in the EU referendum. Two former Prime Ministers, John Major and Tony Blair, warned in one video that Brexit threatened the Peace Process, which was immediately denounced by Vote Leave as irresponsible scare-mongering. Otherwise, it was scarcely mentioned, which now seems strange, because it came to occupy such a pivotal position in the negotiations with the EU that followed. An army general would have immediately spotted that the border between Northern Ireland and the Republic of Ireland might cause problems. It was the only place in the British Isles where the EU met the UK on dry land. There would have to be passport checks, customs and frontier posts. But the Vote Leave campaign was not run by the military, but by marketing gurus, who had decided not to draw attention to this potential fly in the ointment.

The Northern Ireland Act 1998 devolved powers from Westminster to a power-sharing executive in Stormont. It was the consequence of a decades-long peace process, two referendums and the Belfast Agreement, which specified that there would be free movement throughout the island of Ireland.[i] It was internationally binding. When the UK and the Republic were both inside the EU, borderless trade was compatible, indeed essential, to their memberships. If Britain left the EU, her border with the Republic would have to be restored. This, according to the US diplomat, George Mitchell, might unpick the Peace Process, which he had helped to negotiate. This would threaten the return of the paramilitaries and, in the longer run, the unity of the United Kingdom.

To ardent Brexiteers, some in May's cabinet, these matters at first seemed relatively unimportant. There were fewer than two million people in Northern Ireland. Its government in Stormont was deadlocked. Its power-sharing executive had ceased to function as an executive. The province was run on a day-to-day basis by its devolved civil service. Boris Johnson, then Foreign Secretary, likened the border issue to the congestion zones in London. Was it was not possible, he argued, to monitor the border through Automatic Number Plate Recognition (ANPR)? Why should the process of leaving the EU be held back by a few people in a small province, when there were so many larger issues at stake?

From a Continental perspective, this cavalier dismissal of a genuine problem was symptomatic of the Brexiteers' approach. It failed to acknowledge that the Republic of Ireland was a member of the EU, an independent nation, which also had an interest in this matter. If Britain wanted to 'take control' of its borders, it had to acknowledge that the EU might want to do the same. This went to the heart of the dispute between them. If the Republic chose to observe the rules of the EU, but the UK did not, there had to be a border – if only as a temporary measure – while the new trading arrangements were negotiated.

For 45 years, British diplomats had helped in the drafting of EU treaties that gave them their legal status. After Britain left the EU, both sides might be able to start from many points of agreement. But it had not yet left and the sides could not negotiate the terms of future trading arrangements until Britain had become a 'third' country. There was a dilemma. Should there be a 'hard border' between Northern Ireland and the Republic, which would break the terms of the Northern Ireland Act? Or should there be a 'temporary' arrangement, a backstop, whereby Northern Ireland stayed within the EU's customs area, and subject to all of its rules, while the rest of Britain stayed outside? This might threaten the unity of the United Kingdom.

If so, how long would the backstop last and who would decide when it would end?

History casts long shadows. For the ten DUP members, any temporary arrangement that threatened to separate Northern Ireland from the rest of the UK was an anathema. The DUP had agreed to prop up Mrs May's government only on the understanding that no such separation would occur. It raised memories of the first partitioning of Ireland, which provoked the Civil War and the murder of Michael Collins, the revolutionary leader, in 1922. What had once seemed a trivial problem stirred up two sets of tribal loyalties, two opposing national narratives, two cultures, which, according to the Irish Peace Process, should be given 'parity of esteem'.

Nor could it be detached from the bulk of the negotiations and placed in an isolation ward. May's government might insist that the talks to decide the terms of the withdrawal were going well. 95 per cent was settled, but the remaining 5 per cent included the awkward question of the Northern

Irish backstop. Nothing could be agreed, until all had been agreed. Until this issue had been settled, the Irish border would be like an open back door, through which unregulated goods could flood into the Common Market and, from a British perspective, the EU's 'mobility of labour' could proceed unchecked.

More than two years after the EU referendum had been held, within a few months of Britain's planned departure, the problem of the backstop remained unresolved and brought the negotiations to a halt. It added another layer of uncertainty to the Withdrawal Agreement. Other matters might seem to be of greater importance – factories that relied upon 'just-in-time' deliveries, the future role of the City of London and the status of EU citizens – but the backstop was like the loose nail in the horseshoe that, according to legend, led to an army's defeat. It threatened the survival of May's government and the deal with the EU that her team were laboriously in the process of constructing.

Nor should this have been unexpected. It was entirely predictable. The situation on the island of Ireland encapsulated the history of the European movement. It told the story in miniature. As the disputes over the Rhineland symbolised the animosity between France and Germany, so the border between the Republic and Northern Ireland represented ancient quarrels, which had receded into the distance but still retained their power to disrupt.

During the 1930s and World War II, the Republic had been officially neutral but inclined, under de Valera, to support the fascists. It was officially a Catholic country and retained links with other Catholic countries in Europe – France, Italy and Spain. Northern Ireland was Protestant, since the days of the Glorious Revolution in 1688, when King Billy (William III) had arrived from the Netherlands to unite the fragmented British Isles under a new constitutional monarchy. This struggle was never quite over. There were nationalists and unionists on both sides of the border, with caches of arms in both camps, ready to answer the call of the drums. During the Peace Process, which had lasted for thirty years, the levels of violence had much diminished. Belfast was now a safer city but there were still families in mourning, who were seeking vengeance for lives lost in the Troubles.

The dangerous districts in South Armagh, once policed by the Royal Ulster Constabulary, were now farms and villages that stretched across the border. To reinstate crossing points might split them in two and become the slippery escape routes between the two jurisdictions. There were gangs ready to take advantage of this situation and, as elsewhere on the Continent, tribal passions would revive and stir. The EU's philosophy was that peaceful trade, which led to economic prosperity, would keep these hatreds in place. After Brexit, would the reverse prove to be true for that troubled corner of the British Isles?

There were also promises to keep. The EU's backstop proposal was that the border between the EU and the UK would run through the Irish Sea, thus preventing the need for a hard border on the island of Ireland itself. But this would have separated Northern Ireland from the rest of the UK, which May and the DUP ruled out as a solution. Instead, May negotiated an agreement with the European Commission, whereby the whole of the UK should stay within the customs union, until such time as the full trading arrangements had been reached and the backstop was no longer needed. How long would that take?

Michel Barnier, the Chief Negotiator for the European Commission suggested that an additional two years could be added to the transition period, bringing the date of the departure to the end of 2022 or after the next British general election. This was perceived by the Brexiteers as a nasty trick, which might unpick the Withdrawal Agreement. They were not better pleased by the proposal to stay on a temporary basis within the customs union. Who would decide when that temporary arrangement should come to an end? If the UK could decide on its own to end the agreement, this might be acceptable; but, if the EU had to lend its signature as well, the UK would be at the mercy of 27 countries which might have their own reasons for preventing Britain from trading globally.

This would be the worst of all worlds, half-in and half-out of the EU, subject to its rules and restrictions, but unable to influence them. In the Political Declaration which accompanied the Withdrawal Agreement, the negotiators tried to calm these fears. The UK and the EU

> shared [a] commitment to delivering a future Peace Plus programme to sustain work on reconciliation and a shared future in Northern Ireland. . . . The Parties recall their determination to replace the backstop solution on Northern Ireland by a subsequent agreement that establishes alternative arrangements for ensuring the absence of a hard border on the island of Ireland on a permanent footing.

Until that day arrived, the UK would have to observe the EU's rules and could not strike its own trade deals with non-EU countries. But when would it arrive? By whose authority? Who would moderate any disputes, the European Court of Justice?

When the Political Declaration was presented to the Commons on 22 November, the Leader of the Opposition, Jeremy Corbyn, denounced it as 'waffle'. The Brexiteers on the government benches went further. Boris Johnson, Jacob Rees-Mogg and others insisted that it reduced the UK to the level of a 'vassal state', an archaic expression, recalling medieval feudalism, when a vassal was someone who owed allegiance to the Crown. This was over-colourful language. The EU had no wish to humiliate the UK. Its concern was to moderate the language of nationalism and to replace it with something more cooperative. But it had to defend its own interests as well, including those of the Republic of Ireland.

The views seemed irreconcilable, an impasse inevitable, but Mrs May insisted that her deal was the best that could be reached. In Parliament, on radio phone-ins and interviews, she insisted that no other agreement would work, one that maintained the UK's access to European markets and preserved its sovereignty as well. She was asked whether her deal was better than staying in the European Union. Her answer within a BBC interview[ii] was a jewel of evasion: 'It will be a different world outside the EU . . . it's a different sort of environment. . . . It depends upon what we make of it.' She was stonewalling like Boycott.

The stalemate was reaching the level of a Ruritanian farce. Ministers came and left her cabinet. Every day was make-or-break. Brexit was taking up more time than there were days in the working week, spilling over into the weekends and plane trips to Brussels. Yet, from a certain distance, the fuss seemed to be about very little.

For the first time in its recent history, the island of Ireland was relatively peaceful. It may have helped that the memory of the Troubles was so fresh in the mind. Nobody wanted to return to the bad old days. Northern Ireland had voted to Remain by 50 per cent to 44 per cent to Leave and the Democratic Unionists were the only party that wanted to Leave. But the DUP was the largest political party in the province and, under normal circumstances, would be sitting in government with Sinn Fein in the Stormont Assembly. But the power-sharing executive had been suspended, and the only duties that the DUP's representatives had to perform were those of the ten MPs, who propped up the government in Westminster, and they disliked the Withdrawal Agreement as much as anyone else. It threatened the unity of the United Kingdom, which the party was dedicated to defend.

In 2017, 81,752 people from Northern Ireland applied for Irish passports, as they were entitled to under the terms of the 1998 Act. This represented an increase of 28 per cent over the figure for 2016, which (following the EU referendum) was in itself a record year for applications.

Large sections of the population of Northern Ireland were voting with their feet. Apart from holding an Irish European passport which would allow them to travel unrestricted across the Continent, they may have been revising their opinion of the Republic itself. For the first time in its history, there was, according to the polls, a majority in the North for a united Ireland.

After 30 years of EU membership, Dublin was transformed. It had gone through the economic cycle from being 'the Celtic Tiger', then fell prey to the recession and was now a prosperous city. The power of the Roman Catholic Church had weakened, its old abuses exposed and confessed, and in one part of Europe, perhaps the least to be expected, a new liberalism was on the rise. The Irish Taoiseach, Leo Varadkar, of Fine Gael was openly gay, and, in May 2018, there was a referendum, which overturned the previous ban on abortion by 66.4 per cent to 33.4 per cent. Northern Ireland was now the only part of the island, where the ban, supported by the DUP, was still in force. The Republic once held the reputation of being priest-ridden and provincial, whereas Northern Ireland had seemed more open to the world. Now their roles were reversed. Where now were their 'equally esteemed' cultural traditions?

(iii)

On 25 November 2018, after more than eighteen months of negotiations, Theresa May signed the Withdrawal Agreement on behalf of her government with the 27 leaders of the EU at a special convened summit. The deal came in two parts. The Agreement itself was long and legally binding, for it contained the details of the divorce. It totted up the costs and liabilities of the projects in which the UK was involved and allocated an agreed share.

The British contribution to the divorce settlement was calculated to reach £39 billion but this might change, if there were delays or the currencies fluctuated. It calculated the terms upon which Britain would leave the Common Agricultural Policy and the Common Fisheries Policy, ensuring that the country would become a 'coastal state', in charge of its sea as well as its land borders. It covered the Irish backstop, freedom of movement, the rights of British citizens living in the EU and EU citizens living in the UK, and many other matters, amounting to 500 pages of legal minutiae that EU leaders and British MPs were expected to read very quickly.

Accompanying this document was the Political Declaration, which was not legally binding and much shorter. Its intentions were to speculate about the kind of relationship that might exist between the UK and the EU after the divorce had taken place. This envisaged an 'ambitious, broad, deep and flexible partnership' working together to safeguard the 'rules-based international order, the rule of law and the promotion of democracy, high standards of free and fair trade, workers' rights, consumer and environmental protection, and cooperation against external and internal threats to their values and interests'.

There could be no actual treaties until after Britain had left the EU and become a 'third country'. To that extent, the Declaration was purely speculative. It was a benign vision of the world to come, if we all behaved ourselves. The shortcoming of the Declaration was, according to the Brexiteers, that it tied the UK so closely to the EU that there was little reason to leave it at all. It would be hard to escape. It was BRINO, Brexit In Name Only.

Taken together, the Agreement and the Declaration formed the basis of the deal that Mrs May signed with the EU heads of state and brought back to the Commons for its approval, so that the next stage of the negotiations could begin. It was, according to her, the best possible deal. It fulfilled the wishes of the British people to leave the EU, while protecting the economy against the consequences of the departure. In any case, there was no alternative, apart from a Hard Brexit (leaving without an agreement) or 'going back to square one', which could mean anything, no Brexit and civil chaos perhaps.

She acknowledged that compromises had to be made and that the break with the EU was not as clean and definitive as many Brexiteers wished it to be. But her government's website laid out the advantages of the deal. It brought back the 'control of our borders' and stopped 'free movement of people'. Britain would no longer find it necessary to send large sums of money to the EU as its membership fee. It took back control of our laws from the European Court of Justice, safeguarded security and defence arrangements and enabled Britain to strike free-trade deals with the rest of the world. It preserved the integrity of the United Kingdom and, above all, ended uncertainty. Businesses could plan ahead. It was not quite perfect but it was the best that she could do, and there could be no renegotiation.

She presented her Statement to the Commons on 26 November, shortly after her return from Brussels. As soon as she sat down, a formidable battalion of MPs rose on both sides of the House to challenge her compromise agreement. Nobody liked to be told that there was no alternative. There must be other models – 'Norway' or 'Canada'. A full hour passed, before any MP spoke in support of May's Deal and then without enthusiasm. May stuck to her guns and, after three hours of rancorous question-and-answer, the session was adjourned. Five more days of debate lay ahead, before the Commons had to take what was required to be the 'meaningful' decision on the future of the United Kingdom.

This left time for all sides to rally their forces. Mrs May decided to tour the whole country to enlist the support of businesses, farming and fishing associations, and those who feared for their jobs, in the event of a hard Brexit. She offered to debate the issues on television, a chance that she conspicuously avoided during the 2017 General Election. It never took place. Even without her relentless advocacy, the whole country was involved in discussing the future, in or out of the EU, from local newspapers to the international press, from small social media websites to government information services. Seven hundred thousand people marched from Hyde Park Corner to Trafalgar Square to demand a 'People's Vote', a second referendum. It was 'the nation's debate with itself – at flashpoint'.[iii]

In *The Spectator*, a pro-Brexit weekly, Martin Howe QC analysed the Withdrawal Agreement and concluded that it was 'not a bad deal. It is an *atrocious* deal.'

> Once it is ratified, the UK will have no legal route out of it, unless the EU agrees to let us out. . . . Halfway through . . . we find Article 185, which states that a Northern Ireland Protocol 'shall apply from the end of the transition period'. Once the Protocol is in force, the UK cannot leave it except by 'joint decision' of the UK and the EU. . . . The Protocol, which has become known as the backstop, locks the whole UK into a customs union with the EU with no decision-making power.

It merely required the UK to be informed of any EU decision 'in sufficient time for it to align itself with that decision'. It was far worse than staying in the EU.

Those who defended May's deal argued that some degree of leverage had to be given to both sides, as in any divorce. The true negotiations would come later. From a legal point of view, the package was an awkward mixture of the enforceable and the speculative. The British had to accept the protestations of good will in the Political Declaration, if the Withdrawal Agreement were to seem acceptable. All Brexiteers were sceptical, some defiantly so, but what was the alternative? Was it true that 'no deal was better than a bad deal' and, if so, what were the consequences of crashing out of the EU without any kind of agreement?

In the months which preceded the November summit, there were attempts on all sides to model the consequences of a no-deal Brexit. Through Dover, Britain's ninth busiest port, £12 billion of goods passed along Jubilee Way annually – or 17 per cent of the country's import-export business.[iv] Researchers at Imperial College, London, calculated that, if there were customs checks at the border and these delayed the traffic by two minutes per lorry, provision would have to be made for 30 miles of traffic jam. In Kent, work began on giant new carparks. Even greater were the risks to the trade in perishable goods, such as food and medicine, and 'just-in-time' parts for industry. In time, solutions might be found, perhaps involving number plate recognition, and (with friendly cooperation) goods that could be checked at the warehouses; but, in the meantime, there would be delays, frustration and outbursts of very bad temper.

A no-deal Brexit, concluded an analysis in *The Economist*,[v] 'is about a lot more than trade – it would see many legal obligations and definitions lapse immediately, potentially putting at risk air travel, electricity interconnections and a raft of financial services, and throwing into doubt the status of EU citizens in Britain and British citizens in the EU'. A reversion to World Trade Organisation (WTO) rules would solve some problems, but not all. 'To lower tariffs within the WTO rules, you must either enter into a fully fledged trade deal or lower them for all comers', which would rule out a 'deep and flexible' partnership with the EU. In 2017, British exports to the EU amounted to 44 per cent of its entire trade, whereas EU imports amounted to 52 per cent. It would result in, at best, a huge economic shock.

The chair of the Treasury Select Committee, Nicky Morgan MP, commissioned some economic models from the Bank of England. These made gloomy reading. With a no-deal Brexit, the economy would shrink by 8 per cent, house prices would fall by 30 per cent, the value of the pound would fall by 10 per cent, bringing it into parity with the US dollar, and economic growth would stall to 0.3 per cent, a derisory level. Mark Carney, Governor of the Bank of England, stressed that these were not forecasts but models of possible futures, but Brexiteers were quick to point out that the Bank had been proved wrong in the past. Jacob Rees-Mogg MP, leader of the European Research Group, denounced them as 'Project Hysteria' – Project Fear turned mad.

Were there other proposals? Some MPs favoured the Norway option. With Iceland, Switzerland and Liechtenstein – all rich countries, Norway belonged to the European Free Trade Area (EFTA), of which Britain had been a founder member. The EFTA nations could trade within the Common Market on special terms which allowed them to seek deals outside the EU. But to trade within the EU, their largest market, Norway and her EFTA partners had to accept the EU's terms of business. They were rule-takers, not rule-givers. These regulations included mobility of movement, the principle that encouraged many Brexiteers to vote to leave in the first place. It did not deliver on their promise to the British people.

A more ambitious model was 'Canada Plus', favoured by David Davis MP and Boris Johnson MP. According to a report published by the Institute of Economic Affairs, a free-trade think-tank, 'the UK should seek membership of major arrangements, which involve a number of countries, including the Comprehensive and Progressive Trans-Pacific Partnership (CPTPP) and the North Atlantic Free Trade Agreement (NAFTA)'. Britain, it argued, should be 'playing chess on multiple chessboards'.

Unfortunately, in 2018, neither of these trading zones was looking very secure. NAFTA, which came into being in 1994, was an agreement between Canada, Mexico and the US. It was an early casualty of Donald Trump's America First policy. The CPTPP was the successor to the Trans-Pacific Partnership (TPP). This was a trading agreement, signed in 2016, between the US, Canada, Australia, Brunei, Chile, Japan, Malaysia, Mexico, New Zealand, Brazil and Singapore, which also fell apart, when the US withdrew. It was launched again in 2018 without the United States but was hardly a replacement for the European Union, which had been in existence in one form or another for more than half a century.

Perhaps, according to some Brexiteers, we were all thinking along the wrong lines. Instead of seeking formal trading relationships or, worse still, trade linked to social reform, Britain should build upon the informal ties that existed among the English-speaking peoples. According to Graeme Leach, the CEO of Macronomics, a global business and economics consultancy, 'the Anglosphere raises the possibility of creating a new entity which aligns history, culture and politics more closely than with EU Membership. . . . A new world order is evolving in response to the information revolution.' He pointed out that 'around 90 per cent of the top 500 software companies are based in the Anglosphere', and their combined strength rivalled that of China and (if the US were included) other major alignments in the rest of the world. Its nations shared 'economic power, soft power, the strength of its armed forces and English language ascendance'. The UK was its home country, its natural mother.

The 'Anglosphere' was a word coined in the 1990s by the science fiction writer, Neal Stephenson.[vi] It applied to the countries that belonged to the white Commonwealth – Canada, Australia, New Zealand and the UK – and to those countries that spoke English as its *lingua franca* – the US,

South Africa, India and in the Caribbean. – in short, the cricket-playing countries. It excluded those countries like Japan and Brazil, aligned to the West, but not part of the former British Empire.

The Anglosphere was, according to the author and historian, Robert Conquest, 'a centre of hope around the world'. It was the futuristic expression of an ancient longing, *Pax Britannica*. 'God separated Britain,' said Mrs Thatcher in 1999, 'from mainland Europe, and it was for a purpose.' Addressing the English-Speaking Union in New York, she listed the attributes that belonged to countries of the Anglosphere: 'We take seriously the sanctity of the individual', as well as 'religious toleration, democracy, representative government, the rule of law', as if they applied nowhere else.

'This is a once-in-a-lifetime opportunity,' said David Davis in 2016, before the EU referendum, 'to renew our strong relationship with the Commonwealth and the Anglosphere countries.' Could it be revived? Could the UK find partners within the Anglosphere to replace the trading ties that it already had with car manufacturers in Germany? Was there any way in which the economic links that Canada had with the US, or Australia with Japan, could be replicated to include the UK as well? On the other side of the pond? On the other side of the world? 'The new Anglosphere boosters,' concluded a leading article in Prospect,[vii] 'are like the Victorians, bewitched by the belief that technology has dissolved geography.' But the Victorians were very successful in dreaming their impossible dream. Why not us?

The lure of a national narrative should never be underestimated. For many who voted to Leave, it may have been their primary motive. It was reinforced by hundreds of hours of TV programming, history lessons at school, statues in squares and sermons in churches. But for those who voted to Remain, it could be a fatal distraction. The debate was not about the country that we were but the kind of nation we wanted to become.

One political fact was clear. Although May's deal was unlikely to be passed by the Commons, no other proposal was likely to fare better. Parliament might be 'hung', but so too were the two main parties. The EU referendum exposed the deep ideological divisions that were not expressed within the Conservative and Labour narratives. They may have been the wrong parties but they were the only ones with the potential to govern. On this vital question, which affected the whole country, neither could form a government that could command a majority.

Faced by a 'meaningful vote', scheduled to take place on 11 December 2018, which was widely believed to be the last possible date that would allow the government and the country to prepare for our departure on 29

March 2019, the government's Chief Whip went into maximum overdrive. He called in the doubters to one-to-one meetings. It twisted arms and the number of private secretaries was increased on the government's payroll. This was to no avail. Faced with certain defeat in the Commons, the government cancelled the debate on a 'meaningful vote' just before noon on the day it was scheduled to take place.

An alternative date was not announced, but promised.

Faced by the most far-ranging issue of the times, the political process was falling apart in the country that claimed to be the mother of modern democracy.

***

Chapter Fifteen
Square One

(i)

One detail of the 2017 General Election escaped the eye of all but the most dedicated psephologist. The turnout at 68 per cent was 4 per cent lower than that for the previous year's EU referendum. Perhaps the public wanted to leave the EU more than they wanted to elect the government. Perhaps the electorate was suffering from voter fatigue. But it reinforced the impression that the election had been conducted in an old-fashioned way, with debates, manifestos and rallies – unlike the referendum, which Leavers had won by marketing tactics, designed for the Internet age. They were effective and, in the eyes of many Remainers, highly unethical. But unorthodox movements across Europe were starting to use similar tactics to upset the whole applecart of traditional politics.

In 2017, Steve Bannon, the mastermind of Donald Trump's presidential campaign, started 'The Movement', based in Brussels, with Mischaël Modrikamen, the founder of the Belgium People's Party. The Movement is not exactly an organisation. It has no hierarchy, no levels of command. Its aims are to provide 'a connective tissue' between the various ultra-nationalistic movements, and to offer help in polling, Internet messaging and war-room strategy. It does share the bones of an alt-right philosophy and has some common enemies, whom Bannon identified as 'the party of Davos'.

Davos, Switzerland, is where the World Economic Forum holds its annual meetings. World leaders are invited to discuss the challenges that face the world and how they can best be overcome. Bannon identified them as the high priests of an intellectual conspiracy, whose lofty ideals disdained the concerns of the man in the street. They were the ones who preached political correctness, invented globalisation, put miners out of work and switched vast sums of money around the world at the expense of those who could not even afford to pay their mortgages.

He sought to rally the European working classes against them. 'You are the backbone of society', he told a meeting of the Brothers of Italy, a right-wing alliance which embraced neo-fascists as well as dissidents from Silvio Berlusconi's Forza Italia. 'You are the glue. The scientific, managerial, engineering, financial and cultural elite detests you and everything you stand for.' Bannon himself, stocky, roughly shaved and belligerent, was the embodiment of the Common Man. 'I'm not a theologian,' he told Alessandro Bocchi, an Italian freelance journalist, writing in a Catholic newspaper, 'I'm a simple Catholic who grew up in the American South. I was an altar boy from a blue-collar family.'

If the Movement has a coherent political aim, it is to rally the forces of nationalism to take control of the European Parliament in the 2019 elections, and 'drive a stake through the heart of Brussels, the Vampire'. This broad ambition was shared by Bannon, Farage, Banks, Modrikamen, Italy's Interior Minister Matteo Salvini and Hungary's Prime Minister, Viktor Orbán. If it has a common enemy, it is George Soros, the Hungarian-American banker and billionaire philanthropist, who endowed the Open Society Foundation (OSF).

This Foundation supports universities, schools, think-tanks and non-governmental organisations around the world. It promotes multiculturalism, democratic (but not populist) government and the free (and capitalist) press, the full liberal package. Soros has become a hate figure for the right, blamed by Trump for financing 'the invasion' of illegal migrants on the Mexican border, in Turkey, for defending journalists against Erdogan and, in Hungary, Soros' home country, for opposing Orbán's Fidesz party, particularly on immigration.

Orbán sought to close the gates of Hungary against migrants from the Middle East. 'His plan,' according to Soros, 'treats the protection of national borders as the objective and the refugees as the obstacle. Our plan treats the protection of refugees as the objective and national borders as the obstacle.' In saying so, Soros placed the humanitarian crisis of the day within the long tradition of liberal thought. Those who placed the love of their country above their love of mankind were harbouring the seeds of fascism in their veins. Orbán sought to defend patriotic pride and the legacy of Christianity in Hungary against those who, in his opinion, would degrade its integrity. Nationalism should transcend individualism, not the other way round, even to the point of restricting freedom of expression.

Soros passionately wanted the EU to survive and flourish but he saw its limitations. He believed that British political culture was a corrective balance to the top-down tendencies of the EU's founding fathers; thus,

Brexit was 'an absolute tragedy'. He helped to fund the Best for Britain campaign, which called for a second referendum. But this was a desperate measure. He did not believe that it was likely to happen. It was only when British politics became so sunk in the depths of indecision that another referendum might throw a useful lifeline. If a second referendum were won by the Remain camp, it would transform the prospects not just of Europe but the whole world. But that was another very unlikely happening.

His OSF was named after Karl Popper's *The Open Society and its Enemies* (1945), written during the war. During the 1960s, Popper became well-known as the defender of liberal democracy against the threat from totalitarian regimes, linking Marxism and Nazism together as the enemies of freedom. He taught Soros at the London School of Economics. Popper's approach was that of a philosopher, whose political works began with a criticism of Plato's *Republic*. In his view, Plato harmfully influenced Hegel and Marx by pretending that there were absolute values, which could be imposed upon the public for its benefit. Plato had always been anti-democratic, unlike his mentor, Socrates, whose views he was supposed to express. Popper believed that in an open society the values of the ruling classes should always be subject to a rigorous cross-examination by those who had agreed of their own free will to be ruled.

He was concerned with the authoritarianism of science, which asserted that 'facts' could be definitively proved by experiment and empirical reasoning. It was the dark side of the Enlightenment, the belief that any human being could be 'objective'. In his *Logic of Scientific Discovery* (1934), he argued that the 'truth' of any observation could only be established by critical examination. A genuine scientist took into account the possibility the senses might deceive, the models might be wrong and the logic, a delusion. 'Truth' was established by 'falsification', by testing the limits of its veracity, rather than by asserting its absolute validity. Similarly, the health of the open society could only be measured by the way it protected, and sometimes provoked, the right to dissent.

In a world, which by its very nature was uncertain, the individual had to be guided by what he or she believed to be right, although there might be no absolute proof to confirm the validity of the opinion. It was a matter of judgement, common sense and good conscience. This was where Popper joined the mainstream of classical liberalism, which began with the defence of the private conscience. True political activity was never defined by the imposition of set beliefs but by the emergence of a critical culture, in which the better way ahead would become apparent through the process of discussion.

Popper was the John Stuart Mill of modern liberalism but, in the second half of the twentieth century, the stakes of uncertainty seemed intolerably high. The actor, Peter Ustinov, once said that he could never become an army general, because he could never decide whether a certain bridge was worth 30,000 lives. But in a nuclear age, a small, out-of-date, atom bomb might cost 300,000 lives. There are 100,000 more powerful nuclear weapons in the arsenals of East and West.

In the past, people complained about smoky atmospheres but not about the melting of the ice caps. In the past, vital messages went astray, letters fell into the wrong hands and secret codes that controlled submarines were intercepted. But nobody could have anticipated the breakdown of all communication systems, the hacking of the NHS, the betrayals of WikiLeaks or the theft of the Pentagon Papers. The scale of the havoc that might be wrought by new technology falling into the wrong hands simply beggars belief.

The challenge of the times is how to build institutions that can control these terrifying prospects and, at the same time, be controlled by democratic means. The OSF was formed for that purpose. There were no perfect examples, not Athens (too many slaves), not Rome (too imperial), not even France (too prone to indecision), but the closest imperfect one was possibly Britain. The UK was a civilised society, not prone to wild excesses of enthusiasm, and well-used to standing up to dictators. If Britain succumbed to the disease of nationalism, the chances of building a brave new world were greatly reduced. Brexit was in danger of driving a demolition truck through the frail structures that had preserved peace in Europe for 75 years.

Brexit was not just a threat to the EU. It challenged the consensus of educated opinion. These shared views were not a religion. They had no papacy and each university struggled to maintain its form of orthodoxy. They were wedded to the scientific method, peer-group bonding and standards that could be mutually assessed. Most universities in the EU were partly funded by their governments, as well as by big business. Were students trained by the state to meet the needs of the state? In which case, was it not possible that the universities, governments and global business corporations were engaged in some kind of intellectual conspiracy, a giant self-fulfilling prophecy?

The unofficial leaders of Bannon's Movement thought so. Their target was not only 'the party of Davos', but the causes that they represented. Climate change was a myth put around by the environmental lobby or, as Bannon's protégé, President Trump, put it, 'the concept of global warming was created by and for the Chinese to make US manufacturing uncompetitive'. With each spell of cold weather, Trump responded with a jeering tweet: 'Brutal and extended cold blast,' he wrote on 22 November 2018, 'could shatter all records. Whatever happened to global warming?'

Racial theories were revived that many in Europe hoped would never be heard again. Islamophobia joined anti-Semitism. In the US, the leader of the Ku Klux Klan came out for Trump and called for the US to become great again by becoming a white supremacist country. again. According to some conspiracy theorists, the Americans never landed on the moon and the dangers of nuclear catastrophe were much exaggerated. Automatic rifles should be freely available to protect the good people from the bad. The members of the Movement unanimously agreed with Bannon's opinion that the liberal press was a 'cesspit'. The alt-right posts on the Internet should clean them out. The social media buzzed with the politics of denial.

As for Soros himself, according to the alt-right, what was his record? A hedge-fund manager, who made a killing in 1992 by speculating against sterling? Although he might seem to be ultra-philanthropic in the way in which he spent his fortune, this should not conceal how he had gained his money in the first place. He had benefited from a grotesquely unfair system in which the combination of new technology and globalisation had increased the already vast gaps between the rich and the poor. The wealth of Amazon alone already exceeded the GDP of many small countries. If the high priests of capitalism put on the mask of altruism to disguise what they were doing, this was merely the mumbo-jumbo that kept them in power. The EU itself was no more than smoke and mirrors.

What was the answer to this liberal conspiracy? The answer from the nationalists was simple: to stick with what you know, with people that you know and speaking the language that you know. Patriotism begins at home with the defence of those you love. This was not a class struggle but a war of identity. You should feel that your whole being was under attack, where you had come from and the origins of your race. With the strength of your tribe behind you, you could rise up against these existential threats, the monoliths of so-called progress.

Various forms of such nationalism could be found across Europe – sometimes milder, sometimes harsher –- and their assertions could be hard to contradict. How can anyone prove that immigration is not a threat to identity? It depends on what is meant by identity. How can anyone demonstrate that burning fossil fuels is, or is not, a contributory factor towards global warming? For those who were not climate scientists, it was a matter of trusting those that were. It was a matter of trust in institutions as well as academic disciplines.

Whether we want to or not, we rely upon experts, and the integrity of experts, and as our technologies become more complicated, so the levels of expertise pile up, and sometimes collapse like a house of cards, so that we have to rebuild and start again. The strength of the Open Society, according to Popper and Soros, was that it allowed us to do so. The capacity to change was built into the system, unlike authoritarian societies where change was resisted. But this very ability to change exposed the public to the continual threat of uncertainty, which was why, to many of Bannon's supporters, the Open Society could seem a terrifying place.

Problems do not cease to exist, if you stop believing in them. However often Trump withdraws from an agreement on climate change, does not make any difference to global warming, except negatively, by perhaps making it more likely. Brexit would not lessen the dependence that the UK had upon the need for cooperation with her Continental neighbours, in such matters as security, environmental protection and economic development, other than by weakening her capacity to be a reliable partner. Trust is not just a desirable option; it is essential, at every level, everywhere.

But trust was in very short supply.

(ii)

The government was held in contempt. The Commons demanded that it should publish its full legal advice about the Withdrawal Agreement, but the government failed to do so. Instead it published a summary and sent along the Attorney General, Geoffrey Cox, to answer questions in the House. Cox's patriotic oration at their Party Conference in October, delivered like an old-time actor-manager, had stirred the Conservative blood before. He was the man to steady the nerves before May's deal was done at last – if that was going to happen.

Cox started by admitting what many had not wanted to hear. The Irish 'backstop' agreement could not be brought to an end by the UK or the EU unilaterally. It might lock the UK into the EU-controlled customs union indefinitely. This, Cox argued, was most unlikely. It was a matter of good faith and mutual self-interest. The House was still unconvinced and demanded that the full advice be published.

This sets a dangerous precedent. When a government asks its senior lawyer for his or her opinion, it has the right to expect confidentiality. These were exceptional times. The House also claimed the right before voting on May's deal to read the small print in advance. Twice, since the century began, a British government had withheld information to pursue its own course of action. Neither had turned out well. New Labour concealed the advice from its lawyers before invading Iraq. May's government promised to publish impact studies for Brexit, prepared by its own departments, but then refused to do so. How could the elected representatives of the people hold them to account?

The distrust was corrosive. It gnawed into the frail links that held the parties together. An anti-Brexit Conservative might have less in common with a pro-Brexit colleague than with an anti-Brexit Labour opponent. It indicated that the party system was not fit for purpose. It penetrated into the ranks of the civil service, and the trust in its advice to ministers. In the corridors of power, huddles of conspirators queued up to be interviewed. What kept May's government in place was the lack of an obvious alternative.

May appealed for the country to rally. 'We must bring the country together,' she repeated, in a slogan that became as familiar – and as discredited – as 'Brexit means Brexit'. But few liked the deal. It was a dangerous compromise. She ruled out the third option that the government might call for another referendum, a People's Vote, on the grounds that it would be even more divisive. Her government still had to deliver on the first. Who would want to vote again, if the result of the first referendum were to be ignored? The country would be returning to square one, which would mean crashing out with no deal or staying in the EU.

The suspicions penetrated sideways and downwards. 'There is a majority of Remain MPs,' Dr Liam Fox, the International Trade Secretary, told a Parliamentary Select Committee, 'who want to frustrate the Will of the People!' Meanwhile, more than a million people signed a petition that called for a second referendum. Nigel Farage left UKIP on the grounds that the party, under its new leader, Gerard Batten, was Islamophobic. He discovered to his surprise that there were racist elements in his party. Sterling came under pressure. It was thought not to be a currency that could hold its value. Investment in industry was slack. Many matters that required the government's attention had been put on hold. Local councils screamed their frustration. Retirement homes, schools and hospital wings were closing down. Other matters had to be left in the in-trays.

On 18 November, while May was trying to get her Brexit deal through parliament, the United Nations published a report on poverty in Britain. It confirmed the anecdotal findings of the freelance journalist, J.D. Taylor, except that the destitution was now much worse. The report, written by the UN's rapporteur, Philip Alston, found that fourteen million people, one fifth of the population, were living in poverty. Four million were living by more than 50 per cent below the poverty line and one and a half million were destitute. Alston blamed the post-2008 financial crisis, austerity, the changing of the benefits system to Universal Credit and the uncertainty over Brexit. Many were living from food banks. Those living rough on the streets had increased over the year by 58 per cent.

There was deadlock in parliament, frantic activity which led nowhere in particular. This impasse was not merely political: it was constitutional as well. Could parliament exert its will over the government without calling for an election or another referendum, two options that might simply prolong the agony? If not, who would be running the country? Beneath this logjam of unanswered questions, there lay another layer of uncertainty, our fractured culture. Were we held back by our habits of mind that were once widely trusted, but now seemed to lead us astray?

The symptoms were there in our use of the language. When words are employed so vaguely that they could mean almost anything, arguments are hard to express. Who were the 'People' or, in Farage's phrase, the 'real People'? When Brexiteers used the word, they meant the 52 per cent of those who voted to leave, or 37 per cent of the population. When Remainers used the word, as in 'the People's Vote', they usually meant the public at large. In both cases, the word conjured up a vast body of opinion that happened to be on their side. It suggested that those who did not agree with their point of view would find that the nation was against them. It was a menacing phrase, more of a threat than a promise.

The idea that Britain might lose its sovereign independence to a European corporate state had been a source of national anxiety for a very long time. But 'sovereignty' too was an ambiguous word. For Sir Geoffrey Howe, one key element of 'sovereignty' was the right of a government to sign international treaties on the country's behalf with other sovereign states. The Treaty of Rome did not represent the *sacrifice* of sovereignty; it was the expression of it. Thatcher came to a different conclusion. She signed the Single European Act in 1986 in the belief that it would complete the free-trade agreement, Thatcherism on a grand scale, but became suspicious of the rules and regulations that came with it. She treated every one as a threat to British sovereignty.

During the EU referendum campaign, Dominic Cummings simplified this uncertainty into one catchy slogan, 'Take Back Control'. It could be freely applied throughout the debate. 'Take Back Control' of borders, money, laws and immigration etc., as if the EU were an enemy force encroaching upon British territory. This set the tone for the negotiations that followed. Britain behaved as if she were demanding back rights that she had conceded to the Continent. But as the negotiations progressed, it became clear that this was not the case. The UK was in many respects losing control. Britain would no longer sit at the European top table.

If the 'People', 'sovereignty' and 'control' were vague and difficult words, meaning different things to different people, how could that lack of precision be multiplied sufficiently to encompass all the confusions of words like 'freedom', 'democracy' and 'equality'? These grand ideals of Western civilisation were like beacons of hope to many millions of citizens. Blood had been shed for them, prayers raised to the moon, but how differently they might be interpreted, if you were born on one side of the tracks rather than the other.

To some, they were pieties, to others, necessities. To some, they meant no interference from the state, to others, the protection of the state. Bottom-up cultures understood them differently from top-down ones, Eastern from Western. The task of the EU, its burden from Maastricht, was to reconcile them within a framework accepted by all. Political changes start with clarification but how can we decide what we want, unless we know what we mean?

For those who lived in the Westminster bubble, the shades of meaning could be better understood by knowing the opinions of the person who was speaking them. It was a kind of local dialect. For those who lived outside the bubble, the language could be very puzzling. It was rarefied, arcane and surrounded by formal procedures. When Leavers and Remainers cheerfully invoked words like 'freedom' and 'sovereignty' but drew opposite conclusions from them, it was as if they were playing games with the voters. They could not both be right. But voters also had their own world views. Those who grew up before the 1990s and the arrival of the Internet had a certain understanding of what was meant by national borders. Those who corresponded daily across the world through the social media were less likely to see them as barriers to be controlled. The press of Middle England – the *Daily Mail*, the *Daily Express* and *The Sun* – reflected the views of those who grew up in an age of resentment. They could not reconcile themselves to the fact that, after winning a war, we lost an empire.

In Britain, Freeview television was another factor, the 70 channels or so that could be received without subscription by those owning a standard TV licence. With the range of new channels, public service broadcasting lost some of its 1960s power to challenge and subvert; and most of its rivals depended upon advertising as their main source of revenue. They tried to reflect public opinion, rather than, in the words of the BBC's founder, Lord Reith, to 'entertain, educate and inform'. But popular entertainment was still guesswork. How could the scheduling managers know what the masses really wanted? They analysed the polls, learnt by trial and error, and formed their own views of public tastes.

To that extent, TV schedules may be seen as a reflection of British popular opinion during the weeks that saw May's Deal introduced to Parliament. There were many newscasts and debates about Brexit. Those who wanted to watch them were not starved of choice. But surrounding these events and wholly dwarfing them was the parade of adventure movies, documentaries, briefings and comedy series about how the English-speaking peoples won two world wars.

The centenary of the ending of World War I was 11 November 2018, Armistice Day. It was appropriate that on this day, and those that led up to it and those that succeeded it, there should be so many programmes of commemoration. Honouring the dead, however, does not explain the fact that, almost a week later, on Saturday, 17 November, there should be no fewer than twelve programmes on Freeview on how the Anglosphere saved civilisation. These ranged from such sturdy warhorses as the film, 'Where Eagles Dare', to documentaries on the 'Nazi Treasure Hunters' and an episode of 'Dad's Army'. It would have been possible to sit down at 11.00 in the morning and watch programmes about how nasty the Germans were, and how unreliable the French, until well past midnight.[i]

This was not an exceptional day. On 18 November, there were nine such programmes. On 19 November, there were twenty-four; on 20 November, there were sixteen; 21 November, twenty-two; 22 November, ten; 23 November, sixteen; and so on throughout the weeks of the Brexit debate. Most ran for more than 60 minutes. During this one week, there were 120 hours of supercali-patriotic-expialidocious viewing time. It was as if Britain had become locked into her Finest Hour and could not find the key.

Nor were there many programmes to indicate that there might be some alternative narrative. This imbalance has lasted for many decades, 75 years no less. It is something that distinguishes British from French, Italian or German television. This might have been predictable and in some respects desirable. There is nothing wrong with national pride, until it becomes obsessive. When Conservative leaders returned from Brussels, they celebrated their diplomatic achievements by listing the opt-outs that they had obtained – from the euro, the Social Chapter and the Schengen area, where citizens from EU countries could freely travel without visas or passports.

But this semi-detachment was a bit of a posture, more intended to appease the Eurosceptics at home than to describe the treaties that they had signed abroad. Beneath their frozen smiles, there lay a growing dependency. Not only were British manufacturers reliant on their Continental partners, but also our banking and legal services, our universities and research centres, our pharmaceuticals, food, tourism, communications and energy industries, and even our heritage, for Britain's history was always intimately entwined with the family of nations that we now call the European Union.

The British self-image was one of a sturdily independent country, at her best when defending her freedom against those who threatened her. This was part of her narrative, taught in schools and reflected in the 120 hours of war programmes on Freeview television every week. The shelves in British supermarkets told a different story, as did the hospitals, schools and factories. The political impasse was also a spiritual one. It was as if the British could not reconcile what they thought about themselves with how they actually lived.

And so to the logjam in Parliament, how could that be freed? May had secured a Withdrawal Agreement and a Political Declaration from the European Union but it required the approval from Parliament in a 'meaningful' vote. That vote was scheduled to take place on 25 November, preceded by five days of debate. But after three days of intense discussion, it became clear that her deal was very unlikely to be ratified. Her government delayed the vote to allow her to go back to Brussels to see whether she could secure any legally-binding reassurance on the Irish backstop. It was, as most expected, a futile mission.

The 'meaningful' vote was delayed until 11 December and then cancelled at the last minute, showing, according to the Speaker, John Bercow, 'discourtesy to the House'. On 13 December, the Leader of the House, Andrea Leadsom, announced that it would be held early in the following year but no date was given. There were suspicions that May was postponing the moment of decision to prevent any alternative plans from being tabled. The Commons would be forced into an unfairly polarised choice, her deal or no deal.

Meanwhile, the rough sleepers bedded down for another Christmas, more dinghies were rescued from the English Channel and the United Nations issued its sternest warnings on climate change at its summit in Poland. On 16 December, the British broadcaster and natural historian, Sir David Attenborough, warned the delegates that 'the collapse of our civilisations and of our natural environment is at hand'.

Against this background, the Parliamentary games entered another year.

(iii)

The past comes back to haunt us. Little habits that crept into our minds, like orphans from a storm, have grown up into hard-faced tenants, claiming their rights but reluctant to pay the rent. What can be done about them?

How can we politely explain that they are taking up room that might be better contracted elsewhere? How can we reason with them, when reason is part of the problem? How do we kick them out of doors or call up their removal vans which never seem to come? Their baggage piles roof-high in the driveway, blocking out light and access to the world outside, but how do we get rid of them, those care-worn clichés? Equality, democracy and the British way of life.

Which is the worst? Or, rather, if we set aside any matter of moral culpability, which is the least convenient, the most damaging, the largest obstruction? Equality began as a cry against privilege but it became a denial of difference. It does not exist in the real world where no two pebbles are equal, unless we want to call them so. Equality is the devil's magic that turns human beings into bureaucrats. All are treated the same.

In families, equality is a kind of damage limitation. When the children quarrel, we cut the cake into equal portions to stop any grudges, as we do with wills and divorce settlements. In happier times, we take account of what is wanted or needed, for every home is a kaleidoscope of difference. Each member has his or her own strengths, weaknesses and ambitions to fulfil. These are not fixed, but grow or decline, and the roles that we play – and so the patterns of household behaviour – change with every twist of the toy tube. Equality ignores them all. It screws the lid on progress.

Democracy is the expression of equality at a national level. What began as a curb upon tyrants, a social contract, has become the licence of approval for autocrats. It transfers the power of the many into the hands of a few, but implicates us all in decisions over which we have little control. It spreads the dust of complicity across our backs, so that we all feel guilty for the wars we cannot stop, the injustices we cannot curb and the disasters we cannot prevent. Into that grime, it adds layer after layer of excuses, for, when everyone is responsible, nobody is to blame. Democracy is the lemmings' alibi.

Few problems are solved by the head-count of opinion. In daily life, we turn to the experts – the doctor, the plumber or the agony aunt – and we are careful not to trust too much those whom we do not know. When we elect a government, we throw caution to the wind. We vote for political causes that we do not understand, led by people whom we have not met, with consequences that we cannot predict. Elections polarise. Signs of friendship lose their innocence. Whose hand can we shake without taking the leaflet? Democracy tugs at the threads that bind our lives together and where they are loose, unravels them.

In Britain, equality and democracy were quick-fit solutions to the restlessness of change. The walls of an older system loomed over them and mocked them. British equality is modified by ancient hierarchies. We live within a constitutional monarchy but it is still a monarchy and the constitution is unwritten. Our governments are elected by a first-past-the-post voting system, which simplifies the choices that we might want to make into one Clash of the Titans. If things go wrong, we have an unelected House of Lords to act as a safeguard. Evolution not revolution is our watchword.

We have the comfort of knowing that whatever concatenation of circumstances may happen elsewhere, there is something about the British character that makes us immune from them. We believe in fair play. We are pragmatic and warm-hearted. Our cupboards may bulge with collateral corpses but we are too polite to notice them. The difference between the view from the high ground and that of the trenches is one of perspective. When war refugees call to us for protection, they may not appreciate the strain on our welfare services. But we are really sorry for them. That is the British way of life.

It was not always so. Whole chunks of what used to be our philosophical landscape have been chopped off and discarded. Fewer people cycle to church on Sundays and there are fewer churches to go to; many of the causes in which we once believed have been taken over by a benevolent state, helping charities to become more egalitarian and inclusive. But their concern for others cannot be so easily transferred, nor the source of their kindness, for in their eyes, a good deed was a step towards leading a good life. Now every senior citizen in need is granted fifteen minutes of visiting time from a qualified carer, and local authorities are paid to provide them and all that has been lost is the original motive.

Does this matter? What good can be done by one person, when there are continents to be fed and climates to be spared? The causes get bigger every day. They merely start with the planet. The greater the cause, the larger is the conglomerate required to cope with it. One democratically elected government is never big enough. It has to be several, working on a continental or global basis, with agencies of a similar size, filling up space in the public and private sectors for the benefit of mankind, and power is transferred from even more hands into even fewer fingers, for there can be no confusion at the top. That would be anarchy.

In other countries this might lead to dictatorship but in Britain, there are checks and balances – the press, the police, the judiciary, the independent civil service, and public opinion, to add to the other institutions of freedom, such as Parliament, the monarchy and the BBC. When they speak with a united voice, we do not have to worry about the decline of the Church. We have our own papacy in Westminster. Personal goodness gives way to political correctness, for where is the authority of a private conscience against the collective wisdom of the think-tanks that advise the powers-that-be?

At this point, the rest of the world starts to fidget and look in the opposite direction, for few of its faiths carry the confidence of modern management ethics. The twentieth century was the Western century and left its fingerprints on every cracked mirror and dusty window sill of the global village. The parade of its achievements stretches along our Appian Way, from the internal combustion engine to the Apple Mac, from the howitzer to the drone, from selective breeding to bioengineering, and all our lives have been transformed by them, even those who in a generous display of public art now dangle as skeletons by the wayside.

Like all great victories, it came at a cost, for after two World Wars and a Cold War with its plentiful retraining camps, we have finally succeeded in making conflict more democratic. Out went the armies, in came the back-packers. Out went the tanks, in came the car bombs. Out went the command posts, in came the Internet, and the right to bear arms is enshrined in the Constitution of the Leader of the Free World. There are no reliable league tables, but the twentieth century can confidently claim to be the most blood-soaked in human history.

In the cold depths of the ocean, solitary submarines patrol the playground, their only sanction the ultimate one.

The secret of our success lay in science, the faith that has no need of worship. It deciphers Reality through measurement and the application of numbers. It has no conscience. It does not need one. Its theories are right, wrong or speculative. Its motives are immaterial. It is innocent of the consequences, whatever it does, and to that extent is guilt-free. Science was the purifying force that rescued Prometheus from his rock and placed him in charge of his own affairs and liberated the rest of us from the tyranny of Sunday mornings at the altar.

Similarly, the tools of science are without fault. They work, do not work or need to be repaired. How they are used is another matter. The intricate technicians cannot be blamed if more is spent on munitions than medicine. That is the way of the world. Paranoia is a deep hunger that feeds even upon silence and there is always a place for it in the market economy. Whole universities are sustained by the defence requirements of their governments, being more reliable, financially speaking, than the love of learning. Industries are driven, even whole economies, by the need for security at a time when any bunch of migrants – do not be fooled by their looks! – can conceal a terrorist, for even the humble gun can be a weapon of mass destruction, if it is mass-produced and we can be taught en masse how to use it.

Paranoia builds barricades, digs trenches and stores wealth in offshore accounts for fear of an uprising. The more we have, the more we need to hang on to what we have got. What is so odd about that? It staffs the detention centres, the halfway houses and the border crossing points, where watchful soldiers with their assault rifles, upgraded from the ranks, guard the desk clerks, who examine and stamp our papers – or not, as the case may be. When asked what they are defending, they reply, 'Equality, Democracy and the British Way of Life' or words to that effect, as if they were already living in paradise and could not see beyond the cluttered driveway of that confined garden.

But we who are blocked from the rest of mankind by our prosperity can still hear the sounds from the other side of the barriers, the cries and the curses, and we can still smell the tear gas and urine brought over by a trespassing breeze; and, through the CCTV camera which overlooks our front gate, we can inspect at a safe distance the suspicious rubbish bin and the woman who lives inside it with her child, kept not quite warm enough by yesterday's papers; for there are no secrets in today's wall-to-wall, 24-hour media coverage, only excuses.

In our mind's eye we can imagine the vast complexities of the world outside and recoil from them, for we know that, with the flick of a coin, our roles can be reversed, inside out, upside down, as has happened many times before.

And so we wait our turn.

At the arrival of a new year, 2019, we in Britain do not know what will happen. Will we leave or will we stay? Will we find a divorce settlement, whereby we keep the car but lose the chicken shed? Or will crisis follow crisis, while Theresa May, or her successor, strong and stable as ever, 'stands upon the burning deck, whence all but she has fled'?

Or will, by some miracle, a removal van appear from around the corner, to take away the baggage one by one that obstructs our view of the outside world. The saddest feature of the Brexit paralysis is the way in which a national self-absorption has stopped us from facing up to global challenges. The great betrayal of our heritage is that we no longer have time to play our full part in world affairs. Our sense of global responsibility has been diminished.

Nobody is holding a gun to our head. There may be weapons of mass destruction somewhere in the Negev desert but, as far as we know, there are no ballistic missiles aimed at Guildford. Perhaps within all the terrors that confront us, there may still be blessings in disguise. Even globalism is not all wrong. According to the United Nations, prosperity has spread to other parts of the world. Between 2000 and 2017, the number of children suffering from extreme hunger has been reduced from 198.4 million to 150.8 million. Nearly 50 million children are no longer starving.

The Internet may have caused havoc with our electoral systems but makes possible a more responsive level of democracy, in which regular polling can influence our choices without waiting for polling days. This may or may not be of benefit to humanity. We know more about global warming. How we act is another matter. How we adjust to change, how we overcome the gulf between the rich and the poor, has become more, rather than less, within our power to redress.

Now more than ever, the future is in our minds.

***

Appendix
World War Movies and Documentaries from Radio Times Listings

Screened between 17 and 30 November 2018

Saturday, 17 November

BBC 2: *Dad's Army*
More 4: *Nazi Treasure Hunters*
5 Select: *All Quiet on the Western Front*
5 Select: *Supernatural Nazis*
SyFy: *The Final Countdown*
History: *World War II Treasure Hunters*
Film 4: *The Train*
Movies4Men: *The Last Blitzkrieg*
Movies4Men: *One Minute to Zero*
Movies4Men: *The Silent Enemy*
TCM: *Where Eagles Dare*
TCM: *The Dirty Dozen*

Sunday, 18 November

BBC 2: *The Battle of the River Plate*
ITV 3: *Foyle's War*
5 Spike: *Submarine Seahawk*
Yesterday: *Churchill's Bodyguard*
Yesterday: *The World at War*
Yesterday: *'Allo 'Allo* (Triple bill)
Quest: *Wings of War*
Gold: *Dad's Army*
Sky Movie Select: *Casablanca*

Monday, 19 November

BBC2: *Home Front Heroes*
BBC4: *Long Shadow*
ITV4: *Inglorious Bastards*
Paramount Network: *Enigma*
Yesterday: *Nazi Hunters*
Yesterday: *The World at War*
Gold: *Dad's Army*
Sky Arts: *The Pity of War*
PBS America: *The Ghost Army*
Discovery: *World War II in Colour*
History: *Nazis on Drugs*
History: *WWII in 3D*
National Geographic: *WWII's Greatest Raids*
National Geographic: *WWII: Hell under the Sea*
National Geographic: *Nazi Megastructures*
Film 4: *Halls of Montezuma*
Movies4Men: *The War in the Air*
Movies4Men: *The Fall of France*
Movies4Men: *Casablanca Express*
Movies4Men: *Spitfire*
Movies4Men: *Battle for the Skies*
Talking Pictures: *A Family at War*
Sky Action: *Behind Enemy Lines*
TCM: *The Night of the Generals*

Tuesday, 20 November

BBC2: *Homefront Heroes*
BBC4: *Royal Cousins at War*
Gold: *Dad's Army*
PBS America: *Pioneers in Aviation*

PBS America: *Women Air Force pilots and WWII*
Discovery History: *WWII in Colour*
National Geographic: *WWII's Greatest Raids*
National Geographic: *WWII: Hell under the Sea*
National Geographic: *Nazi Megastructures*
Sony: *Saints and Soldiers*
Sony: *Battle of the Tanks*
Movies4Men: *Black Parachute*
Movies4Men: *Surrender – Hell*
Movies4Men: *Stormtroopers*
Movies4Men: *Hawker Hurricane*
Movies4Men: *Blitz on Berlin*
Talking Pictures: *A Family at War*

Wednesday, 21 November

More 4: *Jutland: WWI's Greatest Sea Battle*
Yesterday: *Nazi Hunters*
Yesterday: *The World at War*
Gold: *Dad's Army*
Gold: *Saluting Dad's Army*
Gold: *Dad's Army* (Double bill)
PBS America: *Flying Dreams: Women Air Force Pilots of WWII*
Discovery History: *WWII in Colour*
National Geographic: *Hitler's Death Army*
National Geographic: *Nazi Megastructures*
Film 4: *Stalag 17*
Movies4Men: *Blitz on Cologne*
Movies4Men: *Lost Command*
Movies4Men: *Germany at War*
Movies4Men: *Their Finest Hour*
Movies4Men: *Hawker Hurricane*
Movies4Men: *Allied Fighters*
Talking Pictures: *A Family at War*
Sky Movies: *Darkest Hour*
TCM: *The Night of the Generals*

Thursday, 22 November

BBC4: *The Most Courageous Raid of WWII*
Yesterday: *The Light of Dawn (The Normandy Landings)*
Yesterday: *The World at War*
Yesterday: *Nazi Murder Mysteries*
Gold: *Dad's Army* (Double bill)
Discovery History: *WWII in Colour*
National Geographic: *Hitler's Last Year*
National Geographic: *Nazi Megastructures*
Movies4Men: *Germany at War 1943-45*
Movies4Men: *The Air Campaign*

Friday, 23 November

Yesterday: *The Light of Dawn*
Yesterday: *The World at War*
Gold: *Dad's Army*
Gold: *Saluting Dad's Army*
Discovery: *WWII in Colour*
National Geographic: *Nazi Secrets*
National Geographic: *WWII – The Apocalypse*
National Geographic: *Nazi Megastructures*
Film 4: *The Train*
Movies4Men: *The Blitz on the North*
Movies4Men: *The Battle for the Fatherland*
Movies4Men: *The Avro Vulcan*
Movies4Men: *From Remagen to the Elbe*
Talking Pictures: *A Family at War*
Sky Action Movies: *The Longest Day*
Sky Greats: *Inglorious Bastards*

Saturday, 24 November

BBC2: *Dad's Army*
BBC4: *Blackadder Goes Forth* (Double bill)
5 Select: *Supernatural Nazis*
PBS America: *Hitler's Germany*

PBS America: *Pioneers in Aviation: Aircraft that Helped to Achieve Allied Victory*
History: *WWII Treasure Hunters*
History: *Nazis on Drugs*
History: *Surviving Auschwitz*
Movies4Men: *The Fall of Berlin*

Sunday, 25 November

BBC2: *Reach for the Skies*
ITV3: *Foyle's War*
Paramount Network: *Enigma*
5 Select: *The Dirty Dozen*
Yesterday: *The World at War* (Triple bill)
Yesterday: *'Allo 'Allo* (Triple bill)
Gold: *Dad's Army*
Gold: *Dad's Army Tribute Series*
Gold: *Dad's Army* (Double bill)
Discovery History: *WWII – Germany Invades France*
Movies4Men: *Hell River*
Movies4Men: *Shout at the Devil*
Sky Great: *Empire of the Sun*
Sky Select: *Billy Lynn's Long Halftime Walk*
Sky Select: *The Bridge on the River Kwai*
Sky Select: *Darkest Hour*
Sky Select: *Hatred*

Monday, 26 November

BBC4: *Long Shadows*
Yesterday: *The World at War*
Gold: *Dad's Army* (Triple bill)
Discovery History: *WWII in Colour*
Discovery History: *Unsolved History: Reconstructing Hitler's Bunker*
History: *WWII Treasure Hunters*
History: *Hitler's Circle of Evil*
History: *WWII from Space*
National Geographic: *Nazi Secrets*
National Geographic: *WWII – The Apocalypse*
National Geographic: *Nazi Megastructures*
National Geographic: *Hitler's Last Stand*
Movies4Men: *The Black Parachute*
Movies4Men: *Dive Bombers of WWII*
Movies4Men: *Marine Raiders*
Movies4Men: *War in the Pacific*
Talking Pictures: *A Family at War*

Tuesday, 27 November

BBC4: *Royal Cousins at War*
Yesterday: *The World at War*
Quest: *Wings of War*
Gold: *Dad's Army* (Double bill)
Gold: *Saluting Dad's Army*
Gold: *Dad's Army*
Discovering History: *WWII in Colour*
Discovery History: *Unsolved History: The Shooting Down of Baron von Richthofen*
History: *Hitler's Circle of Evil*
National Geographic: *Nazi Secrets*
National Geographic: *WWII – The Apocalypse*
National Geographic: *Nazi Megastructures*
Movies4Men: *The Panzer*
Movies4Men: *Operation Valkyrie – The Plot to Kill Hitler*
Movies4Men: *The Battle of Crete*
Movies4Men: *Grey Wolves U-Boats*
Movies4Men: *The Fall of Berlin*

Wednesday, 28 November

Yesterday: *The World at War*
Yesterday: *The Day that Churchill Chose War*
Yesterday: *'Allo 'Allo* (Quadruple bill)
Gold: *Dad's Army* (Double bill)
Gold: *Saluting Dad's Army*
Gold: *Dad's Army*
Sky Arts: *Hitler the Artist*
Discovery History: *WWII in Colour*
History: *Hitler's Circle of Evil*

National Geographic: *Nazi Secrets*
National Geographic: *WWII – The Apocalypse*
National Geographic: *Nazi Megastructures*
Movies4Men: *The Hindenburg Disaster*
Movies4Men: *Operation Valkyrie*
Movies4Men: *The de Havilland Mosquito*
Movies4Men: *Grey Wolves U-Boats*
Talking Pictures: *Nine Men*
Sky Greats: *Empire of the Sun*
Sky Select: *The Zookeeper's Wife*
Sky Select: *Darkest Hour*

Thursday, 29 November

Yesterday: *The Forgotten Gunners of WWII*
Yesterday: *The World at War*
Yesterday: *Nazi Murder Mysteries*
Yesterday: *'Allo 'Allo* (Quadruple bill)
Gold: *Dad's Army* (Double bill)
Sky Arts: *Entertaining the Troops*
Discovery History: *WWII – The Complete History*
Discovery History: *Unsolved History: Sinking of the Wilhelm Gustloff*
History: *Hitler's Circle of Evil*
National Geographic: *Nazi Secrets*
National Geographic: *WWII – The Apocalypse*
National Geographic: *Nazi Megastructures*
Movies4Men: *The Battle of Midway*
Movies4Men: *The de Havilland Mosquito*
Movies4Men: *Grey Wolf U-Boats*
Talking Pictures: *A Family at War*

Friday, 30 November

Yesterday: *The World at War*
Gold: *Dad's Army*
Gold: *Saluting Dad's Army*
Discovery History: *WWII – The Complete History*
History: *Hitler's Circle of Evil*
History: *WWII Treasure Hunters*
National Geographic: *Nazi Secrets*
National Geographic: *WWII – The Apocalypse*
National Geographic: *Nazi Megastructures*
Movies4Men: *Tank Commandos*
Movies4Men: *Britain Stands Alone*
Movies4Men: *The Fall of Berlin*
Talking Pictures: *A Family at War*

Endnotes

Chapter 1

i. The phrase, 'English-speaking peoples', is worth noting. Churchill wished to avoid the suggestion of racial superiority. His was a cultural distinction.
ii. Yugoslavia, the federation of feuding Balkan nations formed after World War I, once seemed a stable society with a civil service where Croatians, Serbs, Macedonians and Bosnians worked together in apparent harmony. After Tito's death in 1980, the federation collapsed and, in the 1990s, fratricidal wars returned. Those of a nervous disposition fear that something like this may happen to Europe, if the European Union falls apart.
iii. I have written about the usefulness of rhetoric in *Missing the Point: The Rise of High Modernity and the Decline of Everything Else* (Cambridge: James Clarke & Co., 2007).
iv. J.M.Keynes: *The Economic Consequences of Peace* (1919).

Chapter 3

i. Francis Fukuyama's 1989 essay, 'The End of History', published in the international affairs journal, *The National Interest*, borrowed this phrase from Kojève, but argued that Western-style liberal democracy had, with the ending of the Cold War, achieved the result which Kojève had predicted.
ii. Films such as *The Guns of Navarone* (1960) and *Where Eagles Dare* (1968).
iii. *Disrupt the Spectacle* was the title of a book by Peter Ansorge, which provided a critical guide to the left-wing theatre companies of the 1960s and 1970s.

Chapter 4

i. In *Sizwe Bansi is Dead* (1972)_and *The Island* (1972).
ii. The British sociologist, Anthony Giddens, developed a theory of Structuration in *The Constitution of Society* (Oakland, CA: University of California Press, 1984), which influenced New Labour under Tony Blair; but the word was first used in this context by the French philosopher, Emile Durkheim (1858-1917), a *normalien*.

iii. See Introduction to John Elsom, *Erotic Theatre* (New York: Taplinger Pub. Co., Secker and Warburg, 1975).

Chapter 5

i. See John Elsom (ed.), *Is Shakespeare Still Our Contemporary?* (Abingdon on Thames: Routledge, 2004).
ii. '*Nous sommes quand même avant tout un peuple européen de race blanche, de culture grecque et latine, et de religion chrétienne.*'

Chapter 7

i. I got this job after a disappointment. My play, *Peacemaker*, with music by Sally Mays, received good reviews at the ADC (University) Theatre in Cambridge, where it was staged in two separate runs. But it failed to come to London and one of its potential backers suggested that I should read plays for Paramount.
ii. In her childhood, Lwów was considered to be within Poland but, after World War II, it was brought into Ukraine and is now known as Lviv.
iii. This was first staged in the ILEA's Cockpit Theatre in Marylebone.
iv. Its full title was *The Persecution and Assassination of Jean-Paul Marat as Performed by the Inmates of the Charenton Under the Direction of the Marquis de Sade*, produced at the Aldwych Theatre in 1964.
v. *The Well-Intentioned Builder* has since been restaged several times, most recently at the National Theatre of Craiova, under the direction of a Romanian director, Anca-Maria Colteanu, where it ran in repertoire for three years.

Chapter 8

i. July 1988.
ii. 6 July, in a speech to the European Parliament.
iii. *The Downing Street Years* (London: Harper Collins, 1963) p. 634, *passim*.
iv. *Newsnight*, October 1982.
v. *The Arts: Change and Choice*, Liberal Party Publications, 1979.
vi. *The Guardian*, 5 July 1982.
vii. Published online by the Margaret Thatcher Foundation.

Chapter 9

i. John Elsom, *The History of the National Theatre* (London: Jonathan Cape Ltd, 1978).
ii. *Hansard*, 20 May 1992.
iii. *Ibid.*

Chapter 10

i. Gerald Kaufman MP, formerly Harold Wilson's Press Officer.

Chapter 11

i. Yuval Levin, *The Great Debate: Edmund Burke, Thomas Paine, and the Birth of Right and Left* (New York: Basic Books, 2013).

Chapter 12

i. This work was translated by William McCants, and published by the John M. Olin Institute for Strategic Studies at Harvard University in 2006. *Financial Times*, Henry Sanderson's column, 6 February 2015.
ii. Financial Times – Henry Sanderson's column – February 6, 2015.
iii. I visited Ukraine many times during these years. I wrote about Ukraine as a journalist, gave British Council lectures in Kiev and Lviv and was the Chair of the Awards Committee for the Gold Lion Theatre Festival. I never met anyone who claimed to support Yanukovych.

Chapter 13

i. There is an excellent account in Tim Shipman, *All Out War: The Full Story of How Brexit Sank Britain's Political Class* (London: William Collins, 2016).
ii. Vote Leave on YouTube.
iii. Vote Leave, *Take Back Control*, You Tube.
iv. *Ibid.*
v. Michael Gove, Vote Leave Press Release, 19 April 2016.
vi. The similarity with a National Socialist party poster from the 1930s was detected by the researchers for ITN and widely publicised.
vii. John R. Gillingham, *The EU: An Obituary* (London and New York: Verso, 2016).
viii. *The Observer*, Sunday, 8 July 2018.

Chapter 14

i. There is a fuller description of the peace process in John Elsom,: *Missing the Point: The Rise of High Modernity and the Decline of Everything Else* (Cambridge: James Clarke & Co., 2007).
ii. 23 November 2018.
iii. This was the late Sir Peter Hall's remark about the National Theatre, when he was its Director.
iv. These figures are provided by *The Economist*, 24 November 2018, p. 25.
v. *Ibid.*
vi. In his book *Or, a Young Lady's Illustrated Primer* (New York: Bantam Books, 1995).
vii. February 2017 issue.

Chapter 15

i. I provide the full list of these programmes in the Appendix.

Index

You may also be interested in:

Missing the Point

The Rise of High Modernity and the Decline of Everything Else

John Elsom

In his book, John Elsom considers the drama of international politics from the viewpoint of a theatre critic, someone who sits in life's stalls and takes notes in semi-darkness. He relates how grand narratives of human behaviour grew from the insights of Darwin, Descartes and the ancient Greek philosopher, Plato, to become 'the unacknowledged state religion of the West, High Modernity'. He argues that the primary aim of most European ministries of culture, together with Western media companies, is to promote aspects of this faith.

With a dazzling range of examples, from George Bush's New World Order to the war in Iraq, the Peace Process in Northern Ireland and John Birt at the BBC, Dr Elsom describes how the faith in High Modernity has permeated Western habits of mind. High Modernity may alarm those who do not share its Enlightenment beliefs, but it reassures others who want to believe that the future is something that 'we can, and must, control', according to the mission statement for the Millennium Dome.

Essential reading for anyone willing to open their minds to the realities of international differences in modern politics, this book will challenge readers' perceptions of the world they live in and the role of High Modernity in Western politics and culture.

Paperback ISBN: 978 0 7188 3075 5 / 234x156mm, 172pp / Published: 2007

BV - #0006 - 040419 - C0 - 234/156/14 - PB - 9780718895174